# Capitalism in contemporary Iran

Manchester University Press

**PROGRESS IN
POLITICAL ECONOMY**

**Series editors:** Andreas Bieler (School of Politics and International Relations, University of Nottingham), Gareth Bryant (Department of Political Economy, University of Sydney), Mònica Clua-Losada (Department of Political Science, University of Texas Rio Grande Valley), Adam David Morton (Department of Political Economy, University of Sydney), and Angela Wigger (Department of Political Science, Radboud University).

Since its launch in 2014, the blog Progress in Political Economy (PPE) – available at www.ppesydney.net/ – has become a central forum for the dissemination and debate of political economy research published in book and journal article forms with crossover appeal to academic, activist and public policy related audiences.

Now the Progress in Political Economy book series with Manchester University Press provides a new space for innovative and radical thinking in political economy, covering interdisciplinary scholarship from the perspectives of critical political economy, historical materialism, feminism, political ecology, critical geography, heterodox economics, decolonialism and racial capitalism.

The PPE book series combines the reputations and reach of the PPE blog and MUP as a publisher to launch critical political economy research and debates. We welcome manuscripts that realise the very best new research from established scholars and early-career scholars alike.

# Capitalism in contemporary Iran

## Capital accumulation, state formation and geopolitics

Kayhan Valadbaygi

MANCHESTER UNIVERSITY PRESS

Published by Manchester University Press
Oxford Road, Manchester M13 9PL

www.manchesteruniversitypress.co.uk

British Library Cataloguing- in- Publication Data
A catalogue record for this book is available from the British
Library

ISBN 978 1 5261 9557 9 hardback
ISBN 978 1 5261 6178 9 paperback

First published 2024
Paperback published 2026

EU authorised representative for GPSR:
Easy Access System Europe – Mustamäe tee 50,
10621 Tallinn, Estonia
gpsr.requests@easproject.com

Typeset by Newgen Publishing

*In memory of my late and beloved grandfather, Mohammad-Salim*

# Contents

# Figures and tables

**Figures**

**Tables**

# Acknowledgements

My intellectual pursuit to gain a deeper understanding of the sociopolitical transformations that have taken place in contemporary Iran, particularly regarding the process of class and state formation since the late 1980s, has been the driving force behind this research endeavour. Although I have invested an immense amount of time, effort and dedication towards completing this research project over the course of more than seven years, I am acutely cognisant that no scholarly pursuit can be solely deemed the product of individual efforts. Therefore, I would like to express my profound appreciation for the invaluable assistance and unwavering support that I received from the individuals mentioned below. Their guidance, encouragement, constructive feedback and productive critique played a pivotal role in helping me bring this project to fruition as it stands today.

Andreas Bieler deserves my deep gratitude for augmenting my intellectual capacities, fostering the expansion of my thought processes, and directing me in refining the fundamental arguments of this publication. Through my engagement with his scholarly works, along with his incisive conceptual inquiries, I was able to elucidate the theoretical implications associated with this study, while significantly influencing my perspectives on political economy and historical materialism. Furthermore, his steadfast support and encouragement were key in transforming this research endeavour into its present form as a published book. I am also immensely thankful to Adam David Morton for his invaluable feedback on my work and constant support. The ideas presented in this publication have been shaped in an indispensable way by his pioneering works. Countless hours were spent engaging with Jokubas Salyga through discussions that centred around various theories, notions and issues that form an integral part of this work. His sharp intellect and profound expertise in historical materialism have greatly contributed to advancing my understanding of capitalism. Daniel Ritter's rigorous examination of my work and constructive feedback posed a formidable challenge, yet proved to be immeasurably beneficial in enhancing the quality of my book. I am grateful to Tony Burns for his constant availability, which enabled me to engage in enlightening discussions on various concepts and ideas.

Any scholarly endeavour thrives on a continuous dialogue with a wide range of researchers across different disciplines. Sustained engagement with the works and insights from scholars such as Adam Hanieh, Kamran Matin, Eskandar Sadeghi-Boroujerdi, Roberto Roccu, Hannes Baumann, Payman Jafari, Stella Morgana, Joerg Nowak and Kevin Harris also contributed significantly towards completing this manuscript. In fact, several of them offered their valuable feedback on specific sections of this work which further enriched its quality. Debates and discussions with scholars who actively participated in the Marxist Reading Group, the Classical Political Economy Reading Group, and the weekly seminar series of the Centre for the Study of Social and Global Justice (CSSGJ) at the University of Nottingham were intellectually stimulating and highly beneficial in enhancing my understanding of concepts and issues related to this book. Noteworthy contributors included Jon Mansell, Jamie Jordan, Akif Avci, Oliver Dodd, Thanos Liapas, Basile Boulay, Rumman Khan, Andy Higginbottom, Gorkem Altinors, Kristiyan Peev, Alex Serafimov, Hamish Reid and David Porter. The completion of my book at Leiden University has been an enriching and fulfilling experience. I am grateful to my colleagues in Middle Eastern Studies, MA in International Relations, and BA in International Studies – Sai Englert, Crystal Ennis, Christian Henderson, Jonathan London, Lindsay Black, Vineet Thakur, Karen Smith, Cristiana Strava and Noa Schonmann – for their warm welcome. Constructive conversations with some of these new colleagues helped me refine some central ideas in my book.

Several chapters in the book have been enriched by valuable feedback received during presentations at various academic events. These include talks given at the British International Studies Association (BISA) 2019 annual conference, the International Initiative for Promoting Political Economy (IIPPE) 2018 annual conference, and research seminars hosted by the University of Liverpool's International Political Economy and the State in the Middle East workshop and the Leiden Political Economy Group (L-PEG). The thought-provoking discussions and debates held during the 'Revisiting the Mode of Production' workshop, which I co-organised at the University of Nottingham, on the historiography of global capitalism with prominent scholars such as Silvia Federici, Jairus Banaji, Neil Davidson, Benno Teschke, Alessandra Mezzadri and Andreas Bieler, among others, provided me with a deeper understanding of certain concepts that are pivotal in this book.

The School of Politics and International Relations at the University of Nottingham provided valuable financial support through their Postgraduate

Scholarship initiative to fund a portion of the research for this publication. In addition, various centres within the University of Nottingham offered numerous conference bursaries and field research travel grants, which had a significant impact on advancing the research project. Furthermore, I express my warm gratitude to the Institute for Area Studies at Leiden University for their generous grant, which facilitated the proofreading and indexing of the book. These grants were instrumental in enabling the successful completion of the research project and the subsequent publication of the book.

I would like to thank my parents and siblings for their constant love and support throughout my life. Additionally, I am deeply appreciative of the substantial impact that my uncle, Burhan, had on me, as his critical thinking helped mould my initial academic interests. Moreover, engaging in informal discussions on topics related to political philosophy, political economy and global politics with Aaram, my brother, and Navid, my cousin, has significantly stimulated my intellectual curiosity while assisting me in clarifying my views. Lastly, I am at a loss for words in expressing the depth of my appreciation for the affection and support given to me by my wife, Beatriz Gómez Fariñas. Her invaluable assistance in the editing process of the entire manuscript and her astute recommendations on structuring my arguments have helped me avoid common pitfalls associated with intricate or verbose prose in academic writing. Most noteworthy is her endless patience throughout this arduous undertaking which has enabled me to bring this book project to completion.

# Abbreviations

| | |
|---|---|
| BRI | Belt and Road Initiative |
| BRICS | Brazil, Russia, India, China, and South Africa |
| EMP | EU–Mediterranean Partnership |
| ENP | European Neighbourhood Policy |
| EOI | export-oriented industrialisation |
| FDI | foreign direct investment |
| FIPPA | Foreign Investment Promotion and Protection Act |
| FTZs | free trade-industrial zones |
| GCC | Gulf Cooperation Council |
| GDP | gross domestic product |
| GVCs | global value chains |
| IAEA | International Atomic Energy Agency |
| ILNA | Iranian Labor News Agency |
| IMF | International Monetary Fund |
| IRGC | Islamic Revolutionary Guard Corps |
| ISI | import substitution industrialisation |
| JCPOA | Joint Comprehensive Plan of Action |
| MNCs | multinational corporations |
| NGOs | non-governmental organisations |
| OPEC | Organisation of the Petroleum Exporting Countries |
| P5+1 | five permanent members of the United Nations Security Council plus Germany |
| Setad | Headquarters for Implementation of Imam's Order |
| SOEs | state-owned enterprises |
| SWIFT | Worldwide Interbank Financial Telecommunication |
| TCC | transnational capitalist class |
| UNSC | United Nations Security Council |
| WTO | World Trade Organization |

# Note on transliteration and translation

This book uses the *Iranian Studies* guidelines for the transliteration of Persian words and names. Persian terms are rendered in italics, but commonly used words derived from Persian (e.g., bazaar) are not. Common English spelling for personal, place, organisation and media outlet names (e.g., Khomeini, Tehran, Shargh, Kayhan) are preferred rather than transliteration.

All English translations from Persian sources are mine unless a translator is cited. For academic Persian sources, a translated version of the title in square brackets is included after the original language version. For Persian newspaper and website sources, the original Persian titles are not included.

# 1

# Framing Iran: A historical materialist approach

In the wake of the 1979 revolution with strong anti-capitalist and anti-imperialist propensities that vowed to eradicate class disparity, inequality and poverty, the meaningful study of capitalism in Iran faded. The lack of foreign direct investment (FDI) and the apparent absence of the country in the post-1980s international division of labour – resulting from the internationalisation of capital and associated neoliberal reforms as the latest spatial fix of global capitalism – has further demoted the analysis of capital accumulation and class formation in Iran. In the first place, this has led to the persistence of the cursory view of the external effects of the global economy on Iran through oil revenues. Accordingly, most explanations of the Iranian post-revolutionary state and society have largely hinged upon the key political and economic characteristics of the rentier state theory, as if the country has been immune to the wider space of neoliberal globalisation and the related dual tendency of competition and cooperation between the existing and emerging major centres of capital accumulation (i.e., North America, Europe and East Asia). When economic development in Iran has been at the centre of scholarly investigation, methodological nationalism and exceptionalism have been reproduced in different forms. As part of this effort, the analysis of Iranian neoliberal reforms since the end of the war with Iraq has rarely surpassed shallow Orientalist and Eurocentric canons that regard these measures as 'spurious', 'flawed', 'corrupt', inconsistent with 'true neoliberalism' and incapable of fostering a 'real private sector'. Among a handful of critical scholars who consider capitalism as an analytical category, the internal/external (local/global) dichotomy has not also been sufficiently challenged by locating Iran inside the process of internationalisation of capital and global neoliberalism. Nor has Iranian neoliberalisation been studied as the latest form of capitalist restructuring with conclusive impacts on the regimes of capital accumulation and the processes of class and state formation.

## Deserting the global in conventional perspectives on Iran

The primary focus of those who sideline capitalism as an analytical category is the political structure of Iran characterised by factionalism through which the economic development of the country is surveyed. In these accounts, since the post-revolutionary political factionalism has led to deep-rooted (institutionalised) divergences between revolutionary elites over the most optimal economic policies and blocked the formation of coherent economic planning for industrial and agricultural growth, they tend to document 'ill-considered' economic policies of various governments. Apart from a lack of vision for economic development, it is argued that political factionalism has also enabled rampant corruption as different state institutions and self-interested government bureaucrats have strived to divert state oil rents toward their affiliated economic entities and networks (Amirahmadi, 1990; Siavoshi, 1992; Schirazi, 1993; Baktiari, 1996; Amuzegar, 1997; 2014; Moslem, 2002; Saeidi, 2004; Rakel, 2009; Maloney, 2000; 2015; Mohseni, 2016; Ehteshami, 2017). The underlying assumption of these accounts is that the reliance on oil as the primary source of state revenues has nurtured the Iranian political factionalism that in turn fuels economic inefficiencies and incompetence. This narration largely omits a thorough investigation of how these policies relate to capital accumulation and, more precisely, capitalism as a systemic totality.

Influenced by neo-classical economics, new institutional economics and developmental state theory, the second group of scholars is predominantly concerned with the causes and conditions of the 'failure of development' in Iran. From a neo-classical liberal perspective with strong Orientalist and Eurocentric flavours,[1] Ghaninejad (2017) identifies the resonance of 'Iranian traditional collective values' with socialist and nationalist ideologies for the dominance of 'state economy' and the weakness of 'true capitalism' in Iran. Under this condition of contempt for the 'scientific truth' of the market system, the protection of property rights, the private sector and individualism, it is argued that the privatisation initiative and other market-oriented reforms of the Iranian state have resulted in the continuation of an insecure business environment and widespread corruption. Momeni's new institutionalist approach (2014) more or less accepts the necessity of all neo-classical assumptions and policies for development such as liberalisation, stabilisation and privatisation. However, rather than the traditional Iranian collective values, it lays the blame on the absence of functional national institutions for the 'debacle' of Iranian neoliberal reforms. Drawing on the developmental state theory,[2] Delafrouz (2014) compares Iran's sociopolitical context of development with the newly industrialising Asian countries, claiming that due to the lack of developmentally oriented elites, rational bureaucracy and an autonomous state, elites have become involved in a discursive battle to win the fluctuating social demands of various societal groups through elections. Echoing the negative depiction of Iran's state capacity of the political factionalism argument, it is observed that the plurality and dispersion of elements of power and the populist nature of the electoral system in the Islamic Republic have disturbed the political stability required for grand developmental economic policies. In other words, by following an ideal-type model that implicitly incorporates Weber's concept of bureaucratic rationality (Selwyn, 2009: 166; Selwyn, 2016: 789), this developmental state account accentuates the dis-embeddedness of state autonomy in Iran as the prime culprit behind the failure of development. Like other neo-statist accounts, the study is unable to comprehend that any form of state (including the so-called developmental state) is not completely autonomous from society since its institutional setup and its capacities to implement certain policies and pursue specific long-term objectives are strongly influenced by the class structure of the society and the balance of power between various fractions of capital within the state.

As a body of literature, all the above accounts downplay questions of capital accumulation and class formation in the study of the state and society in contemporary Iran. Not only does this critique apply to political factionalism studies, but it is also true in the case of the 'failure of development' scholarship, despite its primary focus on the question of economic planning and growth. More crucially, the whole literature reinforces the exceptionality of the Iranian socioeconomic and political system by underscoring the significance of internal determinants. While the political factionalism scholarship ultimately reduces everything to the unique characteristics of the post-revolutionary state (its paternalistic power networks, institutions and Islamic revolutionary ideology), the latter similarly gives centrality to domestic factors to evaluate the success or failure of development whether they be pre-modern values and excessive state intervention in the neoclassical liberal perspective, the underdevelopment of national institutions in the institutionalist approach or the lack of state autonomy in the developmental state theory. In other words, what unites them is a reliance on methodological nationalism; that is, 'a focus upon individual nation-states as self-contained, enclosed sets of social relations, separate from the wider region and world market' (Hanieh, 2015: 58). In reality, however, social relations are never bounded with national borders since they 'develop across and through borders within a single global structure' (Hanieh, 2015: 62).

## Inadequacies of the existing critical accounts on Iran

Critical explanations of the sociopolitical transformations in post-revolutionary Iran also do little to investigate capital accumulation and class formation, nor do they transcend methodological nationalism. In contrast to the common perception that views Iran's extensive patronage and welfare system as the product of a top-down means of state control or factional accommodations at the top, Kevan Harris (2017) demonstrates that the struggles from below and threats from outside have resulted in the formation of coalitions around social and economic policies between the poor, working class and middle class and different factions of political elites. In another work that addresses the neoliberal reforms and forms of capitalism in Iran after the war with Iraq, Harris (2013) maintains that the protracted post-war intra-elite conflict and the persistence of the embeddedness of the state within various social groups with opposing interests have generated struggles over the distribution of state resources. These distributional conflicts have formed Iranian capitalism and impeded the state's ability to 'fully implement real privatisation'. Opting for the three ideal types developed by Eyal, Szelenyi and Towneley (2001), Harris thus categories Hashemi-Rafsanjani's restructuring (1989–97) as 'capitalism from without', the reform project (1997–2005) as 'capitalism from below' and Ahmadinejad's project (2005–13) as 'capitalism from above'. Harris's intervention defies the total separation of state and society by incorporating the role of social forces in shaping post-revolutionary Iran. He also attempts to tackle the charge of methodological nationalism by comparing Iran to other middle-income countries. That said, his comparative efforts do not adequately consider how neoliberal global capitalism has shaped developments in these similar middle-income countries. In other words, his welfare state lens overestimates the importance of elite and political structure and underestimates the importance of capital accumulation and class formation. Therefore, as Burawoy (2001: 1001–2) rightly observes in the case of Eyal, Szelenyi and Towneley's work, in Harris's analysis likewise '[neoliberal] capitalism drops out of the picture'.

Two historical materialist accounts of post-revolutionary Iran are susceptible to similar criticisms, despite offering some fruitful insights. In an attempt to statistically navigate the transformations in the class composition of Iran, Nomani and Behdad (2006; 2008; 2009) compare the first decade of the revolution with the post-Iran–Iraq-war liberalisation era. Influenced by Erik Olin Wright's analytical Marxism, the first period is characterised as 'structural involution' due to the expansion of 'petty-commodity production' and the decline of capitalist relations, which resulted in the 'de-proletarianisation and peasantisation' of the economy. As the latter period has revitalised capitalist relations, reconstituted market institutions and proletarianised the workforce, it is labelled as 'structural deinvolution'. Nomani and Behdad's rigid definition of social classes excludes many workers from the working class and makes a clear boundary between the capitalist class and the state, even though lines between public capital and private capital are often obscure and elusive in Iran, as will be shown throughout this book. Above all, neither does the classification of the two periods on the grounds of these conceptual assumptions comprehensively conceptualise the patterns of capital accumulation, nor does it fully incorporate the role of global dynamics into the analysis.

Morady's *Contemporary Iran* (2020) is perhaps the only account of Iranian capitalist development that aims at locating the country within the global capitalist system to challenge 'widespread Orientalist and mainstream approaches'. However, by giving centrality to the oil industry, the influence of global dynamics on Iran hardly moves beyond the argument of the rentier state theory, as Morady vividly notes (2020: 6): 'The Iranian state continues to behave as a "rentier state", receiving its major income from energy, and does not need to impose high taxation. This has been fundamental to shaping the Iranian state and its relationship with domestic social forces and global powers, and its role in the Persian Gulf region.' Indeed, the hydrocarbon industry has been a prominent feature of the Iranian economy, but the ways in which oil and gas revenues have historically been allocated point to the different accumulation strategies of the country, as I will demonstrate throughout this book. Since this reflects the specific context of the various episodes of global capitalism, it seems inadequate to reduce the impacts of global dynamics to an immutable form of incorporation of Iran into the capitalist system through the production of oil and gas. This oversimplification leads to the inability to conceptualise the process of neoliberalisation, the class basis of the state and the different capital fractions of the ruling class.

As part of the historical materialist tradition, this book grants centrality to capitalism as an analytic by tracing the patterns of capital accumulation and changes in class and state formation emanating from it in Iran during the era of neoliberal global capitalism. This analysis proceeds from a relational methodology based on the ontology of the *philosophy of internal relations* that problematises the dualism of material/ideal, politics/economics, state/market, internal/external and local/global. In the first place, this relationality implies that there are inner connections between the nature of contemporary development in Iran, the form of the state, the ongoing sociopolitical transformations in society and the geopolitical tensions with the West. At the same time, it stresses that these issues should be explored in terms of their internal relations to global capitalism as a social system with an overarching power structure and totalising unity. In other words, from this relational approach, to fully grasp the changes in the regimes of capital accumulation and the processes of class and state formation in Iran, we must frame the country inside global class politics and economic processes, more specifically the motions and tendencies of neoliberal global capitalism and resulting geopolitics. Moreover, this relational approach casts doubt on the globalist methodological tendencies that portray the materialisation of capitalism in the Global South inevitably as the imposition of policies from outside. Regardless of the positive or negative depiction of the global as a modernising or destructive force, this globalist methodological orientation problematically leaves little or no room for the agency of domestic forces. Hence, apart from overcoming methodological nationalism and exceptionalism, this relational method accounts for national shaping factors and remains sensitive to the gravity of local dynamics in the process of capitalist development in contemporary Iran. In the next four sections of the chapter, I shall outline theoretical concepts necessary for this relational method that systematically considers the interplay of global and local dynamics and national and international factors and thoroughly historicises and relativises nation-states vis-à-vis subnational, supranational and transnational aspects (van der Linden, 2008: 7).

## Totality, internal relations and capitalism

In the radical social ontology of the philosophy of internal relations, the connection between all spheres of the social world is viewed as internal and necessary, not external and contingent. By opposing the idea that objects are subsistent, pre-existing and independent entities that are similar to billiard balls that might run into one another, this ontology calls for the study of any object as 'relations, containing in themselves, as integral elements of what they are, those parts with which we tend to see them externally tied' (Ollman, 2003: 25, see also Morton, 2013b). With the concept of internal relations, the problem is therefore never 'how to relate separate entities but how to disentangle a relation or group of relations from the total and necessary configuration in which they exist' (Ollman, 1976: 48). What follows from this is that if there is a dialectical interaction between all parts of the social world, we ultimately engage with the notion of the *totality*. The crucial point, however, is that the totality is not simply the sum of all parts, but is an evolving, self-forming whole in which parts/instances are distinct, mutually conditioning moments of this singular phenomenon (McMichael, 1990: 391). In other words, in this perspective, the observation of how parts are conditioned by the whole and how parts condition one another does not lead to the discovery of the whole since parts 'reveal and realise the changing whole' (McMichael, 1990: 391). Rather than being an a priori entity, the whole is thus an emergent totality, which materialises through the action of its parts since this relational understanding does not assume the whole prior to the parts. Against the conventional comparative method that considers the objects of investigation as 'discrete building blocks that can be compared or contrasted', a method of analysis which is advanced from this ontology 'focuses on exploring the manifold relations that exist between things and the movement of these relations over time' (Hanieh, 2018: 15). Accordingly, this relational method argues that parts are only comparable if they are seen as 'historically connected and mutually conditioning', constituted in relation to one another 'and in relation to the whole formed through their inter-relationship' (McMichael, 2000: 671). In a word, this approach does not only imply that 'every phenomenon can be conceived as a moment of a whole', but it also avoids 'hypostatising the whole as a reality above or separate from its parts, by rejecting 'the whole (e.g. the global scale) into an a priori entity that is served from the mutual internal relations of its parts (e.g. other scales), sitting above them like some form of *deus ex machina*' (Hanieh, 2018: 17; Bieler and Morton, 2018: 8–20).

Drawing on the above discussion, I perceive capitalism as a totality. Before proceeding further, we need to define capitalism. In simple terms, 'capitalism is a system of competitive accumulation based on wage labour' (Davidson, 2010a: 88). In Marx's conception of historical materialism, human beings repeatedly and purposefully apply labour to nature to produce necessary elements for their survival. This labour, which is necessarily social, is 'a process between man and nature, a process by which man, through his own action, mediates, regulates and controls the metabolism between himself and nature … in order to appropriate the materials of nature in a form adapted to his own needs' (Marx, 1867/1990: 283). This labour process consists of three elements: (1) purposeful work, (2) the objects of labour or raw materials, and (3) the instruments of work. With the advance of primitive societies due to the development of more efficient tools and methods of production, this social labour produces goods beyond the survival and reproduction needs of humans. Human struggles for control over this social surplus product provide the basis for the development of classes by generating two sets of relations. The '*vertical* relationships of exploitation *between* exploiters and exploited' are the result of the attempts of the minority ruling classes to subject the direct-producing majority to their dominance to produce a surplus. The second set of relations is '*horizontal* relationships *within* between the exploiting and exploited classes themselves, which in both cases involve both cooperation and competition' (Davidson, 2016: 205; Brenner, 1986). Unlike other modes of production where the labour process is organised for the purpose of consumption, under capitalism production occurs for creating value. In capitalism, as Rosa Luxemburg (1913/1951: 42) contends:

> the whole process of production as well as of reproduction is ruled by value relationships. Capitalist production is not the production of consumer goods, nor is it merely the production of commodities: it is pre-eminently the

production of surplus value. Expanding reproduction, from a capitalist point of view, is expanding production of surplus value, though it takes place in the forms of commodity production and is thus in the last instance the production of consumer goods.

The essence of capitalism therefore is this endless production of surplus value or, as Marx (1867/1990: 431) metaphorically expresses, 'Accumulate, accumulate! That is Moses and the Prophets.'

As Marx meticulously explains in *Capital Volume II* (1885/1992: 109–43), the circuit of capital for the purpose of the production of surplus value involves several stages, with the following basic form: $M – C (Mp + Lp) \dots P \dots C' – M'$. The accumulation of capital begins when a capitalist uses their money (M) as capital to exchange it with two sets of commodities (C): means of production such as raw materials, machinery and land (Mp) and labour power (Lp). By combining the labour of workers with machines and raw materials in the process of production (P), a new commodity with an increased value is produced (C'). While the labourer always works under the control of the capitalist and the product of the worker belongs to the capitalist, the worker (Lp) creates this enhanced value because 'the value of labour-power, and the value which that labour-power valorises in the labour process, are two entirely different magnitudes' (1867/1990: 291–2 and 300). In the labour process, not only does the labour power create the value for the reproduction of the worker and their family, but it also has a particular use-value that creates new value, surplus value, for the capitalist through a volume of unpaid labour to the worker (Harvey, 2010: 124). The capitalist then appropriates this enlarged value by exchanging it in the market for greater money (M'), which is higher than the initial capital. Because capitalists are in fierce competition for dominance of the market for a higher realisation of surplus value of their products, competition is thus the inner nature of the capitalist system. This competition in turn intensifies the compulsion to accumulate or the unquenchable thirst for surplus-value extraction. Therefore, rather than being consumed for luxury goods, the extracted surplus value is continuously reinvested in the same circuit for a greater new surplus value.

The bourgeoisie as a ruling class in capitalism is not a homogeneous class as it comprises various groups, considered here as class *fractions*. Based on the above schematic representation of the general circuit of capital, three basic moments or subcircuits can be identified: the productive circuit, the commodity circuit and the finance circuit. In the productive circuit, a section of the capitalist class produces new commodities. In the commodity circuit, another section of the capitalist class realises surplus value by selling commodities. In the finance circuit, banks and other financial institutions deal with money and the reproduction of surplus value (Hanieh, 2011: 18–19).

As such, within the capitalist class, industrial capital, commercial/merchant capital and financial capital fractions can be recognised. As will be shown below shortly, this class could also be divided into different fractions by virtue of the orientation of their activities, including international, internationally oriented and nationally oriented capital. It is also important to point out that the capitalist class as the ruling class cannot be limited to the legal owner of the means of production, nor should we accept a sharp dichotomy between 'private' capital and 'state' capital. Because if we define a capitalist as someone who personifies or gives form to and executes the dictates of capital 'as self-expanding value', many individual personnel of state institutions can be part of the capitalist class. Therefore, many bureaucrats, like the legal owners of means of production, 'function as embodiments of capital, serving its (and, consequently, their own) best interests in whatever way their current positions allow. They all work to expand surplus value and benefit materially when that happens' (Ollman, 2003: 199).

As should be clear by now, the creation of a class of wage labourers is a precondition for capitalist competition and capital accumulation (Davidson, 2010a: 88). The meaning of wage labour needs to be unpacked given the misinterpretations surrounding Marx's definition of the term. By referring to passages in Marx's work that argue that the fundamental conditions of capitalist production depend on the emergence of two types of commodity owners, i.e., the owners of means of production and free sellers of labour power, many assert that 'a wage-labourer is one who, divorced from any means of subsistence, is forced to sell her labour-power to others'. In other words, a 'wage-labourer is dispossessed labour, labour divorced from the means of production, with labour-power as a commodity' (Banaji, 2010: 53). On the basis of this simple abstract/ideal-type model, the proponents of this definition of a wage labourer argue that, for Marx, wage labour always takes 'free' form, i.e., free wage labour. However, at a deeper level of abstraction, as Banaji argues (2010: 54), 'in the process of Marx's analysis, as a "concrete" category, wage-labour was, for Marx, capital-positing, capital-creating labour. "Wage labour, here, in the strict economic sense," Marx wrote, "is capital-positing, capital-producing labour."' This capital-producing labour cannot be reduced to 'free' labour in the marketplace since the commodification of labour power for capital can take several forms. By reference to the history of capitalism that shows significant flexibility in the structuring of production and in the forms of labour for the production of surplus value, Marcel van der Linden (2008: 32–4) correctly points out that 'there is a large class of people within capitalist society, whose labour power is commodified in many *different* ways', including chattel slaves, forced labour, semi-free labour, child labour, share-croppers, small artisans, self-employed, as well as non-wage activities that workers depend upon such as the farming of small plots of land or unpaid family labour. The common denominator for all these subaltern workers is 'the *coerced* commodification of their labour power'. Given this, the position of Marxists who share 'the liberal conception of capitalism which sees the sole basis of accumulation in the individual wage-earner conceived as free labourer' is highly untenable. This liberal understanding of wage labourers 'obliterates a great deal of capitalist history' and erases the contribution of the above-mentioned groups whose labour power has been commodified differently from the classic 'free' form (Banaji, 2010: 145).

For Marx, capitalism thus is not a neutral arena of exchange, but a set of *social relations* between humans – it appears as a relation between things or between humans and things – that constantly reproduces the subordination of labourers to the owners of capital (Selwyn, 2014: 2). In addition to the capitalist class and the working class with numerous fractions and groups, capitalism generates other social classes, including the middle class and petty bourgeoisie. Members of the middle class include senior officials, managers and professionals. Similar to the working class, the middle class is deprived of owning the means of production, but its members exercise some degree of authority and possess relative autonomy in the labour process. This fundamental feature distinguishes the middle class from the working class. The owners of small enterprises, usually fewer than ten workers, who themselves work alongside other workers (paid or unpaid family labour), constitute the petty bourgeoisie. What distinguishes a petit bourgeois from a bourgeois is that the former does not engage in the process of reinvestment at the extended level because the extracted surplus value from the exploitation of workers is used for the maintenance of their small business and unproductive consumption.

Capitalism as a world-historical system subordinates everything to its predominant drive to competitive accumulation, always therefore striving towards universalism. Yet, given that factors such as 'the technology of production, structures of distribution, modes and forms of consumption, the value, quantities and qualities of labour power, as well as all necessary physical and social infrastructures must all be consistent with each other' for the production and realisation of value and surplus value, capitalism produces different territorial and regional configurations (Harvey, 2006: 416–17). That is to say, the logic of capital accumulation contradictorily yields geographical differentiation, resulting in the inevitable uneven development by generating social differences, inequalities and processes. These economic impacts of uneven development in effect block the formation of a single fraction of global capital and a single global state, therefore generating the territorial configuration of the state and the state system (Anievas, 2008: 200–2). At the same time, the structural contradictions of the capitalist mode of production generate periodic crises. The tendency of the rate of profit to fall as the central chronic tendency of the system manifests itself in recurring crises of overaccumulation is defined as 'surpluses of capital and of labour power side by side without there apparently being any means to bring them profitably together to accomplish socially useful tasks' (Harvey, 2004: 63). Thanks to the uneven geographical development of capitalism, one way of averting and overcoming the crises of overaccumulation is spatial reorganisation, or what is often referred to as the 'spatial fix' (Harvey, 2006: 426–38). To concretely demonstrate these dynamics, in the next section, I shall look at the post-1970s spatial reorganisation of global capitalism.

## Internationalisation of capital and neoliberalism

To grasp the post-1970s spatial reorganisation of global capitalism we first need to briefly look at the structure of the post-WWII global economy dominated by the state capitalist model of accumulation. After the Great Depression of the 1930s and the subsequent devastating Second World War (WWII), in the Global North, the Fordist regime of material accumulation was implemented to revive growth, which necessitated the need for direct state intervention in the process of production. Although Fordist methods of mass production – the factory system with standardised mass production lines – led to an initial dramatic rise in labour productivity, it brought a high degree of alienation and deadening boredom at work due to the 'unprecedented degree of unskilled repetitive labour'. To overcome the problem, rising consumption was considered to be the answer. Put differently, under the Fordism regime 'dissatisfaction was transformed into demand and regulated through annual pay bargaining', which further augmented the power of organised labour. After two decades, it became obvious that this method of production was costly for capital because it required investing an ever-increasing amount in machinery and raw materials in the presence of a high cost of variable capital thanks to the effectiveness of working-class struggles. Consequently, despite growing capital investment in mechanisation, the rate of productivity declined sharply between 1968 and 1973 (Holloway, 1996: 24). The refusal of individual capitalists to invest in the absence of profitable opportunities brought about an increase in surpluses of capital and labour, i.e., the crisis of overaccumulation.

During this period, the international context of uneven development fostered the import substitution industrialisation (ISI) model of development for many 'Third World' countries by breaking from the colonial model of the international market. Consequently, under 'autarkic state capitalism' with the objective of building up a heavy industrial base, the colonial institutional configurations were largely dismantled. Unlike the class compromise between capitalists and workers mediated by the state in the Global North, in most of the 'periphery', the state-led fostering of national capital often treated working classes as a mere instrument of accumulation for 'grandiose catch-up development' (Selwyn, 2014: 29–53). Its chief outcome was the nullification of the attempts of subaltern classes to be part of the state's decision-making processes. That said, the struggle of these classes compelled many developing states of the postcolonial order to take a range of measures to improve the living standards of the poor and working classes through the provision of food and other subsidies to the poorest layers of the population and job security in the public sector and state-owned enterprises (SOEs). This development model soon reached a crisis for two reasons. First, the rising material demands of subaltern classes gradually decreased the profit margin of the (new) ruling class in the Global South. More importantly, the ISI regime of accumulation paradoxically relied on the import of productive capital, machines and semi-finished goods from more advanced capitalist states. The central problem was the inability of developing countries to generate adequate foreign exchange to finance the import of these intermediate and capital goods, which often escalated the balance of payment deficits. As import controls gave rise to a crisis of accumulation, borrowing from international money markets was the projected solution. In some countries exporting raw materials and foodstuffs could partially avoid such an outcome, as in the case of Iran since the export of oil was considered to be a reliable source of financing for imports of the ISI-required goods. Nonetheless, the instability of raw materials markets and their price fluctuations did not fundamentally solve the crisis tendencies associated with this accumulation strategy. Ultimately, this structural problem resulted in the debt crisis of the 1980s in the Global South (Yaghmaian, 2002: 195–8).

To revive profit following this global crisis, in recent decades, the internationalisation of production and finance has been implemented in the global economy. The rise of financial offshore markets and the deregulation of national money markets and financial operators have blurred the differences between them. This has led to the emergence of an integrated global financial market with new characteristics:

> (a) the blurring of the line, in terms of ownership structures and market activities, between banking, securities and insurance industries, a process referred to as desegmentation; (b) the liberalisation of traditional cartel arrangements in national sectors through domestic market-orientated reform programmes, understood as marketisation; and (c) the integration of financial markets across traditionally closed national jurisdictions.
>
> Underhill, 1997 cited in Bieler, 2006: 47–8

In a word, this spatial fix has freed the shackles of large financial firms to invest in the world market. In production, the old regime has been replaced by a new flexible model through which different stages of a production process have been placed at several widely scattered locations. This has ultimately altered structures of production in every country and region, resulting in a profound integration of national economies into the global economy. This reorganisation of production has proceeded through two different forms of outsourcing, namely FDI and arm's length. The process of dividing production processes into ever finer vertical and horizontal segments and locating their stages of production in various countries has resulted in the creation of global value chains (GVCs). This new global architecture has mostly been achieved through state-negotiated international trade/investment agreements. Initially, several rounds of World Trade Organization (WTO) negotiations, starting from the mid-1980s, aggressively pursued the opening up of all economies to manufacturing goods, services, public procurement and investment. Since 2003, following the collapse of the Doha Round of WTO negotiations, the extended free trade agenda in the format of bilateral free trade agreements between countries and regions has been enthusiastically promoted (Bieler, 2014: 4). As part of this global restructuring, developing countries have abandoned ISI in favour of export-oriented industrialisation (EOI) to facilitate participating in the GVCs controlled by multinational corporations (MNCs). While through this process the world market as the horizon of capital has been fully realised, this by no means implies the end of the regeneration of spatial differentiations within the world market since the internationalisation of production and finance has paradoxically intensified the uneven pattern of development between different regions, cities and the countryside and within countries (Hanieh, 2018: 10–11; Saull, 2012: 333).

The economic doctrine of neoliberalism has been the ideological backbone of the internationalisation of capital because, as a set of policies, it is envisioned to promote the deregulation of all economic activities to facilitate the free flow of capital across borders (Hanieh, 2010: 82). Under neoliberal policies, efficiency and price stability have become new priorities for governments across the globe. The doctrine has advocated the privatisation of SOEs and the liberalisation and deregulation of the economy at the national level. Furthermore, the rejection of the policy of full employment and universal rights of healthcare and education in favour of market freedom has been at the centre stage of this economic dogma (Bieler, 2000: 22). Overall, this neoliberal economic package includes fiscal policy discipline, removal of public subsidies, tax reform, introduction of market-based interest rates, competitive exchange rates, trade liberalisation, liberalisation of FDI, privatisation of SOEs and a move away from import substitution (in the case of developing countries), deregulation and introduction of private property rights (Hill, Wald and Guiney, 2016: 130–3). Emerging out of 'the systemic needs of capitalist social reality' rather than 'an ideological choice of the capitalist class (or a fraction thereof)', neoliberalism has therefore been a means for the reconstitution and strengthening of class power in favour of capital (Hanieh, 2013: 14; Harvey, 2005: 19).

By viewing capitalism as a totality, neoliberalism cannot be reduced to either certain policies and ideas generated by Western intellectuals and poli-cymakers (e.g., Klein, 2007; Harvey, 2005; Ong, 2006) or a new stage of capitalist development that first emerged in the economy of the United States and Europe (e.g., Robinson, 2001; Duménil and Lévy, 2004).[3] These perva-sive Marxist and poststructuralist articulations of neoliberalism have mean-ingfully contributed to our understanding of the mechanisms and dynamics of capitalism in recent decades, but their heavy focus on North America and Western Europe runs the risk of reproducing what John M. Hobson (2007; 2012) calls 'critical subliminal Eurocentrism'.[4] In contrast, my argument is that some members of the ruling class in developing countries have deployed neoliberal policies linked to the new alternative developmental strategy in order to revive capital accumulation and stabilising/reimposing class order to encounter the post-1970s economic crisis and the related political insta-bilities. This means that global neoliberalism is neither simply 'a projection of Northern ideology or policy' nor 'a by-product of the internal dynam-ics of the global North' (Connell and Dados, 2014: 124). Rather, based on the notion of *emergent totality*, we should view it as 'a re-weaving of worldwide economic and social relations' (Connell and Dados, 2014: 124) whereby both advanced capitalist states and developing countries, more specifically their ruling classes, have participated in the reconstruction of the global economy to tackle the same pressures and crisis tendencies that I explain above.

Nonetheless, subject to the particularity of domestic class structure and hence vertical antagonisms between various capitalist fractions as well as class struggles from below, the outcome of the process of neoliberalisa-tion has been neither predetermined nor inevitable. Consequently, as an inherently struggle-driven process, the product of neoliberal renovation of capitalism in any given society is unique and often hybrid despite sharing universal common features. The notion of hybridity might echo the key arguments of the uneven and combined development school of interna-tional historical sociology (e.g., Rosenberg, 2006; Matin, 2007; Anievas and Nişancıoğlu, 2015). In recent years, by drawing on Trotsky's analy-sis of the development of capitalism in Russia, this intellectual current has made a case for the causal significance of 'the international' in development, proclaiming that the process in any given society proceeds by its interactive relation with other developmentally differentiated societies. In other words, for them, development is 'neither unilinear, nor homogeneous, nor homogenizing but interactively "multilinear" ' (Matin, 2012a: 460). However, it is highly problematic to analyse concrete cases of combinations while remaining at the level of 'the international' – as it is put forward by these scholars – since the territorial confines of states 'are where the specific combinations take place'. This is because if what happens in each society is an example of a universal process, the uneven and combined development school cannot explain the particularity of development in any given society (Davidson, 2009: 19). Put differently, whereas unevenness is the universal feature of capitalism, combinations are a feature of certain societies. This inability ultimately relates to the fact that the uneven and combined development school overlooks 'the spatio-temporal dynamics and causal effects of state and class agents' in the wide variety of processes through which capitalism has become constituted and restructured around the world (Bieler and Morton, 2018: 99). In the next section, I will explore the impacts of the internationalisation of capital on class and state formation.

## Class and state formation under neoliberalism

Being actively parts of this emergent totality, the process of capital accumulation, the patterns of class formation and the nature and functions of the state in both developed and developing countries have been substantially transformed. With regard to class formation, the internationalisation of capital has led to the emergence and reconfiguration of capital fractions. Particularly, three ruling class fractions can be identified: international capital fraction, internationally oriented capital fraction, and national capital fraction. It should be noted that my notion of international capital fraction is different from William Robinson's transnational capitalist class (TCC). For Robinson (2004: 51), the TCC as a global ruling class is both a class-in-itself and class-for-itself since it has developed 'a subjective consciousness of itself'. It is composed of 'the transnational corporations and financial institutions, the elites that manage the supranational economic planning agencies' and 'major forces in dominant political parties, media conglomerates, and technocrat elites and state managers' in the developed countries of the North and the developing countries of the South (Robinson and Harris, 2000: 12). This notion is flawed for several reasons. First, highlighting the increasing level of transnationalised economic processes does not automatically imply the formation of a *single* global fraction of transnational capital that self-consciously pursues a unified objective of a global capitalist project. This conclusion can only be deduced if there is an unsophisticated causal chain of 'class place–class consciousness–class action'. An emphasis on the class place ignores the fact that the constitution of class interests and class actions also requires cultural and political mediation. While there might be some political, ideological and economic conditions for the formation of a TCC globally, these conditions largely remain unconnected (Hirsch and Wissel, 2011: 9, 14–15 and 23; Anievas, 2008: 197). Second, due to intense competition between individual capitals, the idea of a monolithic and relatively homogeneous capitalist class even at the national level has been contested both theoretically and empirically. Surely, for the same reason, a unified TCC cannot be recognised 'as it underestimates the horizontal socioeconomic and political competitiveness and contestations between individual capitals' (Taylor, 2017: 29; Block, 2001: 218). Underestimating this factor leads to the following problematic statement:

> the emergence of a transnational capitalist class (TCC) meaning that it is no longer possible to simply speak in terms of a rivalry between 'German' capital, 'French' capital, or 'American' capital, etc. Transnational capital, too, relies on the legal and institutional support by states and international institutions of global governance, but different fractions of capital are no longer defined by their particular relationship to a specific state.
>
> Bieler and Morton, 2015: 105

In contrast, if we assume that competition continues between and among capitalists in an international environment, for these international capitals it 'would be damaging to abandon their national bases because of the many advantages these bases provide, for example contracts with the military, export subsidies and access to intelligence information' (Hack, 2002 cited in Hirsch and Wissel, 2011: 11), especially in times of crisis when struggles for domination and conquest of particular markets intensify between various capitals. Hence, instead of using the transnational capitalist class, it seems more appropriate to speak of international fractions of capital in plural as they are transnationally oriented but still nationally rooted. This means that it is more convenient to talk about international fractions of the German capital, French capital, American capital, etc.

The internationalisation of capital does not imply the disappearance of national production, but it has enormous impacts on capital fractions that are more nationally rooted than international capital fractions, i.e., national capital and internationally oriented capital fractions (Bieler, 2000: 47). National capital fractions are spawned by national production that produce for the domestic market. While internationally oriented capital fractions still largely stem from national production that mostly produces for export, they advocate EOI strategy and aim to integrate into GVCs. Internationally oriented capital fractions, similar to international fractions, advocate and support neoliberal policies, while national capital fractions vehemently oppose the entrance of foreign capital and international competition despite advocating and implementing some neoliberal policies. Equally, the internationalisation of capital has reconstructed and reshaped other social classes, particularly the working class. As well as creating new international strata of workers employed by MNCs who operate through global chains of production and distribution, privatisation and deregulation of the labour market have directly contributed to the expansion of informalisation of work and the creation of the precariat as a growing segment of the working class (Bieler, 2014: 1–2). Again, as neoliberal renovation of capitalism is subjected to the domestic class structure and the balance of class forces in a given society, which are often unique, we thus need to consider the particularity of the reconfiguration of these capital fractions and other social class forces in each state.

The internationalisation of capital has equally had major repercussions for the state. The state is a set of institutional forms, which is internally related to the process of capital accumulation as well as capitalists' class interests (Ollman, 2003: 201–2). This means relating the imperatives of capital accumulation and its associated class formation to the potentialities of politics in order to understand changes in the nature and form of the state (Ayubi, 1996: 14). In other words, any restructuring of the economic sphere and the subsequent reconfiguration of the capitalist class is thus reflected in state institutions. Since the internationalisation of finance and production has engendered and reconfigured various class fractions, these ruling class forces have been involved in the reorganisation of state institutions for the realisation of their class interests. This conceptualisation of the state renounces the 'common sense' perception that views neoliberalism as an anti-statist endeavour. While the state and its agents are accused of being 'wasteful', 'self-serving' and 'irrational', the state is paradoxically viewed as the key instigator of reform under neoliberalism (Davies, 2018: 273–4). Since 'the state is already dedicated to the defence of capitalism in a general sense', neoliberalism, as a form of capitalist restructuring, thus demands that 'the activity of the various state institutions needs to be decisively turned in a specific and different direction' (Davidson, 2017: 618). Hence, rather than being about 'institutional retreat or subordination of public and private actors to the discipline of disembedded markets', neoliberal practices aim to create, legitimise and consolidate new institutional capacities and mechanisms of control (Konings, 2012: 618). It is also important to point out that state institutions should not merely be limited to formal apparatuses. As a result, alongside attempts for the reorganisation of the formal institutions of the state, civil society organisations are either created, attacked, or banned and the 'capillary networks' of various organisations of civil society (publishing houses, newspapers, magazines, periodicals, news agencies and so forth) are utilised by ruling class fractions for the articulation of this strategy of class power in the neoliberal era (Bieler and Morton, 2018: 72–3).

Broadly speaking, whereas in the Global North, under neoliberalism, the priority has been given to the abolition of the post-war class compromise and the dismantling of the institutions of the welfare state, in the Global South, the ruling classes have endeavoured to eliminate the provision of food and other subsidies to the poorest layers of the population and end job security in the public sector and SOEs, which were achieved as a result of struggles of the working class and the poor. To realise these objectives, the reorganisation and substitution of the institutional forms of previously dominant state capitalism have been pursued through re-tasking the role of the state in the name of good governance and efficiency. That is to say, while there has been a push for 'better governance', 'accountability' and 'transparency' everywhere, there is no pure instance of the neoliberal state as the particularity of class structures and the balance of class forces in different societies have produced a unique form of a neoliberal state in any given society.

So far, by focusing on the spatial dimension of global neoliberalism, I have endeavoured to challenge several pervasive methodological tendencies. To counter methodological nationalism and exceptionalism, I called for situating national development projects and their associated class and state formations within the broader context of crisis and transformation in global capitalism. Moreover, to recover the significance and agency of the Global South, I argued that it is essential to survey dynamics beyond the Global North to show that the periphery is another significant space of global capitalism where neoliberalism has evolved. By conceptualising neoliberalism as a global response to the crisis of the late 1970s and the early 1980s with the participation of the ruling classes of all states, I also intended to accentuate that there is necessarily agency unfolding beyond America–Europe. However, this focus on the spatial dimension does not mean ignoring the hierarchical structure of the global economy and the ranked geopolitical balance of forces because of the time dimension in capitalism. Indeed, these factors have placed certain states/actors in privileged positions to shape global neoliberalism to perpetuate the hierarchical order and international inequality. This links us to the relationship between the internationalisation of capital, imperialism and geopolitics, which is the topic of the next section.

## Neoliberalism, imperialism and geopolitics

Historical materialism traditionally positions geopolitics within the wider concern/question of the relationship between capitalism and the international system of states. This mode of inquiry has resulted in the return of the study of empire and imperialism since the beginning of the new millennium. For Negri and Hardt (2000), the deterritorialised character of the reconstitution of contemporary global capitalism as an empire means the end of imperialism and geopolitical competitions. On the other hand, Panitch and Gindin (2004; 2012) assert the significance of the formation of an informal empire under the leadership of the American state that has successfully reconstructed states around the globe to accept responsibility for managing their domestic capitalist order in line with the direction of the international capitalist order. Despite occasional US military interventions in 'rogue' states to shore up the capitalist system, for Panitch and Gindin the cooperation between states is the key product of the increasingly integrated American-led international economic order. Accordingly, this US policing role has nothing to do with geopolitical competition between states, particularly rivalries between advanced capitalist powers.

The US invasion of Iraq has further generated a debate among other Marxists regarding the relations between the 'logics' of capital and state and the notion of imperialism. A group of Marxist scholars argues in favour of the existence of a fusion of the two logics but cautiously calls for accepting some degree of autonomy in the interlinking of the logics of capital and state (Callinicos, 2007; 2009; Harvey, 2003). This 'new imperialism' literature, influenced by the 'Lenin–Bukharin' thesis, stresses that imperialism should be 'understood as the intersection of economic and geopolitical competition' and rivalries among great powers arising from the changes in the structure of capitalism (Callinicos, 2009: 16; Harvey, 2003: 26). According to this account, as the post-WWII restructuring of global capitalism led to the rise of Germany and Japan and, in recent years, China, the United States has been eager to deploy military power to warn off potential 'peer competitors' as in the case of the Iraq War which meant to maintain American hegemony through the control of the supply of oil in the global market (Harvey, 2003: 19–24; Callinicos, 2009: 15).

In contrast to the two logics thesis, political Marxism emphatically defends a divorce between the logics of capital and state (Teschke and Lacher, 2007; Teschke, 2003; Lacher, 2002; Brenner, 2006). From this perspective, 'capitalism is structured by an international system because it was born in the context of a pre-existing system of territorial states', meaning that 'there simply is no straight line from capitalism to any specific geo-territorial matrix or set of international relations' (Teschke and Lacher, 2007: 574). The theory of uneven and combined development in its transhistorical formula agrees with political Marxism that 'the plurality of the geopolitical spaces is not co-emergent with capitalism, and in contrast to the logics of power approach, it refuses to derive geopolitics from within a theory of capital' (Tansel, 2016: 499). However, to explain the existence of the political multiplicity of geopolitical systems, the uneven and combined development theory proposes a universal structure of social development (Rosenberg, 2005, 2006; Matin, 2013b), which in turn reduces its explanatory power to analyse capitalism, imperialism, and the relations between capitalism *and* geopolitics (Tansel, 2016: 499; Smith, 2006: 182).

From a neo-Gramscian perspective, Andreas Bieler and Adam Morton (2013/2014; 2015; 2018) provide another alternative historical materialist account built around three main propositions: the internality of the dynamics of capitalism and geopolitics, the constant need of capital for an outward expansion to create hothouse conditions for capital accumulation, and the importance of examining the formation of specific forms of state. In the case of the Iraq War, they thus focus on the analysis of the class struggles between different transnational and national fractions of capital inside the US state within the structural context of the constant pressure for capitalist expansion, claiming that the invasion was 'the spatial ordering of the built environment through militarism and other mechanisms of finance linked to specific fractions within the U.S. state form' (Bieler and Morton, 2018: 215–16).

Whilst this reinvigorated debate on the concepts of imperialism and materialist geopolitics to decipher contemporary conflicts has hugely contributed to our understanding of global capitalism, a number of pitfalls can be identified. First, the two positions on the relations between the 'logics' of capital and state are not convincing from the standpoint of capitalism as a totality. Political Marxism's pure historical contingency on the grounds that the current state system as a social form incapable of incorporating into and adapting to the capitalist mode of production makes little sense given that capitalism has triumphantly seized and fundamentally reconstructed many pre-modern relations, social forms and institutions (Callinicos, 2009: 80). As Bieler and Morton (2013/2014: 26) rightly point out, articulating imperialism as 'a hypostatisation of the two logics of capitalism and geopolitics … which are conceived as always-already analytically separate elements that are then subsequently combined' is equally problematic. More importantly, this formulation ultimately goes against the theoretical assumptions of the fusion of the two logics power thesis. This is because if one argues that the state system 'can and should not be deduced from the concept of capital', and then stresses that 'it exerts its own set of determinations, quite independently of capital', in effect it denies the notion of totality (Pozo-Martin, 2007: 556–7; Davidson, 2010a: 82). Second, the rejection of any specific geo-territorial matrix in capitalism or formulating the relations between states, specifically advanced capitalist powers, as either continuous rivalry or amicable cooperation does not correlate well with the reality of neoliberal global capitalism. Rather, the dialectic of rivalry and cooperation better explains this relationship. Third, these accounts often highlight military domination, but imperialism is equally '*a question of exploitation–one that necessitates, and is principally bound up in, forms of economic domination*' [emphasis in original] (Hanieh, 2013: 13). Relatedly, alongside the use of military force, we need to include other geoeconomic mechanisms and tools such as economic sanctions as complements or partial substitutes of political/military domination. Finally, these accounts do little to challenge the unsophisticated narratives of viewing peripheral states as only passive battlegrounds and victims of Western domination. The inadequacy of incorporating the agency and resistance of peripheral states/actors thus makes these theories susceptible to the charge of 'critical subliminal Eurocentrism' (Hobson, 2007; 2012; Brewer, 1990: 89).

Based on this critical engagement, I propose four propositions/claims which will be central to my analysis. First, in the age of the internationalisation of capital, imperialism needs to be perceived as 'the tendency of dominant capital to increasingly draw the world market in on itself, forcibly extracting profits from all corners of the globe' (Hanieh, 2013: 12). Second, drawing again on the philosophy of internal relations, the 'logics' of state and capital or corporate and policy-planning networks should not be treated as things that are externally related to each other, but we need to situate the full meaning of each in its internal relationship with the others (Bieler and Morton, 2015: 100; Morton, 2007: 606). Taking these two propositions together, we can then argue because of this relation of interiority between capitalism and geopolitics, in the contemporary world, geopolitical confrontations should be viewed in relation and response to the international movement of capital and the processes of neoliberalism at national, regional and global levels. Third, as explained above, to counter recurrent crises in capitalism, spatial fixes are often pursued, but these constant reorganisations for the facilitation of endless capital accumulation, in turn, generate the dialectic of competition and cooperation between states. As Adam Hanieh (2013: 13) succinctly points out with reference to the neoliberal era:

> On the one hand, the internationalisation of capital has generated heightened levels of competition between the large corporations that dominate the global economy, and this is refracted through increased interstate competition. Consequently, inter-imperialist rivalry remains a salient feature of the world market. On the other hand, the very nature of internationalisation demands greater coordination and cooperation between states in order to maintain the required conditions for accumulation as a whole.

Finally, some peripheral states, particularly regional powers, exploit the geopolitical spaces generated as a result of this dual tendency of rivalry and cooperation between the global centres of power to exercise agency. Though this allows us to incorporate the agency of peripheral states/actors in the analysis of the relationship between capitalist development and geo-politics, we should not overlook the hierarchal structure of contemporary capitalism, which I now turn to examine.

Due to the weight of historical time, the United States and the European Union are still at the apex of the system with more effective tools at their disposal to utilise global neoliberal restructuring to reproduce the dominance of the West over the 'Rest'. In the period between the early 1980s to 2007, alongside pushing for neoliberal free trade agreements, the United States used military actions (most notably the invasion of Iraq) and economic sanctions against 'rogue' states to consolidate its hegemonic power under neoliberalism. Likewise, the European Union on behalf of its international capital deployed free trade agreements and economic sanctions to materialise its interests which were often in line with the United States, despite occasional noticeable disagreements and conflicts. In this period, because economic sanctions as a punitive tool were largely employed against small economies or those with a limited integration into the global economy, the cost of joining these sanctions for other states was minimal. Moreover, the sale of oil due to its importance for stabilising global capitalism and the total block of targeted countries' access to the global financial system were often exempted from sanctions.

In recent decades, because of the internationalisation of capital, new centres of capital accumulation outside this historic core of the capitalist system have emerged. In particular, the 2008 global financial crisis has acted as a catalyst for the rise of China and, to some degree, Russia. China and Russia are not yet dominant imperial powers but can be viewed as 'nascent empires' or 'empires in formation'. In contrast to the United States, China's economic pre-eminence does not yet have a military correlate and Russia still lacks the required economic weight, despite having the geopolitical-military element of imperialism (Katz, 2022: 173–9). The case of China requires some attention here. Following the 1978 economic liberalisation of Deng Xiaoping, China had become the major destination of FDI and the workshop of the world based on low-wage and high-labour content forms of production. Although the 1999 'Going Out/Going Global' policy (Gallagher and Qi, 2021: 260) resulted in a ninefold upsurge in China's outward direct investment and a triple rise in its outward direct investment stock from 2003 to 2007 (Zhang, 2009: 81–2), the real transformation occurred after 2008. To recover from the 2008 crisis with the loss of around 30 million jobs in the export industries, instead of pursuing a politics of austerity, China started major infrastructural investments (particularly in the built environment) and initiated plans to transform its economy to produce high-value goods through capital-intensive means (Harvey, 2020: 64–8). This led to a flood of China's export of capital abroad, especially after the launch of the Belt and Road Initiative (BRI) in 2013 (Gallagher and Qi, 2021: 260). China allocates considerable financial resources for the initiative, including the New Silk Road Fund and the Asia Infrastructure Investment Bank with US\$40 billion and US\$100 billion funds respectively. Other financial development institutions such as the China Development Bank, the Bank of China, Industrial and Commercial Bank of China, China Construction Bank, and the Agricultural Bank of China 'are also financing various projects along the BRI' (Kamel, 2018: 77). By 'lending money to countries to buy up surplus Chinese product (steel, transport equipment, and cement)', the BRI aims to earmark China's surplus capital through commercial loans 'to rebuild the transport and communications connectivity of the Eurasian continent with offshoots across Africa and into Latin America' (Harvey, 2020: 92 and 94). While commercial loans constitute most of China's overseas investment flows, China's FDI has also increased exponentially since 2008. In 2019, in terms of FDI stock, China was 'the largest investor in least-developed countries, the top investor in developing Asia, the fourth-largest investor in Russia, Eastern Europe, and Central Asia, and the fifth-largest investor in Africa' (Gallagher and Qi 2021: 261). According to Ye (2022), 'in 2012, China's outbound foreign direct investment (FDI) was \$82 billion, but in 2020, it was \$154 billion, ranked as the world's number one overseas investor'. As well as solving China's capital surplus problem, the BRI has a geopolitical angle since it has the potential to substantially grow the influence of China in Africa and Latin America and facilitate its control over Asia (Harvey, 2020: 93–5). Despite the success of China's Going Global strategy, some cautions need to be considered as this does not imply dominance of the world economy. This is because

> US capital, multilateral institutions and European investors have more strength, prestige and networks worldwide than their Chinese counterparts. Western loans and investments are still preferred to China's, whether in Europe, Africa or Asia. In addition, the US and its allies, such as the European Union (EU), Japan and South Korea, have technological strength, developed economies and sustainable infrastructure.
>
> Ye, 2022

In the context of the economic rise of China and the return of the military power of Russia following the 2008 global crisis, the United States has more and more relied on economic sanctions to reassert its power mostly through the weaponisation of the dollar. For the United States, economic sanctions have thus served 'as partial substitutes for military power' (Davis and Ness, 2021: 1; Karuka, 2021: 57). The threat of using military power has also often been used 'as an important adjunct to the implementation of sanctions' (Beal, 2021: 33). Since 2008, the deployment of sanctions by the European Union has equally amplified. Accordingly, the United States and the European Union have more regularly attempted to block the entire world from trading with targeted 'unfriendly' and 'rogue' states 'as a means to foment dissent in hopes of destabilizing leaders and governing parties (often referred to in the parlance as "regimes")', overthrowing them from power and replacing them with 'political leaders who are supportive of US policies'. More meaningfully, the United States and the European Union have applied economic sanctions against China and Russia during this period (Davis and Ness, 2021: 2; see also Capasso, 2021). The American unilateral extraterritorial sanctions and secondary sanctions have also drastically increased in recent years thanks to the significance of its MNCs in globalised value chains, and more importantly 'its immense control over the international financial system and banking, and the traditional use of the dollar as the unit for international trade, and as a reserve currency' (Beal, 2021: 40). Although China and Russia are still way behind the United States and the European Union in terms of control over financial and capital flows, they have become more active in confronting increasingly aggressive Western sanctions. They have facilitated the circumvention of the US and EU sanctions through, for example, the development of transnational grey markets. At the same time, they have intensified their geoeconomic and geopolitical cooperation with each other and with other targeted countries. As well as increasingly refusing to collaborate with the United States on sanctions (Beal, 2021: 33), China also began to devise its own sanctions policy by 'issuing new rules against global companies that comply with US sanctions against its industries' (Bridenthal, 2021: 326). More significantly, China and Russia have endeavoured to de-dollarise international finance by resorting to trade in local currencies, reducing their holdings of US treasury bonds and hoarding gold to prepare for a possible future of a multi-currency monetary system. For instance, China's holdings of US debt dropped to less than $1 trillion in 2022 (Cox, 2022) and 25 per cent of Russia's trade with China was in their national currencies in 2021 (Bridenthal, 2021: 325). China also attempted to create 'a digital gold-backed Renminbi which it plans to launch as a real rival to the US dollar in international trade' that can also avoid cross-border payments through the American-dominated Worldwide Interbank Financial Telecommunication (SWIFT) network (Bridenthal, 2021: 327–8).

The rise of these nascent empires more than anything else implies a dialectic of rivalry and unity of interests between major capitalist states rather than an outright inter-imperialist competition. This is because a total instability of integrated global capitalism does not serve the interests of these global centres of power against the backdrop of the internationalisation of capital. This fact is perhaps even more important for China than for Russia given the deeper enmeshment of Chinese capital in the global trade and capital flows. We should also bear in mind that there is little evidence that the accumulation model of these powers moves beyond neoliberalism. Put differently, it is true that the Chinese BRI and the Russian military intervention in Syria and the invasion of Ukraine have posed serious challenges to the United States and the European Union in various regions of the world, but we need to remember that the infiltration of Chinese and Russian capitals into these regions similar to other major Western states has been predicated upon the intensification of neoliberalism rather than a qualitative break with it (Hanieh, 2013: 44).

Whilst a great number of developing countries still reside at the bottom of the capitalist system, in the hierarchy of contemporary capitalism after these imperial powers and nascent empires, there are a number of countries with noticeable accumulation processes and regional projections that can be called 'peripheral' powers or 'sub-imperial' states (Alexander, 2018; Katz, 2022: 163–9). Three determinants have been crucial in the rise of these peripheral powers. In the first place, the gradual reduction of the gap between the core and the periphery since the second part of the twentieth century has played a role in the emergence of these regional powers. Secondly, the geoeconomic and geopolitical actions of the great powers (e.g., trade agreements, economic sanctions, military actions) to integrate different regions of the world into global patterns of trade and investment have not only acted to augment the position of the advanced capitalist states but have also reproduced power hierarchies within these regions in favour of 'friendly' states. For instance, the facilitation of regional accumulation in the Middle East has led to the rise of Gulf capital under neoliberalism. Apart from consolidating US power through stronger linkage with Western capital, petrodollars, and military sales, among others, the rise of Gulf capital has equally augmented the influence and power of the Gulf monarchies in the region (Hanieh, 2013: 33–42). Thirdly, the dialectic of rivalry and unity of interests between the global centres of power have provided some spaces for these peripheral powers to utilise geoeconomic and geopolitical tensions and cooperation for deepening or halting the international movement of capital linked to the major accumulation centres (i.e., North America, Europe and East Asia). The periodisation of neoliberal global capitalism can also help to reveal the level of agency of these sub-imperial states. In contrast to the early stage of global neoliberalism, where the Western powers appeared triumphant, the rise of China and Russia as competitors to the US hegemony has fertilised the grounds for these peripheral/regional powers to exercise more agency in recent years. All things considered, we can assume that these sub-imperial states are not always in a position to exert a constant degree of influence in their region. Since the capitalist class formation in these peripheral powers has increasingly been tied to the ebbs and flows of accumulation at the global level due to the internationalisation of capital, the dynamics of competition and cooperation between major capitalist states have still to some degree conditioned and shaped their actions (Alexander, 2018; Katz, 2022: 163–9). Given this, we should view these peripheral powers as adjuncts or autonomous associates of great capitalist powers that often pursue independent actions in coordination and conflict with them.

\* \* \* \*

So, how does the above conceptual discussion help us to grasp capitalism in contemporary Iran? The developed theoretical framework equips us to answer the following question: Why were neoliberal reforms instigated following the end of the war with Iraq in 1989? How has neoliberal restructuring in Iran been shaped in and through the state both from above (transformations in the global political economy) and from below (social forces)? What are the structural changes experienced by the Iranian economy because of this process? How has the state itself, both institutionally and ideologically, been transformed? What has been the role of geopolitical tensions with the West in the process of Iranian neoliberalisation?

At the outset, the approach makes a case for the importance of dialectical interactions between external and internal dynamics and international and national factors. Herein, by situating Iran within the broader process of neoliberal restructuring of the global economy, it accounts for shaping international determinants in the country's economic development as well as other sociopolitical reformations/transformations since the late 1980s. Simultaneously, the approach draws resolute attention to the particularity of its domestic class structure to put a spotlight on the conflict of interests between different national centres of political-economic power over these changes. In this way, the notion of development as a 'technical' process is problematised in favour of a politically charged process, which proceeds through struggles and resistance from above and below by external and domestic forces. Notice that the Iranian state also cannot be any longer theorised as a passively external entity that has implemented a set of 'non-ideological' economic policies on behalf of the 'public interest', nor as a set of formal and informal institutions separated from struggles over the process of capital accumulation. Rather, this framework opens a way to perceive the state as a form of social relations with 'capacities' and 'institutional endowments' which is strongly influenced by wider patterns of class formation (Kiely, 2007: 185). Likewise, this mode

of inquiry challenges the separation of the market from the state by attesting
that neoliberal restructuring is 'a form of State "regulation", introduced and
maintained by legislative and coercive means' (Gramsci, 1971: 160). It further
casts doubt on the treatment of material and ideational structures as well as
(geo)politics and the economic as distinct, separate spheres. Accordingly, this
approach demonstrates how ideological factions within the state structure,
various major episodes of political turmoil and social upheavals as well as
geopolitical tensions with the West (e.g., the nuclear programme, international sanctions and regional interventions) in the last three decades are internally related to the opposing economic interests within the society and the
state produced by the process of neoliberalisation, and how these economic
interests are themselves generated in relation and response to the advance of
the international movement of capital.

## The arguments and plan of the book

The key object of inquiry through which all the aspects come together is the
Iranian ruling class. The book argues that the process of Iranian neoliberalisation since the late 1980s has brought about the *internationally oriented
capital fraction* and the *military–bonyad complex* as the two wings of the
ruling class that have pursued opposing accumulating strategies (bonyads
are charitable trusts that play a major role in Iran's economy). Not only have
these competing strategies resulted in the unstable hybrid neoliberal form of
development, but they have also generated an intense struggle within the
state due to the historical importance of the state in Iran to capital accumulation. Apart from changing the function and operation of numerous state
institutions, this intra-class confrontation has provided the material bases
for the realisation of the liberal/democratic discourse and the revolutionary
interpretation of Islam, and in turn they have aided the two wings of power
in their struggle for societal hegemony. The book also demonstrates that
the struggles from below by workers and the poor and geopolitical tensions over the nuclear programme and related international sanctions have
shaped the process of Iranian neoliberalisation.[5]

These arguments unfold in the next six chapters. As a historical background of the study, Chapters 2 and 3 periodise the development of capitalism in Iran from the beginning of the nineteenth century until the instigation
of neoliberal restructuring in 1989. Due to the importance of understanding
the state and class formation during the late Pahlavi reign for the study of
contemporary Iran, Chapter 2 scrutinises the wide-ranging land reform and
the rapid industrialisation programme of the Shah under the name of the
White Revolution. It contends that the shakeup of global capitalism and

the shift in power from Britain to the United States in the global political economy after WWII laid the foundation for the restructuring of capitalism and the reorganisation of the state form in the developing states linked to the Western Bloc through the promotion of ISI strategy. Besides the structural conditions of the international system, it shows that the national class structure and the relation of political forces equally influenced this restructuring. In Iran, in the context of the Cold War, the Shah's modernisation project, as an example of state capitalism, was geared toward the creation of modern industries. The chapter demonstrates that both the financial and technological support of the United States and the growing foreign reserves of the country due to the increasing oil revenues crucially aided the financing of the imports of machinery, components and other inputs needed to build up Iran's industrial base. It consequently substantiates that the process generated a new, small, protected capitalist class with close ties to foreign capital, who controlled the whole apparatus of the state.

Chapter 3 first explains how the White Revolution led to the forming of an unwritten alliance between the powerful traditional mercantile class of the bazaar, the petty bourgeoisie, the growing working classes and the urban poor of shantytowns that aimed at overthrowing the Shah's regime. The main objective of the chapter, however, is to understand the patterns of state and class formation during the first decades of the revolution from 1979 to 1989. It claims that the 1979 revolution did not destroy the socioeconomic foundation of the society since the ISI state-led development even expanded in the first decade of the revolution, albeit against the backdrop of US hostility and under the name of the national liberation of the 'downtrodden'. Accordingly, a range of measures in favour of the poor and the working class, including the provision of food and other subsidies as well as job security in SOEs, was implemented by the revolutionary state. The chapter argues that these measures, nonetheless, were secondary to the interests of the new ruling class with two fractions. By examining the confiscation of the property of the old ruling class and the extensive nationalisation of the first decade of the revolution under 'government' and 'public' ownership as two forms of state ownership, it traces the emergence of the *stratum of government managers* and the *bonyad–bazaar nexus* as the two fractions of the ruling class in the first decade of the revolution. The chapter emphasises that the legacy of state capitalism and the class character of the revolutionary state have had an indispensable impact on the process of neoliberalisation and the development trajectory of contemporary Iran.

Chapter 4 aims to comprehend the process of neoliberalisation in the aftermath of the war with Iraq. It maintains that the process was part of a response to the 1970s' global crisis of overaccumulation that hit the Global South in the form of the debt crisis arising from ISI strategy in the 1980s.

In Iran, the revolutionary state continued the ISI in the context of turmoil and chaos generated by the revolution and the war with Iraq. Whilst delaying the neoliberal restructuring until 1990, the revolution and the war further aggravated the crisis associated with ISI. Aiming to revive capital accumulation through integration into the new global world economy characterised by the internationalisation of capital, accordingly, some members of the ruling class viewed the EOI strategy and its associated neoliberal policies as an alternative developmental strategy that would generate economic growth and mitigate external geoeconomic and geopolitical pressures. The chapter demonstrates how the first phase of neoliberalisation (1989–2005) led to the metamorphosis of the stratum of government managers into the *internationally oriented capital fraction*. While this wing of power has controlled a big chunk of the national market, in line with the EOI, it has viewed integration into GVCs of Western capital, particularly European capital, as a guarantor of its long-term existence. The chapter further shows that the transfer of the shares of many large government-owned enterprises to economic entities affiliated with the military forces and the revolutionary foundations (bonyads) during the second phase of neoliberalisation (2005–13) led to the emergence of the *military–bonyad complex* out of the bonyad–bazaar nexus. This fraction has hindered the entrance of Western capital under the name of 'economic resistance' and 'self-reliance'. The chapter substantiates that while the uneven development of capitalism, the movement of international capital and the international rivalries between the United States and China/Russia have drastically influenced Iranian restructuring, the struggles of these class forces have equally shaped the process. As the process has not eliminated the ISI strategy, it concludes that the amalgamation of the ISI and EOI strategies has generated a particular form of hybrid neoliberalism.

Chapter 5 argues that most explanations of the post-revolutionary state still heavily rely on the key political and economic characteristics of rentier state theory. By challenging the reliance of these accounts on contingent factors such as religion, resource endowment, patronage networks, leadership styles and institutional arrangements, it maintains that the specificity of the nature of capital accumulation and its associated class formation needs to be given weight for understanding the state's form. As a set of institutional forms reflective of social relations of production, the chapter stresses that the state cannot be understood with reference to national space in the era of the internationalisation of capital. By including civil society organisations in the analysis of state institutions as well as internally relating ideas to the material structures, the chapter argues that both formal state institutions and civil society organisations have been the zones of the struggle for mastery of the emerging internationally oriented capital fraction and the military–bonyad complex. It first documents how the struggles between these fractions have constructed some new institutions and changed the operation of existing institutions. It then highlights the internal relationship between the formation and crystallisation of the new discourse of 'democratic Islam' and the rearticulation of 'revolutionary Islam' to the process of neoliberalisation. Although these discourses have been articulated through civil society organisations, it demonstrates that the realisation and relevance of these ideas have been dependent on the availability of material organisations provided by the aforementioned fractions while the historical existence of the different interpretations of Islam is acknowledged. The chapter asserts that this conspicuous institutional reorganisation and ideological change since the end of the war with Iraq are the upshots of the reconfiguration of the class basis of the state, which is internally related to the process of neoliberalisation.

Chapter 6 first documents how the process of neoliberalisation has reshaped the subaltern classes and then explores the struggles of workers and the poor in contemporary Iran. With regard to the former, the chapter identifies two substantial transformations in the composition of the subaltern classes, namely the rise of the precariat as the largest section of the working class and the genesis of the new poor consisting of unemployed educated young people. Concerning the second objective, the chapter documents the resistance of workers since the early 1990s against privatisation, casualisation, redundancies and overdue pay through various means, including the establishment of independent labour unions and networks for the first time since the 1979 revolution. After reviewing the revolts of the poor against the rising cost of living and the elimination of state subsidies in the 1990s and 2000s, the chapter turns its attention to the post-2017 waves of popular uprisings known as the Dey and Aban protests. These impromptu nationwide protests and riots of the new poor are understood as the opposition to the deterioration of the economic crisis generated by the combination of the aggressive neoliberal policies of the government and crippling US sanctions. Although these structural causes were integral to the development of the Women, Life, Freedom revolt in 2022, the chapter argues that this new round of mutiny achieved greater success in galvanising a varied range of societal groups when compared to the post-2017 uprisings. In light of the recent struggles from below, while pinpointing the signs that illustrate the Iranian subaltern classes have been somewhat successful in transcending their divisive particularities, the chapter outlines several central obstacles to the formation of working-class identity and a broad-based subaltern coalition under the leadership of the working class. These include state repression and the persistence of a 'workerist' understanding of the class struggle that reduces the working class to blue-collar workers and disregards that the capitalist rule advances through the hierarchal re-ordering of the working class along the lines of gender, race, nationality and ethnicity.

Chapter 7 explores the internal links between the Iranian nuclear programme, international sanctions and regional policy with the processes of neoliberalism in Iran, the Middle East and globally. By situating Iran within the geoeconomic and geopolitical policies of the United States, the European Union, China and Russia since 1990, the chapter shows how these global centres of power have utilised the Iranian nuclear programme and economic sanctions to shape neoliberalism in the region and Iran in two different periods (1990–2007 and 2008–present). With the aim of establishing Iran's agency as a regional power, the chapter also demonstrates the ways in which the different fractions of the Iranian ruling class have pursued different policies regarding the nuclear programme, international sanctions and regional interventions in line with their long-term interests by utilising the dialectic of rivalry and unity of interests between these major capitalist powers. More specifically, the chapter documents that the internationally oriented capital fraction has been bargaining with the West for economic integration into the global political economy through pursuing conciliatory policies regarding the nuclear programme and the Middle East. On the other hand, the chapter reveals that the military–bonyad complex has strategically utilised the nuclear programme, interrelated international sanctions and Iran's influence in the Middle East to hinder the permeation of Western capital, halt further integration of Iran into the Western-centred world order and push Iran into the orbit of China and Russia. The concluding chapter attempts to sketch the possible determinants that could impact the future paths of the Islamic Republic in the context of the global crisis of neoliberalism, the changing global order and the intensification of struggles from below.

## Notes

1 For a comprehensive definition and various aspects of Eurocentrism see Matin (2013b) and Tansel (2015; 2016).
2 Some key works that constitute developmental state theory are Chang (2002), Wade (1990), Evans (1995), Amsden (1989; 1990), White (1988) and Kohli (2004).
3 For a substantial critique of these accounts see Connell and Dados (2014).
4 Hobson (2012: 234) defines critical subliminal Eurocentrism as a feature of neo-Marxist theories 'wherein the West is viewed as the supreme agent of world politics/economics that lies at the very centre of all things, while the East is denied progressive agency of any sort and is portrayed as a hapless

down-and-out, condemned for the foreseeable future, if not for all eternity, to eke out a miserable existence in the ghetto of the periphery'.

5 The book largely relies on a documentary and archival method of data collection by using the following primary sources: (a) the databases and archives of various Iranian ministries and international organisations; (b) documents produced by the Iranian government, employers, political parties and labour organisations; (c) documents produced by the United States and the European Union regarding Iran; (d) newspaper and periodical reports, mostly in Persian. These primary materials have been complemented by secondary sources.

# 2

# Modern Iran from Pax Britannica to Pax Americana: The emergence and consolidation of capitalism

This chapter explores the development of capitalism and the forms of state in Iran from the mid-nineteenth century until the 1979 revolution. This investigation proceeds in line with the conceptual framework of the study outlined in the previous chapter that calls for a relational approach that incorporates the dialectical interaction of global and local dynamics and international and national shaping factors. The approach maintains that comprehending capitalist development and the form of the state in each society in any period requires adopting a world-historical perspective. While in this framework analysing the structure of the global economy is the essential point of departure, this does not imply that the global capitalist order simply predetermines the outcome of the process of development and form of state in the given society. Rather, the structure of global capitalism in each epoch creates a terrain through which a particular model of development and state form can be more favourably articulated. That is to say, despite the dominance of a specific model of global capitalism in each era, the outcome of the capitalist restructuring and form of the state in each society are often unique owing to the particularity of the domestic class structure and its specific forms of class struggle. Analysed through this theoretical perspective, the chapter investigates the trajectories of economic restructuring and the processes of state formation in Iran during Pax Britannica and Pax Americana as the two successive structures of the global order since the mid-nineteenth century. While the emergence of capitalism in Iran during the supremacy of Britain in the global order offers the necessary historical background for understanding modern Iran, the primary focus of the chapter is the delineating of the process of state-led development under the strategy of ISI during the reign of Mohammad Reza Shah in the era of Pax Americana, which led to the consolidation of capitalist social relations and rapid industrialisation in Iran. The legacy of this restructuring has had an indispensable effect on the process of development and the emergence of the ruling-class fractions and political agents in the first decade of the 1979 revolution as well as the post-1989 neoliberal era.

The remainder of the chapter consists of two main parts. The first section begins with a brief discussion on the mode of production and the form of state in pre-modern Iran, but its chief objective is to scrutinise the ways in which Iran integrated into the British-led global economy under the liberal free trade international economic order of the nineteenth century, which is also referred to as free trade imperialism (Kiely, 2010: 42–52). The section thus surveys the instigation of capitalist social relations and the institutionalisation of the modern state in Iran, conceptualising it as a passive revolution. The second section unpacks the consolidation of capitalism in Iran by examining the wide-ranging land reform and the rapid industrialisation programme of the second Pahlavi state during the order of Pax Americana under the name of the White Revolution. Relatedly, it also breaks down the process of state-led development based on the ISI strategy. After summarising the key points, the conclusion outlines the centrality of this history of the emergence and consolidation of capitalism in Iran for the subsequent chapters.

## Pax Britannica and the *longue durée* of the emergence of capitalism in Iran

Between the early nineteenth century and the early to mid-twentieth century, Iran's pre-modern social structure had gradually transformed from the tributary mode of production to capitalism. In addition to the external pressure from the capitalist West, domestic actors, conditions and structures had challenged these tributary social relations. In particular, the Qajar empire and the first Pahlavi state along with the incipient domestic social forces – mostly generated because of the incremental privatisation of land – had been actively involved in this transformation. Iran's pre-modern tributary mode of production was the product of an amalgamation of Turkish tribal nomadism of Central Asia and the Iranian sedentary-agricultural society. This resulted in the formulation of 'patrimonial-absolutist states' founded on the institution of *uymaq* or 'household-state' and the lack of private property on land (Matin, 2007: 430). *Uymaqs* as mini states with political and administrative authority collected tax from peasants and urban merchants 'in return for partaking in "national" defence or external expeditions' (Matin, 2007: 434). The *uymaqs* were appointed by the king, who was himself the leading *uymaq*. The instability of the system as a single *uymaq* could overthrow the ruling dynasty led to the process of state centralisation under the Safavid rule (1501–1736), during which the *uymaqs'* structure was replaced by the *ghulaman* slave army. The process intensified the conquest of new territories since the centralised state needed greater taxes, tributes and above all population to recruit more slaves. Granting land to the new military commanders-cum-state officials presupposed the king's formal ownership of the land, but this was the first step in the long process of privatisation of the land, which in turn facilitated the spread of non-tributary social relations in agricultural production. Furthermore, nullifying the *uymaqs*' political power through the centralisation process unintentionally brought new sociopolitical forces to the state structure, namely the Shi'a ulama and the mercantile class of the bazaar (Matin, 2007: 437–8). The Usuli Shi'a ulama[1] gradually became the state functionaries in the battle with the *uymaqs*, whose ideological basis was Sufism,[2] by taking over the judicial system in accordance with their interpretation of Islam. Aimed at augmenting their positions in the state bureaucracy, vast areas of land in the name of the non-taxable charitable property (*vaqf*) were assigned to them by the later Safavid kings – they eventually became quasi-owners of this land after the fall of the Safavid empire. Furthermore, to marginalise Sufism, the Shi'a ulama forged close ties with the mercantile class of the bazaar (Matin, 2013a: 41–2).[3] In addition to these internal developments, the growing military power of Russia and the domination of Asia–Europe trade routes by the Western capitalist powers through the sea sounded the death knell of the tributary mode of production.

Throughout the Qajar rule (1794–1925), because of the combination of external and internal factors, state officials incessantly but gradually continued the appropriation of large parts of state land and its conversion into 'de facto private property' that was 'inheritable and alienable by sale' (Lambton, 1991: 139). The launch of the *Nizam-e Jadid* reforms for modernising the tribal army and state institutions by Abbas Mirza at the beginning of the nineteenth century was crucial for the process. As a result of the two successive defeats in the Russo–Persian wars of 1804–13 and 1826–8, Iran lost its northern territories. Losing the tax revenue of the northern territories made the financing of the modernisation project difficult. This necessitated an austerity programme through which state pensions to the courtiers, provincial elites and ulama were substantially reduced (Matin, 2012b: 48–9; Matin, 2013a: 59–60). The backlash from these powerful groups compelled the state to pursue the intensification of the sale of crown and state lands, titles and government offices. This transformation sequentially accelerated the emergence of a class of large landowners, which was already instigated in the late Safavid era at a slow pace.

Since the selling of state and crown land did not generate enough surplus to materialise the reforms, the state also adopted a policy of selling commercial and economic concessions to Britain and Russia by lowering import duties, authorising both superpowers to open trading agencies everywhere in the country and exempting their merchants from local laws and tariffs.

Whilst the policy prevented the formal colonisation of Iran, it facilitated the integration of the Iranian economy into the global capitalist system under the liberal international regime of free trade that Britain aggressively promoted from the mid-nineteenth century onwards (Kiely, 2010: 42–52). By the late nineteenth century, the free trade regime had reduced the export of traditional manufacturing products (Karshenas, 1990a: 48) and increased the position of agriculture due to the global demand for raw agricultural goods, such as cotton and opium. Therefore, some merchants of the bazaar turned to purchase land since investment in the agricultural sector promised healthy returns (Keddie, 2003: 26). The reform of the educational and judicial system as part of the modernisation process also spawned new strata of the administrative staff of the state and a relatively small but influential stratum of the modern intelligentsia. Despite being engendered as a result of the *Nizam-e Jadid* reforms, these groups denounced the Qajars' arbitrary rule for the 'backwardness' of the country and advocated a more comprehensive modernisation of the state (Ashraf, 1981: 22).

Throughout this period, the privatisation of land and the growing commercial relations with the West facilitated the emergence of capitalist social relations, even though modern industrial activities were not developed until the early twentieth century. At the beginning of the century, in addition to some Russian and German entrepreneurs, a small group of Iranian merchants invested their capital in modern industry by establishing small-scale modern workshops and medium-sized factories. Besides this domestic capital, large British and Russian firms invested in 'the fisheries, lumber industry, railway construction and oil industries' (Ashraf, 1981: 20). Together, these developments in the early twentieth century led to the emergence of an industrial working class of approximately 12,000. This was one-tenth of the total non-agricultural labour force, of whom only 4 per cent were employed by the burgeoning national bourgeoisie (Ashraf, 1981: 21). At the same time, a considerable number of peasants and urban poor migrated to the trans-Caspian regions to work in modern industries due to the worsening of economic conditions in their homeland. These immigrant workers imported working-class revolutionary ideas that were influential in the politicisation of the peasantry and the working class during the Constitutional Revolution of 1906–9 (Keddie, 2003: 69).

This slow emergence of capitalism created precarious sociopolitical conditions in Iran by the late nineteenth century and early twentieth century. Eventually, the deterioration of the economic situation and the disturbance of the balance of class forces crystallised themselves in a series of revolts between 1890 and 1914 (Keddie, 1991: 192–212). These periods of unrest, particularly the Constitutional Revolution, attempted to establish a constitutional monarchy and a modern state with the support of the *bazaari* classes and their political allies and the nascent capitalist class and their intellectual forces. After a period of uncertainty and chaos following the revolution, two important events, the discovery of oil and the October Revolution of 1917, paved the way for the intensification of reforms from above that led to the formation of a modern centralised state after 1921.

In 1901, William D'Arcy secured a sixty-year concession for the exploration and export of oil from Iran with the help of the British authority (Issawi, 1991: 606; Stork, 1975: 8). The discovery of oil in 1908 in southern Iran led to the establishment of the Anglo-Persian Oil Company in 1909,[4] the first shipment of oil in 1912 and a dramatic climb in the output of oil by the beginning of the 1920s (Issawi, 1991: 607). The company initially supported and cooperated with the local rulers in the absence of a powerful centralised authority following the revolutionary turmoil. However, in order to protect wells, rigs, pipelines and installations against unrest in the countryside and to provide trained domestic personnel, Britain recognised the importance of cooperation with the Iranian ruling class for the institutionalisation of a modern centralised state. This desire was explicitly stressed by a senior member of the management of the Anglo-Persian Oil Company: 'Our salvation lies in a strong Central Government … it is in our common interest [the company and the Iranian ruling class] to assist a proper central government' (cited in Ferrier, 1991: 643). To this end, Britain entered negotiations with the Iranian cabinet, resulting in the 1919 Agreement in which Britain agreed to provide a loan and military and civil advisers to modernise Iran's army and state administration. Since the newly established Majles (Parliament) refused to ratify the agreement, Britain supported the coup of 1921 by an Anglophile journalist, Saayed Zai Tabatabai, and an army officer, Reza Khan (Katouzian, 1981: 77–80). The prime ministerial era of the former lasted less than 100 days, but Reza Khan, who initially acted as the Minister of War, eventually became king in 1925 (Arjomand, 1988: 59–62). The 1917 October Revolution had a dual influence on the process. On the one hand, it intensified the British ambition to stabilise Iran to safeguard the production of oil. On the other hand, the protection of the country from the diffusion of the Bolshevik creeds that might have galvanised the peasants, the urban poor and the working class, unified all fractions of the ruling class around the idea of the formation of a strong centralised modern state (Katouzian, 1981: 77). Because one of the objectives of the Constitutional Revolution was to form a modern state, it was also popular among most of the constitutionalist leaders even though some of them loathed Britain (Arjomand, 1988: 62). The new king did not disappoint as his state-centralisation programme shrewdly managed the balance of the external and internal social and political forces.

In the first step, the new Shah completed the conversion of land into private property. By violently disarming the tribes, which constituted around 25 per cent of the population in 1920, the new state finally ended the policy of the abolition of land assignments a century after its inception (Arjomand, 1988: 63–4 and 69). In addition, Reza Shah introduced successive land and property laws and regulations that converted 'a variety of conditional, de facto and tribal – often communal – holdings' into 'unconditionally held private property' (Arjomand, 1988: 70–1). The reform made large private landlordism the dominant form of land ownership, therefore completing the creation of a homogeneous class of large private landlords. The policy further consolidated the integration of the Iranian agricultural sector into the global economy (Ashraf, 1970: 330). The confiscation of a significant amount of land by the Shah made him the biggest single absentee landlord of the country by the time of his abdication in 1941 (Hooglund, 1982: 40). Consequently, during his reign, the government blocked all attempts at agrarian reform, which was triggered during the Constitutional Revolution, either in favour of the industrialisation of the agricultural sector or the distribution of land among peasants.

In the second phase of Reza Shah's reign from 1931 to 1941, the state intervened strongly in the economy and introduced a series of measures to protect the national economy in line with the new direction of the global economy in the interwar period. The Great Depression of 1929 caused a slump in foreign trade and the devaluation of the Iranian currency because of the drop in the price of silver. This forced the government to monopolise the right of all foreign trade of valuable agricultural products, including cotton, tobacco, opium, tea, sugar and dried fruits, in 1931 (McLachlan, 1991: 608–38). Relatedly, the government unveiled a system of high tariffs on importing cheap manufacturing goods. Furthermore, the D'Arcy concession for oil exploration and extraction was cancelled by Reza Shah in 1932. After the degree of control in trade and output and the modest increase in the oil revenue after signing a new agreement with the Anglo-Persian Oil Company (Abrahamian, 1982: 144), the state intensified its expenditure on the modern transport system and directly invested in the industry (Halliday, 1979: 148). The construction of the Trans-Iranian Railway, the building of 12,000 miles of highway, the investment in ports and the establishment of a new national bank and other banks for agriculture, industry and mortgages led to the augmentation of the national market (McLachlan, 1991: 611–12). The government also contributed approximately half of the £58m investment in the industry. Thanks to the subsidising measures to promote the growth of the industry in the form of tariff exemption, preferential exchange premium and exemption of transport fees for imported machinery and the high level of protection of the home market from international competition, private investment in manufacturing became highly profitable. Accordingly, by the end of the 1930s, there were more than 260 private and public industrial plants in textile, sugar, cement, and chemicals, among others (Karshenas, 1990a: 76; Ashraf, 1970: 329–30), which directly contributed to the expansion of the Iranian industrial working class. Due to the flirtation of Reza Shah with Nazi Germany to counterbalance Britain during WWII, the Allies occupied Iran in 1941. The main upshot of the occupation was the crowning of Reza Shah's son as a new king.

The class basis of the modern state, established during the reign of Reza Shah, was a coalition comprising the landed gentry, the comprador bourgeoisie, the emerging national bourgeoisie and the modern petty bourgeoisie. Ending all talk of land reform strengthened the position of the landowners. The modernisation of infrastructure and transportation and a modest investment in national industry satisfied both comprador and national capitalist classes (Moaddel, 1986: 535). The abolition of tribal nomadism and the unification of the country based on the forced policy of 'one people, one nation, one language and one culture' (Abrahamian, 1982: 142) appeased all the modern social class forces, in particular the embryonic middle class, which was composed of the few but resolute Western-influenced intelligentsia and the growing state bureaucratic middlemen. In addition, the new state became popular among this modern petty bourgeoisie due to the introduction of a secular system of national primary and secondary schools, the constitution of the first modern university (the University of Tehran) and the use of the French civil codes instead of Shari'a law in the new legal system that brought more non-clerical members to the judiciary (Matin, 2013a: 87).

How should we theorise this process of the instigation of capitalism and the formation of the modern state in Iran? For this, a conceptual discussion on transitions between modes of production as well as trajectories of restructuring within capitalism, especially the concepts of social, political and passive revolution, might be necessary. A social revolution involves 'the transference of political power to a new class; and this change in ruling class tends to entail a basic change in the social system (mode of production)'. It is 'a process, more or less extended in time' because 'such a sweeping change cannot be conceived as a mere act or event' (Draper, 1978: 19). In contrast, a political revolution is 'a social-revolutionising drive toward the transference of state power to a new class' without revolutionising the socioeconomic foundation of the society. In this case, we witness a change in the personnel of the ruling class without a transformation in the class power since the new ruling class maintains the socioeconomic foundation of the society by thwarting the initiatives of the exploited majority for the creation of a new society.[5] A social revolution can take three different forms: bourgeois revolution, proletarian revolution and passive revolution.

However, due to its importance for my argument, I only focus on the notion of passive revolution.

By analysing the unification of Italy (*Risorgimento*) in the 1860s and Italian fascism and Fordism in the early twentieth century, Gramsci articulated the concept of passive revolution as instances of the establishment of modern states on the basis of the institution of capitalism or the expansion of aspects of capitalist social relations (Morton, 2010: 318). During these processes, the 'State replaces the local social groups in leading a struggle of renewal' since 'these groups have the function of "domination" without that of "leadership": dictatorship without hegemony' (Gramsci, 1971: 105–6). Inspired by Gramsci's articulation of these processes, Adam David Morton (2013a: 38–9) argues that passive revolution can follow two different processes: 'a revolution without mass participation' (revolutions from above) and 'revolutions-restorations'. The former involves 'elite-engineered social and political reform that draws on foreign capital and associated ideas while lacking a national popular base'. The latter explicates 'how a revolutionary form of political transformation is passed into a conservative project in which popular demands of class struggle still play some role'. As this interpretation results in its application to different situations and contexts, Alex Callinicos (2010: 505) warns that the concept could lose its specificity to the extent that it might become 'a distinction without a difference'. By identifying the problem of over-extension of the concept in the *Prison Notebooks*, Callinicos stresses that fascism and Fordism were instances of '*counter-revolutionary projects*' that sought 'to manage the structural contradictions of the capitalist mode of production'. On the other hand, because 'the *ancien régime* has given way to a society in which the capitalist mode of production prevails', Callinicos (2010: 498) contends that the Risorgimento can only plausibly be described as 'revolution without revolution'. In his account, the application of the concept of passive revolution is thus reduced to the examples of transition between modes of production. While Callinicos's interpretation restricts the significance of the concept for the understanding of the dynamics within capitalism, Morton's twin definition is also problematic since passive revolution may apply to all elite-engineered reforms with the purpose of the reorganisation of capitalist social relations in the absence of an 'antithesis' from below.

Against these interpretations, to qualify as an instance of passive revolution, restructuring must be carried out during a socioeconomic crisis that might bring about a revolutionary rupture from below. In other words, the extension of the role of the state in modifying the relations of production has to be seen as an attempt to tame and pacify the participation of the masses in the process of social upheaval through which subaltern demands are displaced and partially fulfilled at once. To be precise, a passive revolution occurs if four key elements exist, as outlined by Roberto Roccu (2017: 547):

> First, the international as a source of both material pressures towards transition, in light of the uneven development of capitalism, and of events and ideas that become inevitable reference points of an epoch. Second, a structurally necessary transformation whose specific form and content are determined by a specific relation of political forces, and particularly by the presence of a non-hegemonic dominant class and a weak, or weakly organised and articulated, subaltern bloc. Third, the extensive use of state power as a surrogate for hegemony on the part of the ruling class to effect a transformation for which it cannot win the consent of the ruled. Finally, an outcome whereby popular demands are simultaneously partly fulfilled and displaced in a way that essentially consolidates the political *status quo*.

Accordingly, in the absence of 'a vigorous antithesis prior to a passive revolution and the partial fulfilment of popular demands' following the process of restructuring, a transition within capitalism in the form of reforms from above could simply be called 'capitalist restructuring' (Roccu, 2017: 549–50) (see Figure 2.1).

Drawing on these concepts, the emergence of capitalism and the establishment of the modern state from the mid-nineteenth century to the early twentieth century in Iran can be seen as an example of passive revolution. The *Nizam-e Jadid* reforms to modernise the state and the integration into

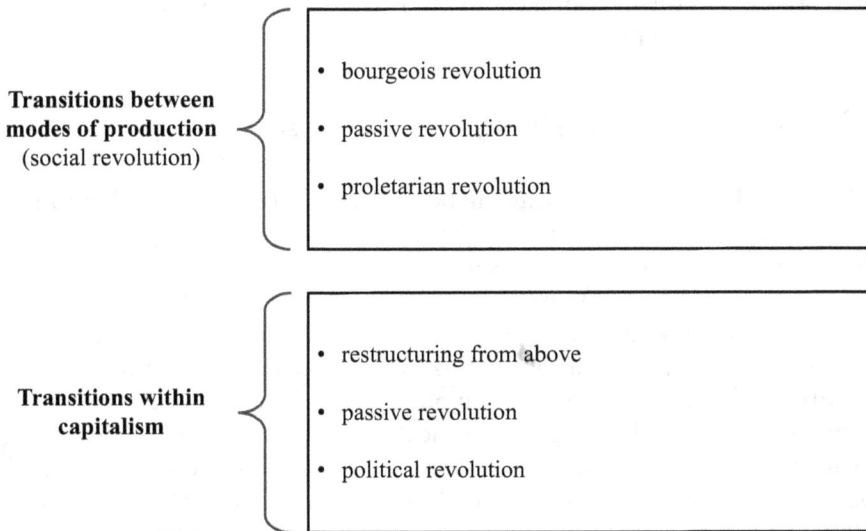

**Transitions between modes of production** (social revolution)

- bourgeois revolution
- passive revolution
- proletarian revolution

**Transitions within capitalism**

- restructuring from above
- passive revolution
- political revolution

Figure 2.1 Transitions and revolutions

the free trade order of Pax Britannica from the middle of the nineteenth century onwards generated sociopolitical upheavals. The reforms continued at the beginning of the twentieth century in the context of the growing importance of petroleum to the global economy. This eventually led to the completion of the constitution of the modern state during the reign of Reza Shah. This social revolution in the form of passive revolution, which resulted in far-reaching changes in social relations, was a long process. While the global transformations induced the reorganisation of the Iranian state and the transition to a capitalist mode of production, the process was mediated by the domestic class structure and internal factors. In particular, the active agency of the Qajar empire and the first Pahlavi state must be acknowledged given the relation of political forces in which the ruling class was not hegemonic. Throughout this period, the subaltern classes had failed to develop a radical political project to win power. However, the revolts and uprisings of the late nineteenth century and the early twentieth century and the fear of a radical alternative socioeconomic order from below in the context of the Bolshevik October Revolution were critical for the implementation of these prolonged and top-down social and political reforms from above by the state. This is because the reforms aimed to displace and partially fulfil the demands of urban subaltern classes and gained the support of the nascent middle class. Through this molecular, top-down process of change, the modern state with a commitment to global capital accumulation was established. These reforms further expedited the expansion of capitalist relations and the development of the national market in Iran despite the persistence of some non-capitalist social relations.

## Pax Americana and the consolidation of capitalism in Iran

After WWII, qualitative transformations in the global economy led to the emergence of the United States as the leading capitalist power. As the early steps towards the internationalisation of capital, this period was marked by the drive of capitalist firms, especially American companies, to oversee expansion and international exports. The reconfiguration of the transport sector for the realisation of this international expansion along with the growing demand for mass automobile production and the emergence of new industries such as the petrochemical industry necessitated the replacement of coal with oil and later gas due to their greater energy density and portability. Indeed, oil gradually replaced coal after the 1920s, but it was after WWII that oil became a strategic commodity for the global economy. This made the Gulf region of the Middle East (Iran, Iraq, Saudi Arabia and other small Gulf states) one of the most strategic zones of the global economy. As a result, after the war, the United States attempted to shape the trajectories of change in the Middle East by relying on pro-Western monarchs and elites in the context of the rise of the Soviet Union and regional anti-colonial struggles for popular sovereignty and national independence. To achieve this, the United States viewed Iran, Turkey, Saudi Arabia and Israel as strategic partners for confronting communism and anti-Western nationalism in the Middle East (Hanieh, 2013: 19–22). In addition, like its policy in Latin America, the United States advocated a rapid modernisation of the economies of its allies, especially Iran and Turkey (i.e., land reform and ISI). They perceived this policy as the best means for neutralising potential peasant revolutions and integrating these economies into growing US international firms.

Nevertheless, the United States was very quickly confronted by the nationalisation of the Iranian oil industry movement. Apart from the dominance of the anti-colonial atmosphere in the Global South, the new agreements between US companies and Venezuela and Saudi Arabia on the base of 50–50 sharing profits emboldened some Iranian state elites to pursue the nationalisation of oil. Moreover, many urban elites and the national bourgeoisie viewed the nationalisation of oil as the only path to redirect the failed attempt of the state-centralisation programme in the 1930s and 1940s to overcome so-called Iranian 'backwardness'. Under these conditions, the National Front under the leadership of Mohammed Musaddiq (Prime Minister between 1951 and 1953) enlarged the basis of the movement by fostering a loose alliance of 'various progressive, moderate, conservative, and even some reactionary political groups' (Hooglund, 1982: 44). The principal objective of the movement was to direct the oil revenues towards establishing national industries and creating an independent state without any plan for implementing a radical change in the socioeconomic composition of the Iranian countryside. Musaddiq mistakenly perceived the oil nationalisation as a dispute between Iran and Britain. Hence, to encourage Washington to hold a 'neutral' position, he signalled his inclination to work with the United States by appealing for a $120-million loan (Alamdari, 2005: 207). By assuming the required domestic and international support, the pro-National Front Majles thus ratified the bill of nationalisation in 1951, leading to a British-enforced boycott of Iranian petroleum with sweeping economic consequences. Under the severe financial deficit, the government thus proposed the policy of the 'non-oil economy'. In this connection, the government attempted to tighten the control of foreign trade and issued two decrees to implement modest land reform in 1952. This policy eventually broke down the already loose alliance of the National Front as it alienated the mercantile class, the big landlords and the Shi'a ulama (Matin, 2013a: 91–2; Hooglund, 1982: 43–4). The disunity and the

imminent collapse of the coalition provided an ideal situation for overthrowing the Musaddiq government in a coup on 19 August 1953 with the heavy
involvement of MI6 and the CIA (Katouzian, 1999: 177–94; Katouzian,
1981: 171–9). Following the coup, the new oil agreement led to the loss
of the BP monopoly position in favour of a new US consortium (Halliday,
1979: 142). With the growing influence of the United States in Iran after
the coup, the launch of a reform programme to secure the stability of the
Iranian state and industrialise the country in line with the new American-led
global economy seemed inevitable.

In light of this, US economic aid and military grant aid to Iran reached
$366.8 and $133.9 million respectively between 1953 and 1957. The aid
aimed to stabilise the discontented population and rekindle economic growth
as the United States considered Iran a strategic part of the world capitalist bloc against the threat of communism. To fundamentally restructure the
Iranian economy, these figures notably hiked under the second seven-year
plan between 1955 and 1962. This economic plan had a $1.2-billion budget,
which was a combination of US aid and loans, World Bank loans and oil
revenues. The plan was administered by the Plan Organisation that 'assem-
bled some of Iran's best-trained personnel and hired additional foreign advi-
sors financed by the Ford Foundation'. The chief objective of the plan was
the construction of 'dams, roads, telecommunications, power plants and a
large-scale irrigation project' (Richards, 1975: 7–10). It was the second phase
of a comprehensive national scheme advised by the Americans and World
Bank officials after WWII that 'aimed at increasing the degree of integration between the foreign-financed export-orientated sector and the rest of the
economy' (Afshar, 1981: 1098). Although the Iranian Point IV Programme
was 'one of the largest in the world' and despite the boom of the mid-1950s,
the economy was in a severe crisis in the late 1950s due to the combination of
easy credit, the exhaustion of the country's foreign exchange caused by unre-
stricted imports and rising prices in the absence of purchasing power of the
population (Richards, 1975: 10–11). In accordance with the International
Monetary Fund (IMF) and the World Bank's prescription to mitigate the
crisis, the government implemented an unsuccessful stabilising programme,
including a ban on importing luxury goods, restriction on bank credit and
the sale of foreign exchange (Parsa, 2009: 6).

In addition to this economic crisis, the July 1958 revolution in neighbouring Iraq drastically affected the direction of change in Iran. In the context
of the Cold War, some landlords gradually accepted the necessity of land
reform to prevent an 'impending peasant revolution' and resist the 'menace
of communist encroachment'. However, due to a number of factors, above
all the class structure of Iranian villages that will be explained shortly, the
emergence of a coherent peasant community capable of overthrowing the

regime was something of a myth (Ashraf, 1991: 278–80; see also Kazemi and Abrahamian, 1978). In fact, the severity of the threat of an Iranian peasant revolution was largely deduced from the victory of the Chinese Revolution a decade earlier and the Cuban Revolution in 1959, as well as several Soviet-backed peasant movements in the region rather than the history of the peasant movement in Iran. Against this backdrop, the fall of the monarchy in Iraq made the threat of peasants and communists more tangible for the Iranian elites, especially considering that the Soviet Union propagated the idea that Iranian social conditions would be fertile for a revolution by referencing the case of Iraq. This in turn aided the United States to augment the pressure on the Shah to implement land reform. The Kennedy victory in 1961 was a turning point in this regard because the new US administration made it clear that its economic and political support for the Shah depended on the launch of a reform programme with a particular emphasis on the overhaul of the Iranian countryside and agricultural sector (Halliday, 1979: 26–7). The threat became real when the Ford Foundation removed its advisory group from the Plan Organisation and thus the Economic Bureau of the Organisation practically collapsed following the departure of its best-trained local personnel (Richards, 1975: 10). These national, regional and global determinants ultimately convinced the Shah and the Iranian ruling class that launching a radical agrarian reform and a programme of rapid industrialisation in line with the new American-centred global capitalism was the only viable option for their survival.

Accordingly, in May 1961, the Shah appointed Ali Amini, who was ambassador to the United States from 1956 to 1958, to materialise the land reform programme (Hooglund, 1982: 47–8). At the same time, the Shah dissolved the Twentieth Majles in order to thwart potential threats against the new government from the landlords. In the absence of the Parliament, Amini and his enthusiastic anti-landowner Minister of Agriculture, Arsanjani, proposed much tougher legislation (Ansari, 2001: 7–8). The reform, therefore, launched officially in January 1962 with six provisions: 'land reform, nationalisation of forests, sale of public enterprises, profit-sharing schemes involving workers, female suffrage, and foundation of literacy corps'. Following the dismissal of Amini and Arsanjani in July 1962, the programme, extended to twelve points, went under the direction of the Shah and was renamed 'the White Revolution of the Shah and the People' (Ansari, 2014: 192–8).

The most important component of the project was land reform to eliminate the remaining agrarian non-capitalist relations, neutralise any possible peasant revolt, and mechanise agriculture. As well as increasing productivity, the industrialisation of the agricultural sector was viewed as necessary for the creation of a reserve army of labour, which was essential for the development of national industries (Najmabadi, 1987: 9–10). The Shah also gradually recognised that the land reform not only made his regime popular among the peasantry but also negated the political agenda of the leftist groups and the National Front (Ashraf, 1991: 282). To convince some discontented landlords, the government encouraged them to invest their gained capital from the selling of their land in what the Shah called 'Persia's expanding industry and commerce' for 'quicker returns' because 'landowning as such no longer commands quite so much profit or prestige/value as formerly' (Pahlavi, 1980: 204).

Land reform was a crucial stage in the consolidation of capitalism in Iran. Since the initiation of the modernisation project in the early to mid-nineteenth century, land had been steadily utilised for the accumulation of capital and the commodification of labour gradually expanded in Iranian agriculture. The land reform simply finalised this process. Before examining the phases and outcomes of the land reform, we first need to explore the land tenure system and social relations in the countryside until 1962. There were five types of landholdings before the land reform: large-scale private landed estates, state lands, crown lands, endowment lands, and peasant proprietorship. The owners of the large-scale private landed estates – including absentee landlords (majority), settled nomadic tribal leaders and clergy – owned around 69 per cent of all land. The state possessed approximately 6 per cent of land, 8 per cent belonged to the crown, and around 12 per cent were endowment lands. The small proprietors owned roughly around 5 per cent of the land. As part of these small proprietors, around 7 per cent of the Iranian peasants owned more than three hectares of land each (Alamdari, 2005: 188–95). These small proprietors constituted the middle peasants, who cultivated their land with the help of family labour. The remaining 93 per cent of the Iranian peasants were either cultivating rights holders (*nasaqdār-hā*) or paid agricultural and non-agricultural labourers (Kazemi, 1980: 32–3). The cultivating rights holders had the customary right of cultivation on particular lands (*nasaq*) and constituted approximately 40 per cent of all inhabitants of villages. In contrast, the agricultural workers without this right provided peak-season labour and non-agricultural labourers engaged in service activities for the village, including barbering, blacksmithing, shoemaking, etc. (Hooglund, 1973). They made up 40 to 50 per cent of the total population of the countryside. As the agricultural labourers did not have any regular work, they constituted the poorest of all villagers (Katouzian, 1974: 26–7; Hooglund, 1973: 230). There was hostility between the *nasaq* holders and the agricultural workers mainly because of the conflict of economic interests, which resulted in the exclusion of the latter from membership of the elected village and rural tribunals as well as the discouragement of social relationships such as marriages between the two (Hooglund, 1973: 238). This practically hindered the formation of a coherent peasant community as well as an organised peasant movement capable of jeopardising the interests of landowners.

Let us now turn to the various phases of the land reforms. The first stage aimed at transferring the arable lands to the cultivating peasant house-holders (*nasaqdār-hā*). The state paid the landlords and arranged annual instalments for farmers to repay their loans through the Agricultural Bank. Overall, it is estimated that in this stage around 17 per cent of the ownership of total villages was transferred. The second phase began in 1963 and per-mitted the landowners to hold 30 to 150 hectares of their non-mechanised land in return for managing their land based on a number of given options. Their favourite method was renting their properties to the *nasaq* holders for thirty years contingent on the average income of the preceding three years (Ajami, 1973: 123–5). For farmers to receive land under phases one and two, the government preconditioned membership in newly introduced cooperatives. A government body under the control of the Agricultural Bank, which lent money to the richer peasants, managed these coopera-tives (Halliday, 1979: 121). The outcome was the creation of a considerable number of middle landlords, whose economic activity was lending money to poorer farmers and non-agricultural workers. These new middle landlords along with village tradesmen constituted a new rural petty bourgeoisie with a close link to the urban bazaar (Matin, 2013a: 111).

The major transformation began in the third and fourth stages after 1968, which completely discarded any pro-peasant elements of the first two stages. These phases intended to eliminate 'tenancy, new tenants, and the remaining old relationship between landlords and peasants'. To this end, the third and fourth phases envisaged the formation of three different agricultural companies: joint-stock agricultural companies, farm corpora-tions and large agro-industrial complexes (Alamdari, 2005: 251; Yeganeh, 1985: 78). The government stressed that the establishment of larger and mechanised units of farming would be more productive than the breaking down of farms into smaller parcels (Carey and Carey, 1976: 364). Hence, nearly half of those 1.3 million farmers who had received land in the thirty-years agreement of the second stage lost their rights and became landless labourers (Alamdari, 2005: 252). In the joint-stock agricultural companies with an average size of 2,000 hectares, farmers as members received wages and dividends (Katouzian, 1978: 358–9; Weinbaum, 1977: 438). For the creation of farm corporations, some former landlords and the state elites, including several members of the royal family, either purchased numerous fertile large farms from peasants cheaply or even used force to expel them from their land. To compensate high-ranking officials who were given bar-ren land, the government through the Agricultural Development Bank of Iran offered them a tremendous amount of low-interest loans. In addition, the government considered several thousand private commercial farms and orchards as farm corporations. It exempted them from land redistribution because farms were categorised as highly mechanised land. The principal plan of the state was the creation of several 5,000 to 25,000-hectare farms as 'agro-businesses'. Some of these agro-businesses were owned by the government, some were run by the private sector and the rest were joint ventures between foreign, mainly American, and Iranian firms that could be either private or state-owned. Apart from the direct investment, foreign firms also invested in other activities related to agriculture, for example, dam construction and building of irrigation systems, among others (Weinbaum, 1977: 438–9; Alamdari, 2005: 271–82).

The land reform successfully abolished the remaining pre-capitalist social relations by completely converting land into a commodity, directing its production for accumulation and expanding exchange relations between the cities and the countryside. In contrast to the government propaganda that the land reform would improve productivity in agriculture, the value of the agricultural export dropped by 36 per cent in 1976 and Iran's food imports climbed by more than three and a half times between 1970 and 1975 (Weinbaum, 1977: 445). The real shock, however, was in the socio-economic conditions of the peasants. The Shah claimed that the reform would create a large class of small capitalist farmers loyal to the regime, but only 27 per cent of peasants with cultivating rights received seven hectares of property, which was the minimum amount of land that a peasant household required to provide their means of subsistence. Most importantly, all agricultural workers without cultivating rights did not receive land since the government used the pre-existing *nasaq* arrangement in the land redistribution programme. This meant that more than 40 per cent of Iranian villagers were not in any way eligible to receive land even before the start of the reform (Afshar, 1981: 1103; Matin, 2013a: 110). By the mid-1970s, the army of jobless peasants reached more than 60 per cent of the rural population, forming an enormous impoverished rural proletariat due to two key determinants. First, the mechanisation of farming exacerbated their economic situation because it led to a sizeable decline in employment in the agricultural sector (Karshenas, 1990b: 261). Second, the emergence of the small-size peasant holdings after the reform eliminated opportunities for the landless workers to cultivate as agricultural labourers on those lands. The combination of the two factors forced them to migrate to the urban areas where the urban industrial sectors unceasingly demanded a substantial 'reserve army of labour' because of the industrialisation programme that was initiated simultaneously with the agrarian reform. Therefore, in 1972, rural immigrants formed approximately 14 per cent of the urban population (around 4 million). The incessant immigration of a substantial number of jobless farmers to the major cities had become a common trend throughout the 1970s (Bayat, 1987: 33).

As a result of the land reform, many landlords invested the money from the compensation for their land as capital in the newly established industrial agro-businesses while others became part of the financial and industrial bourgeoisie. Besides the agrarian reform, the significant amount of capital of this new class came from oil revenue. The new oil agreement of the post-1953 coup increased Iran's share slightly, but a fundamental change took place after it joined the Organization of the Petroleum Exporting Countries (OPEC) in the early 1970s. Not only did the revenue precipitate the state investment in industry, but it also provided the funds for the augmentation of the industrial capitalist class. Furthermore, fiscally, the government imposed high rates of duty on imports to promote domestic production to protect and nurture this class (Halliday, 1979: 142–50). This set of policies, known as the ISI strategy, was widely adopted by the so-called Third World states linked to the Western Bloc (Nasr, 2000: 101–2). The industrialisation project was carried out in a series of development plans, namely the third (1962–8), the fourth (1968–73) and the fifth (1973–8) plans. A fundamental development was the formation of influential industrial finance banks, including the Industrial Credit Bank and the Industrial and Mining Development Bank of Iran. The Industrial Credit Bank specialised in small to middle-sized loans and provided approximately 30 per cent of the funds for the private sector throughout the 1960s and the 1970s. The Industrial and Mining Development Bank of Iran, which was created by the Iranian government and the World Bank capital in 1959, was the largest supplier of funds for the private sector. Additionally, it was critically involved in the formulation of the government industrial policies and the promotion of new investment projects and functioned as an intermediary between state, domestic capital and foreign capital. As Karshenas (1990a: 101) points out:

> The structure of capital and ownership of IMDBI [Industrial and Mining Development Bank of Iran] highlights one of the salient features of the post-1953 capitalist development in Iran, namely the emergence of a small group of businessmen with clientelistic ties to the state, who, by virtue of their monopoly access to the state funds and close collaboration with foreign capital, managed to multiply their capital in a hothouse manner.

Large Western firms usually provided technology, managerial skills and finance capital in return for forging profitable partnerships with the local industrial bourgeois to access the domestic market with minimum competition (Pesaran, 1982: 510–11). Hence, with the average annual industrial growth of 15 per cent between 1965 and 1975, it is estimated that 6,000 manufacturing units with more than 10 employees were established by

1977. Many of them were major plants in the petrochemical sector, steel sector, car, truck and bus industry as well as machine-tool factories and electronic assembly plants (Halliday, 1979: 148). In the same year, there were 1.7 million modern industrial proletariat and 700,000 agricultural labourers, while still nearly half a million worked in traditional manufacturing units (Abrahamian, 1980: 22).

We wrap up this chapter with the conceptualisation of this major restructuring that consolidated capitalism in Iran based on earlier discussions on the forms of transition within capitalism (see pp. 39–41). After the Great Depression and the subsequent devastating WWII, the international context of uneven development fostered the ISI model of development for the periphery by breaking from the nineteenth-century model of the international market. This went hand in hand with the change in the configuration of global hegemony from Pax Britannica to Pax Americana. In contrast to Britain's strategy of integrating the peripheral states into the global market through raw materials for its industrial needs, the United States was promoting industrial productive relations in line with the rise of its international firms. Accordingly, the shakeup of global capitalism and the shift in power from Britain to America in the international political economy laid the foundation for the restructuring of capitalism and the reorganisation of the state in the developing countries linked to the Western Bloc. In addition to this push for a state-led establishment of national industries, in the Gulf Middle East, the United States under the Truman Doctrine and later the Eisenhower Doctrine committed to intervening in the region to safeguard the flow of oil to the global economy because petroleum became the essential energy source of new industries and transport networks and key to powering modern navies and armies. While the United States put pressure on these countries to go down the path of 'modernisation', this restructuring cannot be reduced to the agency of the outside imperial power. This is because many ruling elites in these countries initiated and embraced this transformation to counter the threat of communism and peasant revolts. Moreover, the outcome of the postwar restructuring was rather different in these societies as it was conditioned by the domestic class structure and the relation of political forces.

In Iran, initially, the United States orchestrated a coup to overthrow the Musaddiq government in order to block the nationalisation of the oil industry. In addition, the central agencies of the US government and the international institutions, in particular the World Bank, functioned to accommodate domestic social tensions with the requirements of the global economy by providing financial and advisory assistance as well as elements of political pressure whenever required. Nonetheless, many ruling elites shared the US position that land reform and simultaneous rapid industrialisation to create labour-intensive production plants could only undercut the revolutionary threat from the Iranian pro-Western state. Accordingly, the agrarian sector was mechanised and new industries through the ISI model were built and protected. As an example of state capitalism, the Shah's modernisation was specially geared towards building up a heavy industrial base. Due to the inability of the state to mobilise from within its own borders the financial and technological resources and machinery for the creation of modern industries, particularly the heavy industries, the project profoundly relied on the United States and to some extent other advanced Western states. Along with the financial support of the United States and the investments of some large American firms, the large foreign reserves of the country thanks to the oil revenue, especially at the beginning of the 1970s, crucially aided the financing of the imports of machinery, components and other inputs needed to build up the country's industrial base. This transformation placed Iran among the eight developing countries that produced roughly two-thirds of the growth in the value of Third World manufacturing between 1966 and 1975 (McMichael, 2014: 64). The state played the leading role in this process of managed transformation. These reforms from above thus restructured Iranian capitalism and generated the new protected capitalist class of around 2,000 families with close ties to foreign capital – among those were many former landlords – who controlled the whole apparatus of the state. The most influential faction of this class was the Pahlavis, including 'sixty-three princes, princesses, and cousins of the royal family' who 'controlled one-fifth of the private assets of Iran, with shares in 207 companies involved in agriculture, housing, hotels, autos, textiles, insurance, and publishing companies, among others' (Foran, 1994: 169). It is not unreasonable, therefore, to use the term 'monarcho-bourgeoisie' to describe this small 'modern' capitalist class.[6]

The White Revolution can best be conceptualised as an instance of capitalist restructuring from above. The agrarian reform and industrialisation to a great degree reorganised and revolutionised the social relations through which the old ruling class continued to restore its domination in the state. It reimposed class order, revitalised capital accumulation and generated wealth for the monarcho-bourgeoisie as a result of 'Persia's expanding industry and commerce', in the words of the Shah. But the White Revolution miserably failed to partially incorporate and realise the demands of the peasantry despite the Shah's propaganda that the land reform would give peasants a prosperous future and augment his popularity among them. In fact, as I shall demonstrate in the next chapter, these top-down reforms of the second Pahlavi state spawned a highly uneven development that induced absolute growth inequality and poverty in the society by engendering a colossal class of urban poor and worsening the socioeconomic conditions of the working class, the middle class and the traditional petty bourgeoisie. Not only did the White Revolution alienate the powerful traditional mercantile class of the bazaar, but the land reform and the rapid industrialisation based on the ISI strategy also precipitated the forging of a coalition among all social classes against the monarcho-bourgeoisie, which eventually toppled the Pahlavi state in 1979.

## Conclusion

This chapter has narrated and conceptualised the emergence and consolidation of capitalism and the establishment of the modern state in Iran over the *longue durée* by attesting to the centrality of the dialectical relations between global and local dynamics and international and national shaping factors. It began with a brief sketch of the demise of the tributary mode of production in the late eighteenth and early nineteenth centuries. It then explained the introduction of a series of reforms under the name of *Nizam-e Jadid* to modernise the army and state administration in the early to mid-nineteenth century under severe geopolitical pressure and domestic crisis during the global order of Pax Britannica. The series of reforms led to the gradual spread of capitalist relations and the integration of Iran into the global free trade regime, which generated a wave of revolts that destabilised the state and society. The discovery of oil and the intensification of the inter-class and intra-class struggles against the backdrop of the volatile international milieu, especially the diffusion of revolutionary ideas of Bolshevism, necessitated the speeding up of efforts for the constitution of the modern state at the beginning of the twentieth century. The institutionalisation of the modern state and sweeping reforms under the Reza Shah reign committed the Iranian state to the imperatives of capital accumulation and further spread of capitalist social relations in Iran. Conceptualising this long process of the emergence of capitalism and the formation of the modern state in Iran as an instance of social revolution in the form of passive revolution, the chapter called for situating it in the wider context of the global order under the supremacy of Great Britain while remaining sensitive to the particularity of Iranian class structure.

The second part of the chapter narrated the consolidation of capitalism in Iran in the context of the rising power of the United States during the Cold War. It showed that, after WWII, the restructuring of the global economy along new lines necessitated a radical land reform and comprehensive industrialisation programme in Iran to counter the so-called imminent peasant revolt and integrate the economy into the American-led global economy since the country was considered a vital member of the Western Bloc. Rather than being passive recipients of the new order, the Iranian ruling class actively participated in this process of capitalist restructuring and the domestic class structure equally shaped the process. The successful agrarian reform and the rapid industrialisation in accordance with the ISI strategy annihilated the remaining pre-capitalist social relations in the countryside and directed all relations towards the accumulation of capital. This major restructuring had two contradictory results. First, the White Revolution exceedingly destabilised the balance of class forces and generated a united front against the Shah, which ultimately led to the fall of the monarchy following the popular revolution of 1979. Second, despite the overthrow of the Pahlavi state, to a large degree, the new revolutionary state continued the Shah's ISI state-led development in the first decade of the revolution between 1979 and 1989. The next chapter will examine these two processes.

## Notes

1  The Usuli School of Shi'aism believes that reliance on the Quran and the traditions of Prophet Mohammad and the Imams is not always enough and the active intellectual exercise of the qualified Shi'a jurisconsults (*foqa-hā*/*faqihān*) is necessary for establishing legal standards. The doctrine of the guardianship of the jurisconsult (*velāyat-e faqih*), which was reconstructed by Khomeini, was introduced first during this era. For Khomeini's interpretation of the Usuli School, see Abrahamian (1991).

2  Sufism (*tasavvf*) is an esoteric, non-scriptural and non-legalistic form of Islam in which 'Muslims seek to find the truth of divine love and knowledge through direct personal experience of God' (Schimmel, 2022).

3  Understanding the hierarchical social structure and politics of the bazaar and the class basis of Shi'a ulama is necessary to conceive the interactive politics of the bazaar and Shi'a ulama in the modern history of Iran. The bazaar was a bounded space in cities for the production and particularly exchange of specific commodities with their own value chain that generated a hierarchical class structure. At the top of the pyramid were big merchants who imported consumer and intermediate goods and exported handmade products, in particular hand-woven carpets. They also had some links with the countryside as some agricultural goods were exported by them. The multilayered wholesale class, mainly based on the Tehran Bazaar, distributed imported goods by big merchants through their networks across the country. In the middle of the pyramid, there were the owners of retail stores who directly sold goods to customers. These retailers/shopkeepers, with over 100 guild-like associations as well as the headmen and the masters of artisans being involved in traditional manufacturing productions, constituted the traditional petty bourgeoisie. At the bottom of the hierarchy, there were 'the masses of apprentices and footboys, with some marginal elements such as poor peddlers, dervishes and beggars' (Ashraf, 1989; Keshavarzian, 2007: 78–84). Due to its spatial concentration – the central

bazaar was located in a single location in most cities – and trade specialisation, there was generally a strong sense of solidarity among the various classes of the bazaar (Parsa, 1994: 147). Nevertheless, this did not generate a comprehensive class unity as the conflict of interests between merchants and the petty bourgeoisie of the bazaar existed throughout history. Whilst some influential ulama became part of the landowning class through controlling endowment lands after the collapse of the Safavid Empire, the others were in an instrumental relationship with the powerful classes of the bazaar. The merchants and traditional petty bourgeoisie paid a substantial amount of the income of this faction of clergy through religious taxes (*khoms va zakāt*) and contributions to charitable funds. In return, this wing of ulama defended the interests of the bazaar against foreign economic interests and the urban poor (Moaddel, 1986: 524; Ashraf, 1988: 542). Accordingly, rather than constituting a class, from the beginning of the Qajar empire until the 1960s' land reform, different segments of Shi'a ulama had allied with landowners, merchants and the traditional petty bourgeoisie. They thus often acted as 'the political representatives of each, or a combination of some or all, of these classes' (Moaddel, 1986: 520–1).

4  The company was renamed the Anglo-Iranian Oil Company (AIOC) in 1935. In 1953, the name was changed to British Petroleum Company (BP) following three years of conflict over the nationalisation of the oil with the Iranian government at the beginning of the 1950s (BBC News, 1998).

5  Skocpol (1979), Trotsky (1936/1972) and Davidson (2010b) provide invaluable arguments about the distinction between social and political revolution.

6  The term 'monarcho-bourgeoisie' is cited by Matin (2013a: 117) from Ahmad (2008) who notes that the term has been actually used for the first time by Ervand Abrahamian in *Iran between two revolutions* (1982).

# 3

# 1979 revolution and war with Iraq: The expansion of state capitalism

In the previous chapter, we showed how the context of post-WWII global capitalism laid the foundation for the restructuring of capitalism in Iran through the promotion of the ISI strategy. By taking the impacts of the domestic class structure into consideration, we also demonstrated that the relation of political forces in the state and society enormously influenced the White Revolution. Under these conditions, the Shah's modernisation, as an example of state capitalism, resulted in the development of national industries and the emergence of the new protected monarcho-bourgeoisie, comprising many members of the royal family and ex-landlords. With close ties to foreign capital, the monarcho-bourgeoisie controlled the whole apparatus of the state.

Building on these findings, this chapter has two objectives. It substantiates that the top-down White Revolution of the second Pahlavi state spawned highly uneven development that significantly increased growth inequality and poverty in the society. Besides engendering a colossal class of urban poor and exacerbating the socioeconomic conditions of the working class, the middle class and the traditional petty bourgeoisie, the chapter reveals that the Shah's attack on the autonomy of the traditional market also significantly alienated the powerful tradition mercantile class of the bazaar from the mid-1970s onwards. The first objective is to display how the formation of a coalition among all social classes against the monarcho-bourgeoisie toppled the Pahlavi state and the Islamic forces won the post-revolutionary battle. The second objective is to disclose the processes of class and state formation during the first decades of the revolution from 1979 to 1989. It conceptualises the 1979 revolution as an instance of political revolution since the ISI state-led development even expanded in the first decade of the revolution, albeit against the backdrop of US hostility and under the name of the national liberation of the 'downtrodden'. As a political revolution, however, the 1979 revolution replaced the old ruling class with the new one. To unpack the class basis of the Islamic State during the first decade of the revolution, the chapter

traces the ways in which the extensive nationalisation of the first decade
of the revolution led to the emergence of two fractions of the new ruling
class, namely the *stratum of government managers* and the *bonyad–bazaar
nexus*. Looking at this legacy of state capitalism and the class character
of the post-revolutionary state is important for our story because grasping
the process of neoliberalisation and the trajectories of change in contemporary Iran heavily relies on this historical period.

The arguments of the chapter unfold in two parts. The next section scrutinises the impacts of the White Revolution on the non-ruling classes and
the formation of an unwritten alliance between these classes with the objective of overthrowing the Shah's regime. The second section examines the
processes of the establishment of the Islamic revolutionary state and of the
expansion of state capitalism, initially through the confiscation of the assets
of the old ruling class and the nationalisation of industries and later due to
the war with Iraq from 1980 to 1988. The second section thus conceptualises the 1979 revolution, unveils the 1980s' social contract and pinpoints the
class locations and ideological basis of the fractions of the new ruling class.

## Revolution from below against the White Revolution

As the White Revolution immensely expanded modern industries, it generated a powerful bourgeois class. Likewise, it amplified the population of the
urban blue-collar proletariat and the modern service sectors with 1.25 million white-collar workers, of whom 68 per cent were employed in the state
sector thanks to the expansion of the state bureaucracy (Bayat, 1987: 26–7).
The reforms also deepened inequality and poverty. According to an
unpublished report by the International Labour Office, Iran was already
'one of the most inegalitarian societies in the world' in 1959–60, but the
White Revolution exacerbated the level of income inequality as 'the top
20 per cent of urban families accounted for as much as 55.5 per cent of the
total expenditures' while 'the bottom 20 per cent for as little as 3.7 per cent'
in 1973 (Abrahamian, 1980: 23). Politically, the Pahlavi state also antago-
nised the working class because it aggressively dismantled labour unions,
professional associations and political parties after the 1953 coup as a necessary step for implementing economic reforms that largely favoured the
monarcho-bourgeoisie. Another zone of antagonism was the looming precarity of newly unemployed labourers generated due to the massive influx
of peasants to cities. Their labour was provisionally absorbed by the construction sector, but the sudden burst of the sector caused by the mid-1970s'
crisis eventually forced these new urban workers to seek employment in the
bazaar as day labourers, small shopkeepers and street peddlers. Many of

them also found employment in the small-scale workshops and medium-sized units linked to the bazaar. The economic boom and the growth of the urban population partially aided the small-scale units and medium-sized enterprises to flourish since the modern industrial firms were unable to cover all traditional production. As a clear indication of this trend, there were 200,000 small workshops with fewer than ten workers and only 830 factories with 500 or more employees in 1977 (Matin, 2013a: 112). A small number of these small-scale units utilised machines and modern methods of work while most of these units relied on craft techniques and employed migrant workers in poor working conditions with low wages and job insecurity (Bayat, 1987: 31–2).

Many of these small and medium-sized enterprises still heavily relied on the merchants and moneylenders of the bazaar despite the relocation of their units outside the bazaar over the course of the twentieth century. Historically, the bazaar was not just a site for commerce but also a site for production. Due to Reza Shah's modernisation in the 1930s, artisanal and small-scale manufacturing of the bazaar declined. In addition, the second Pahlavi's reconstruction of the economy forced the remaining traditional production lines to move away from the Tehran bazaar to the other parts of the city where the production of goods was less costly (Keshavarzian, 2007: 45–6). That said, the merchants and moneylenders of the bazaar kept their links with both small manufacturing workshops and medium-sized plants by financing them as most of these manufacturing units were not eligible to access the subsidised credits of the state-owned commercial and development banks. Since the government prioritised the large industries, the big businesses received generous 6 per cent interest rate loans of the state-subsidised banks while the small firms borrowed from private moneylenders of the bazaar at very high interest rates, sometimes 40 per cent per month. As a result, the internal credit system of the bazaar flourished throughout the 1960s and 1970s. Keshavarzian (2007: 86) notes that 'in 1963, the bazaaris in Iran were estimated to loan as much as all the commercial banks put together. In 1975, the Tehran bazaar was estimated to control 20 per cent of the official market volume, or \$3 billion in foreign exchange and \$2.1 billion in loans outstanding'. The astronomical interest rates of these loans compared to the official banks' loans did not put the national bourgeoisie and the artisanal wing of the traditional petty bourgeoisie against the bazaar financiers because it was a win-win for both sides during the economic boom. More importantly, they blamed the government not the moneylenders of the bazaar since its economic policies in favour of the protected foreign-affiliated large industries enabled the discriminatory commercial regulations and tax laws and their exclusion from the state's generous credit schemes and loans.

The ISI strategy also strengthened the commercial activities of the bazaar. A major issue with ISI was the shortage of foreign exchange but this was not a problem in Iran owing to the oil revenues. Given this advantage, Iran was reluctant to put strict limits on imports, unlike most middle-income countries associated with ISI. Combined with the high levels of liquidity due to the 1970s' oil boom, the fetishisation of Western goods, the modest rise of incomes and the growth of population, it resulted in a substantial surge in imports during the 1960s and 1970s. Accordingly, the import of consumer goods and intermediate goods as the key activities of the bazaar witnessed a steady rise in the early stage of industrialisation and an astonishing fivefold increase from 1973 to 1978 (Keshavarzian, 2007: 138). The geographical unevenness of industrialisation and urbanisation made Tehran a convenient destination for the absorption of most of the national investment (60 per cent of all industrial investment) and employment in retail and wholesale activities. Moreover, the construction of new business districts and modern shopping malls outside the Tehran bazaar did not reduce the influence of the bazaar because these modern economic centres still depended on the bazaar wholesalers and merchants. Therefore, thanks to its historical and locational advantages as well as the growth of imports, the Tehran bazaar maintained its commercial supremacy as it still controlled a third of imports and as much as two-thirds of the retail trade in the country (Keshavarzian, 2007: 144–5; Abrahamian, 2008: 24). In short, the bazaar benefited enormously from the economic boom of the mid-1960s to mid-1970s even though the state intended to construct economic policies in favour of creating modern large industrial and commercial entrepreneurs.

This unintended economic boom of the bazaar was not something that the state predicted, nor viewed positively. But instead of launching an offensive move against it, in the words of Abrahamian (1980: 24–5), the state pursued the policy of 'let sleeping dogs lie' towards the bazaar prior to the mid-1970s' crisis. In line with the ideas of a simple linear development embedded in the pervasive modernisation theory of the post-WWII era, the state assumed that the construction of modern banks, industries, supermarkets and shopping stores would automatically replace the traditional credit system and moneylending, destroy small-scale manufacturing and oust the bazaar-located retail stores. Hence, despite the contempt of the state towards the bazaaris, the government intentionally chose not to meddle in the politics of the bazaar, regulate its activities or directly restructure it (Keshavarzian, 2007: 133–4).

The economic crisis of 1975–77 forced the state to change this policy towards the bazaar and amplified its pressure on political organisations linked to the working class and the middle class. An enormous increase in the oil price after the OPEC meetings in 1973 generated huge revenue for the

Shah's ambitious industrial modernisation. This induced rising wages and new employment opportunities which in turn encouraged rapid migration and shortages in housing and other goods and services. The result was escalating inflation (Skocpol, 1982: 270; Keddie, 2003: 163). OPEC's decision in September 1975 to decrease oil prices caused a massive decline in foreign exchange receipts and thus a major drop in revenue that threw many workers out of employment. Together with the quick rise in the costs of production and labour that jeopardised the non-oil exports, Iran was on the verge of bankruptcy (Afshar, 1981: 1104). Unable to control the economic crisis, in 1975, the Shah declared a one-party system with two options, either joining the newly formed Resurgence Party (*hezb-e Rastākhiz*) or leaving the country. This was an attempt to tighten the state's control over the growing urban poor and working classes and terminate the autonomy of the bazaar. The state specially targeted the bazaar as a scapegoat, as the Shah acknowledged in his memoir: 'The bazaaris are a fanatic lot, highly resistant to change because their locations afford a lucrative monopoly. Moving against the bazaaris was typical of political and social risks I had to take in my drive for modernisation' (Pahlavi, 1980: 156). The state thus opened branches of the Rastakhiz party in bazaars across the country and replaced the traditional High Councils of Guilds with the tightly government-controlled Chambers of Guilds. Moreover, as the bazaaris were accused of hoarding and price-fixing practices that triggered and intensified inflation, the government launched an anti-price-gouging campaign. This led to the imprisonment of 8,000, the exile of another 23,000, and the fining of as many as 200,000 businessmen, shopkeepers and peddlers of the bazaar in several stages (Skocpol, 1982: 272; Abrahamian, 1982: 242–433; Abrahamian, 1980: 24–5; Moaddel, 1996: 337).[1] This onslaught that targeted all social groups of the bazaar augmented their solidarity against the state and was 'one of the most decisive factors in instigating the bazaaris to join the revolution of 1977–79' (Ashraf, 1988: 557; see also Moghadam, 1987: 11).[2]

The White Revolution also united the two wings of ulama against the state, namely those clerics who were part of the landowning class and those with links to the mercantile class of the bazaar. As explained in the previous chapter, many big landowners were gradually included in the new capitalist class following the land reform, but an influential wing of the ulama, as part of the landowning class, denounced the White Revolution. This dissatisfaction resulted in the June 1963 uprising under the leadership of Khomeini, which was ruthlessly suppressed by the state.[3] Another wing of the ulama with a close bond to the mercantile class and the petty bourgeoisie of the bazaar, however, did not join the uprising at least until the Shah, in defence of the modern industrial class, endeavoured to eradicate the bazaar economy after the economic crisis of the mid-1970s.

In sharp contrast with the conditions of Gramsci's integral state (1971: 238), in Iran, the 'primordial and gelatinous' civil society was incapable of producing a protective buffer to taper class antagonism. Hence, the second Pahlavi state was accused of all the social tensions spawned from the creation and distribution of material wealth. Under this condition, the dissatisfied urban working class, the urban poor of shanty towns, the petty bourgeoisie, the ulama and the bazaar forged an unwritten alliance; that is, the whole society against the small monarcho-bourgeoisie with tight links to the metropolitan capital. The central objective of this unwritten alliance was the overthrowing of the Shah's regime, which was unconditionally supported by Western imperialist powers. This does not mean that the economic positions of these classes automatically determine their class identities and strategies against the regime. As Stuart Hall (1986: 43) correctly argues, the economic structure provides the repertoire of categories as outlined above and has constraining effects on the strategies of classes. Yet 'what the economic cannot do is (a) to provide the contents of the particular thoughts of particular social classes or groups at any specific time; or (b) to fix or guarantee for all time which ideas will be made use of by which classes'. Hence, it is an untenable proposition to claim that an analysis of the objective places of social classes in the economic structure 'can produce empirically-constituted "whole classes"' because 'the political, juridical and the ideological also have *their own* effects, just as they have their own, determinate, conditions of existence, not reducible to "the economic"' in a narrow sense (Hall, 1977: 55–6). This understanding of determinacy crucially justifies 'the necessary "openness" of historical development to practice and struggle' of the agency of classes and fundamentally problematises the deterministic interpretation of history, which results in 'absolute predictability' of the practice of the agency (Hall, 1977: 44). E.P. Thompson (1978: 149) provides a clearer explanation of this process:

> Classes do not exist as separate entities, look around, find an enemy class, and then start to struggle. On the contrary, people find themselves in a society structured in determined ways, they experience exploitation (or the need to maintain power over those whom they exploit), they identify points of antagonistic interest, they commence to struggle around these issues and in the process of struggling they discover themselves as classes.

In our case, although these classes identified points of antagonistic interest with a common enemy due to the uneven nature of Pahlavi's modernisation, their mobilisation required an oppositionist discourse to form and transform their identities. Throughout the revolutionary upheaval and its immediate aftermath, there were several oppositional discourses, but ultimately it was the Khomeinist interpretation of Islam that resonated most with the masses to confront the late Pahlavi state.[4]

Khomeini's militant Islamic discourse was an amalgamation of using particular modern vocabulary, including 'colonialism', 'the West', 'the Third World' and 'Westoxification' and substituting others such as 'proletariat' and 'bourgeoisie' with 'downtrodden' (*mostaz'afān/mostaz'afin*) and 'oppressors' (*mostakberān/mostakberin*) to fight for a just Islamic state ruled by the Shi'a clerics (Matin, 2013a: 130–41). The industrial proletariats amenable to secular left politics were relatively small compared to the workers employed in the bazaar who were 'generally exposed and amenable to the Islamists' ideological appeal' (Matin, 2013a: 118). Likewise, the radical reading of Shi'a doctrine resonated with a significant proportion of white-collar workers and the unemployed urban poor of shanty towns. While admitting the popularity of Khomeinism, we should remember that the Islamist groups widely used violence to purge secular political opponents, especially after the fall of the Shah. Up to the victory of the revolution alongside the Islamic groups, particularly those that adopted the dominant discourse of the militant Islam of Khomeini, the secular left parties and organisations played a key role in the toppling of the Pahlavi regime through various revolutionary waves between 1977 and 1979.[5] However, in the vicious political battle after the revolution, the followers of Khomeini successfully marginalised and destroyed all secular rivals through an enormous level of violence and terror from 1979 to 1982. The Iraqi invasion of Iran and Khomeini's 'Jihad' against Kurdistan further solidified the ascendancy of the pro-Khomeini Islamists (see below). The result was the creation of the Islamic state based on Khomeini's notion of the guardianship of the jurisconsult (*velāyat-e faqih*). In the next section, we shall explore the economic policies and class and state formation during the first decade of the revolution.

## Extensive nationalisation and war: The volatile first decade of the revolution

### Nationalisation and the creation of revolutionary foundations

Soon after the revolution, many foreign firms affiliated with the Iranian capitalist class pulled out of Iran and a few members of the old ruling class fled the country with their capital and assets.[6] However, the Revolutionary Council and the Revolutionary Islamic Courts confiscated most of the property of the monarcho-bourgeoisie through two distinct forms of state ownership, the so-called 'government' and 'public' forms.[7] In the first form, all private banks, insurance companies and all heavy industries were brought under the control of the government. In the initial round of the seizure of the banking sector, twenty-three private banks (around half of them owned by foreign firms) were nationalised in June 1979, followed by the nationalisation of the remaining thirty-six financial institutions in October 1979. Consequently, the nationalisation of the entire banking sector led to the creation of nine government-owned commercial and specialised banks. In July 1979, the nationalisation of the heavy industries, including mining, petrochemical, metals, shipbuilding, automobile and aircraft manufacturing, was justified by the Revolutionary Council on the basis that these industries were strategic and vital to the revolutionary state (Maloney, 2015: 117–18). Furthermore, the provisional government nationalised those industrial firms whose owners and managers fled the country as well as those companies that owed more than half of their assets to the banks and were on the verge of bankruptcy (Ehteshami, 1995: 86). In order to supervise all industrial activities, the Revolutionary Council approved the establishment of four ministries, namely the Ministry of Petroleum, Ministry of Mines and Metals, Ministry of Heavy Industry, and Ministry of Industry (controlled industries involved in food processing, textiles and pharmaceuticals) (Maloney, 2015: 118). The nationalisation was seen as a process to realise one of the principal objectives of the revolution, namely political and economic independence from the West and in particular the United States in order to accomplish 'true economic self-reliance'.

To materialise the redistribution of wealth and income among the 'downtrodden' as another principal aim of the revolution, 'non-profit para-governmental foundations' (*bonyād-hā-ye enqelābi*) were created. To fund these new revolutionary organisations, the Revolutionary Islamic Courts expropriated the assets of the royal family and its close associates, who were considered 'corrupt on earth', and categorised them as 'public' properties separated from government properties (Behdad, 1996: 101). According to Islamic law, this meant that they were at the disposal of the Imam[8] despite the intertwining of political and religious authority in post-revolutionary Iran. The Islamic revolutionary forces considered the bonyads invaluable vehicles because they could maintain the hegemony of the Khomeini conception of just governance over the subordinated classes. Besides the Pahlavi Foundation holdings, the substantial assets of those industrialists owned by the industrial complexes of the country[9] were transferred to these newly created revolutionary foundations, in particular the Foundation for the Oppressed and Self-Sacrificed (*bonyād-e mostaz'afān va jānbāzān*)[10] and Martyrs' Foundation (*bonyād-e shahid*). The Imam Khomeini Relief Committee (*komiteh-ye emdād-e emām khomeyni*) was also formed to provide 'medical, educational, and social assistance to the rural poor, women and orphaned children'.[11] In addition to these public foundations, some religious endowment foundations under the control of the Imam and outside the government authority and regulation were formed with similar goals. Endowment bonyads existed before the revolution, but their economic power and political influence were substantially augmented after the revolution. The Imam Reza Shrine Foundation (*bonyād-e āstān-e qods-e razavi*) is an example of a pre-revolutionary foundation. After the revolution, the most significant endowment foundation was the Fifteen Khordad Foundation (*bonyād-e panzdeh-e khordād*), which was established in memory of the Khomeini-led 1963 uprising against the White Revolution (Amirahmadi, 1995: 235). Along with the revolutionary and endowment foundations, the bazaar merchants formed private bonyads to utilise their private funds for 'non-profit' purposes, including the Islamic Economic Organisation (*sāzmān-e eqtesād-e eslāmi*), the Interest-Free Loan Fund (*sanduq-e qarz-ol-hasaneh*), the Eternal Foundation (*bonyād-e jāvid*), the Foundation for Growth of Islamic Republic (*bonyād-e rajā*) and the Welfare Foundation (*bonyād-e refāh*) (Moaddel, 1993: 248; see also Amirahmadi, 1995: 235).

As indicated above, the initial assets of the bonyads mostly came from the confiscation of the properties of the royal family and the capitalist class who fled the country after the revolution. In the following years, due to the expansion of their economic activities thanks to the war with Iraq, which allowed them to enter the front line of relief and reconstruction work, these foundations were transformed into giant semi-private monopolies by controlling hundreds of companies across dozens of industries. Most bonyads have been involved not only in domestic production but also in imports, distribution of goods and services and banking and credit (Farzin, 1996: 177). According to Behdad (1989: 328–9), the holdings of the Mostazafan Foundation 'in 1982 consisted of 203 mining and manufacturing enterprises, 472 commercial farms, 101 construction companies, 238 trading and other service enterprises, and 2,786 real estate properties'. A year later, the director of the Mostazafan Foundation admitted that his organisation 'is one of the largest conglomerates in the world and the largest Islamic entity in Iran' (Amirahmadi, 1995: 236). Similarly, the Martyrs' Foundation became involved in economic activities under the pretext of providing basic needs, housing, medical insurance, student admission to higher educational institutions and employment through its subsidiaries for the families of the martyrs and war-disabled of the revolution. It is reported that, in 1985, 'the total number of firms and factories under its control included 68 industrial units, 75 commercial companies and agencies, 21 construction companies and 17 agricultural units'. In addition to more than 6,000 units of real estate in Tehran, the Martyrs' Foundation also controlled 140 orchards and plots of land (Amirahmadi, 1995: 237). On top of receiving direct funds from the annual budget, the Imam Khomeini Relief Committee also became engaged in economic activities and owned a considerable amount of property and land holdings. According to Maloney (2015: 123), approximately 4 million poor Iranians were under the support of the Imam Khomeini Relief Committee by 1989. The Imam Reza Shrine Foundation was financed in large part through donations from pilgrims to the tomb of the Eighth Imam of Shi'a before the revolution, but its state annual budget and its economic activities climbed drastically as a result of the revolution. It also owned a large number of properties and controlled numerous trading companies, industrial units and social service delivery centres following the establishment of the Islamic Republic (Amirahmadi, 1995: 235). By engaging in profit-making activities in the following years, the private bonyads became important economic institutions. Although these bonyads were not as powerful as the revolutionary and endowment foundations, the example of the Islamic Economic Organisation indicates that we should not disregard their impact. As reported by Amirahmadi (1995: 235), the loanable fund of the Islamic Economic Organisation 'stood at 50 billion Iranian rials, roughly equal to 5 per cent of the country's total liquidity' in 1987. The para-governmental foundations have resisted scrutiny from parliament and the government and have been exempted from taxation despite being under pressure at certain stages since the establishment of the Islamic Republic (Mazarei, 1996: 299).

## Contestations and the social contract of the first decade of the revolution

Control of the large confiscated industrial, commercial and financial firms by the government and the revolutionary bonyads did not occur without a struggle from the labour movement. The strike of the oil industry workers was a crucial factor in the overthrow of the Shah in the final stage of the revolution (Fesharaki, 1985: 99). Given the significance of this modern industrial sector, the Common Syndicate of Employees of the Iranian Oil Industry coordinated the constitution of workers' councils (*shurā-hā-ye kārgari*) in numerous industrial units across the country. For several months after the revolution, the workers' councils managed most factories, which led to a reduction in working hours, increase in wages, improvement in working conditions, control over the production process and creation of independent labour unions and organisations (Moaddel, 1991: 323–4; 1993: 233–4). Concerned with the increasing role of the labour movement and the secular left, the new Islamic revolutionary state and Islamic militias attacked and eliminated the workers' councils in the summer of 1979. Hence, out of around 300 workers' councils at the beginning of the revolution, only a few of them remained somewhat active in 1983 (Moaddel, 1991: 327). The Islamists formed the government-sponsored workers' Islamic associations (*anjoman-hā-ye eslāmi-ye kārgari*) to replace these independent workers' councils (Maloney, 2015: 125–6).

Another area of major contestation was centred around the legacy of the land reform. Following the revolution, some peasants seized the land of the old ruling class who had escaped the country but at the same time some former landlords reclaimed their old land. To nullify the leftist forces who advocated redistribution of all land among farmers, the Islamists formed over 15,000 Islamic Associations with the same goal which gained the support of some prominent figures inside the Revolutionary Council. In contrast, other powerful clerics and their allies in the Majles fundamentally opposed this reform by referring to the Islamic law that only gives authority to endowment administrators (i.e., clerical landholders) to determine asset disposition. Despite the opposition of these conservative clerics, the Centre for the Transfer and Revitalisation of Land, which enjoyed the backing of the Revolutionary Council, distributed 150,000 hectares of barren land and 35,000 hectares of arable land among small holding and landless peasants in November 1980. The centre also allocated 60,000 hectares of barren land to the creation of rural productive cooperatives and leased 850 hectares of disputed land to farmers on a temporary basis (Moaddel, 1991: 320–3). This was an ephemeral victory because Khomeini used the outbreak of the Iran–Iraq war as an excuse for halting the redistribution of land. In the end, the government and the bonyads, not the ex-landlords, largely possessed the land that was transferred to peasants through the Transfer and Revitalisation of Land (Maloney, 2015: 157).

While the post-revolutionary power struggle sidelined leftist secular organisations, independent labour movements and peasants, Khomeini's militant Islam widely resonated with a significant proportion of the population, especially the poor and non-industrial workers, and the new revolutionary state attempted to address their material needs. On the eve of the revolution, the secular left was in a feeble position due to two factors. The Pahlavi policy primarily to target Third Worldist/communist political forces in the context of the Cold War decisively debilitated the organisational and discursive power of the left. In addition, Khomeini's radical interpretation of Islam largely nullified the discourse of the already frail secular left by shrewdly sketching a state-led distributive programme in favour of the 'downtrodden' and against 'oppressors' and 'global imperialism' (*estekbār-e jāhāni*). Against this backdrop, the Islamist forces were successful in violently purging secular political opponents in the aftermath of the revolution. Two political developments further facilitated the ascendancy of the pro-Khomeini Islamists and aided them in forming the new revolutionary state with a new social contract that ideologically and materially united a large segment of the poor and working class in the centre against the demands of the non-Shi'a oppressed nations/ethnic minorities: the 'jihad' against Kurdistan and the Iraqi invasion of Iran.

Following the fall of the Shah, two popular Kurdish political parties, the Democratic Party of Iranian Kurdistan and Komala, filled the power vacuum and mobilised Kurdistan around a demand for regional autonomy. As the establishment of the religious system was considered detrimental to this objective, the Kurds overwhelmingly rejected the two referendums on a choice between the Islamic Republic and monarchy and the constitution of the Islamic Republic in the early months of the revolution. This renunciation of the legitimacy of Islamists by Kurdistan, which became at the same time a safe refuge for purged secular leftists, provided a pretext for Khomeini to declare a 'jihad' in August 1979 under the name of combating 'separatists' and 'anti-revolutionists' who jeopardised the 'national territorial integrity' and the 'revolutionary state' (Soleimani and Mohammadpour, 2020). The centralised modern state in the early twentieth century in Iran was constructed around a patrimonial Persian-centred nationalism. Hugely influenced by Orientalist scholarship on ancient Persia, this forced state-building project of 'one people, one nation, one language and one culture' disregarded the pre-modern multinational Iranian empire and the rights of non-Persian ethnic groups (Kurds, Azeri Turks, Baluchis, Turkmens and Arabs, among others) (Vaziri, 2013; Zia-Ebrahimi, 2016). Since the state rested on this fragile ground, preserving national integrity became sacred in the state's ideology and practice. To deal with 'Kurdistan sedition', the Islamist forces tapped into this Iranian nationalist psyche, therefore successfully diverting the massive revolutionary grassroots energy by rallying the centre around the threat of a national disintegration under a modified version of Iranian nationalism that accentuated Shi'ism (Soleimani and Mohammadpour, 2020).

The Iraqi invasion that resulted in an almost decade-long war further inflamed this new form of Iranian nationalism and precipitated the institutionalisation of the new Islamic state. As discussed above, after the revolution, to achieve 'true economic self-reliance' and distribute wealth among the 'downtrodden', the assets of the old ruling class were nationalised and handed over to the government ministries or the newly established revolutionary foundations. The new economic direction thus addressed some of the deprivation that the poor and the working class had encountered under the Pahlavi state through the provision of food and other subsidies and job security in growing SOEs. The eight-year war with Iraq served to expand the significance and power of these bonyads, as it afforded them greater latitude in delivering a range of initiatives and undertakings geared towards social welfare. These efforts aimed to satisfy 'the needs of low-income groups, improvements in the conditions of families of martyrs, former prisoners of war, needy rural dwellers, guardian-less households, the disabled, and the handicapped' (Saeidi, 2004: 488). In other words, the war with Iraq deeply fortified the pro-poor economic approach by means of food rations, cash stipends and the expansion of access to public amenities and services, while at the same time making it easy for the state to justify its inability to meet all the material demands of the poor and working class.

In short, the post-revolutionary power struggle and the war with Iraq generated a new social contract that integrated millions of previously excluded and impoverished poor and the working class into a vast but rudimentary welfare state. In addition, the anti-capitalist/anti-imperialist rhetoric and the Persian and Shi'a-centric nationalist ideology of the Islamic revolutionary state harvested popular support for the new state. However, this was achieved notwithstanding the presence of political repression, the lack of real democratic participation or control of the subaltern classes, and the marginalisation of non-Shi'a oppressed nations/ethnic minorities. Put differently, throughout the 1980s, 'state-making and war-making were intertwined, turning the Islamic Republic into a politically and economically authoritarian warfare-welfare state' (Matin-Asgari, 2022).

## The class basis of the new revolutionary state

Through the ruthless suppression of secular and anti-Islamic militant organisations as well as incorporating a large section of the poor and the working class into a rudimentary welfare state, the new state became the area of conflict between two emerging ruling fractions with different views about the role of the government in the economy and private property. In addition to the aforementioned post-revolutionary land reform, a new labour law presented a significant point of contention between the two fractions, despite their shared opposition towards leftist organisations and workers' councils. In 1982, based on the freedom of contract in Islam, a draft bill proposed by the Labour Minister, Ahmad Tavakkoli, dismissed the government's right to interfere in the labour market and rejected workers' collective bargaining, job security and right to strike. The strong opposition from the Islamist statist members of the Majles, who had the majority in the house, led to the rejection of the bill and the resignation of Tavakkoli. Yet the reluctance of the Guardian Council to ratify a revised bill by the Majles halted the approval of the new labour law until 1987 when Khomeini issued a *fatwa* endorsing the right of the government to intervene in the labour market (Maloney, 2015: 160).

Probably the most intense struggle inside the Islamic revolutionary state manifested itself in the bill for the nationalisation of foreign trade.

The Majles passed the first version of the legislation that demanded complete nationalisation of foreign trade in six days in March 1980. The Guardian Council initially considered the bill as un-Islamic, but it eventually ratified the revised version in 1984. The bill resulted in 'a mixed system of foreign trade in which the public sector [the government and enterprises under the control of the revolutionary foundations] imported necessary goods and the private sector [big merchants of the bazaar] all other goods' (Valibeigi, 1994: 5). Between 1979 and 1982, the share of the merchants in imports was nearly 65 per cent and in 1983 they controlled 90 per cent of commercial activities (Mozaffari, 1991: 386). The bill reduced the power of the merchants in trade, but they still had a substantial share in imports throughout the 1980s. The National Iranian Industrial Organisation and the commercial units within various ministries secured the import of raw materials and capital goods for their enterprises. On the other hand, merchants continued their commercial activities by acquiring import licences through the Ministry of Commerce. Besides licensed merchants of the bazaar, bazaar-affiliated officials ran the largest trading firms under the control of the Ministry of Commerce. Furthermore, since some state organisations, in particular bonyads, had access to 'special licenses' for which they could freely import, they easily bypassed bans on the import of specific goods (Keshavarzian, 2007: 165–8). Above all, the bonyads and merchants vastly benefited from the policy of the system of multiple exchange rates. The demand for foreign exchange in the first year of the revolution increased due to the capital flight, the freezing of Iran's foreign assets in the West and the summary repayment of the country's foreign debt. In the mid-1980s, the shortage of foreign exchange was exacerbated because of a sharp decrease in oil revenue following the worldwide oil glut. To manage this severe shortage, the government introduced a system of multiple exchange rates (the controlled official exchange rate and the black-market rate) and institutionalised the rationing of available foreign exchange (Mazarei, 1996: 294–5; Lautenschlager, 1986: 32). This resulted in a substantial gap between the two rates since 'the premium on the black-market rate, which increased rapidly from low levels at the time of the revolution from 200 to 300 per cent by the early 1980s and 500 to 600 per cent by the mid-1980s, reached phenomenal rates of over 2,000 per cent by 1989' (Karshenas and Pesaran, 1995: 98). Those who had access to the official exchange rate, namely licensed bazaar merchants and the para-governmental organisations, were the primary beneficiaries of the system. Merchants and the revolutionary foundations imported goods at the official exchange rate and often sold them later at the market price. Ghafari (1995: 95) estimates that the merchants realised 'a rare return of between 2,140% and 3,140% per item'. Particularly, at the peak of the Iran–Iraq war, the government attempted to augment its direct intervention in the operation of trade and the market by introducing a system of rationing and direct subsidies for a number of commodities to mitigate the impacts of the soaring inflation. However, the bazaar merchants and their allies maintained their influence on the economy throughout the 1980s. As such, by the end of the decade, they still had a significant 37 per cent share of imports (Valibeigi, 1994: 5). It is important to note that import licences, official foreign-exchange rates and tax and duty shelters were available only for specific merchants with clientelistic ties to the revolutionary state, not all bazaaris (Keshavarzian, 2007: 166). In addition to this factor, the growing power of the bonyads in international and domestic trade and distribution restructured the institutional and physical settings of the bazaar. As the well-positioned merchants and the bonyads took control of the large-scale commercial activities, the traditional networks of commerce, wholesale and retail of the bazaar (particularly the Tehran bazaar) lost their monopoly. The upshot of this transformation was the irrelevancy of the historical and locational advantages of the bazaar and the marginalisation of its commercial networks.

So, who were these two fractions of the ruling class of the revolutionary state in the first decade of the revolution? What were their class locations and ideological basis? And how do we conceptualise the revolution and this new economic structure? The first fraction highlighted the egalitarian aspects of Islamic religion, advocated a radical statist approach towards the economy and downgraded individual rights to private property. They managed government-owned enterprises and most of the government bureaucracy during the first decade of the revolution. With the political support of the powerful Revolutionary Council and some junior Ayatollahs, they forged an influential power bloc that can be called the *stratum of government managers*. Considering their influence within the state and Khomeini's subtle disposition towards them, the stratum of government managers enjoyed relative supremacy throughout the first decade of the revolution. The revolutionary foundations, which controlled publicly owned enterprises under the guidance of the supreme leader with exemption from the government's regulation, were the main actors of the second wing. Despite the gradual importance of the traditional networks of the bazaar, some merchants with clientelistic ties with the state enlarged their power and became members of the second fraction of the new ruling class. By controlling revolutionary foundations, a few government ministries – including the Ministry of Trade and Commerce, the Ministry of Labour and the Ministry of Education – and the influential Guardian Council (*shurā-ye negahbān*), this wing of power inside the state was in favour of a conservative interpretation of Islamic law. It thus contested the growing interference of the government with the market and its direct involvement in economic activities (Valibeigi, 1994: 2–4).

Importantly, there were visible links between merchants and the newly created bonyads since most of the directors and high-profile figures of the bonyads came from the bazaar. The first director of the Mostazafan Foundation was Mohandes Khamoushi whose brother headed the bazaar's Committee on Guild Affairs.[12] Following Khamoushi's resignation due to a corruption scandal inside the bonyad, Mohsen Rafigh-Doust, a wealthy bazaari from Tehran and one of the founders of the Islamic Revolutionary Guard Corps (IRGC),[13] was appointed the head of the Mostazafan Foundation (Mozaffari, 1991: 388).[14] Furthermore, for many years after the revolution, the head of the Imam Khomeini Relief Committee was Habibollah Asgar-Owladi, who was the leader of the bazaar-affiliated Islamic Coalition Party (*hezb-e mo'talefeh-e eslāmi*) and the Minister of Trade and Commerce from 1980 to 1984 (Maloney, 2015: 123). That said, the affiliation between the bazaari merchants and the conglomerate network of the revolutionary foundations should not be perceived solely through the social class origins of the key figures of these revolutionary organisations. Above this, the interconnection between them represents 'the articulation of the synergy between the structure, activities, methods of operation, and interests of the bazaar with those of the bonyads' (Maloney, 2000a: 159–60). Hence, the second product of the revolution was the emergence of this new class fraction inside the state, which I call the *bonyad–bazaar nexus*. Despite their differences, both fractions committed to the revolutionary idea of aiding the 'downtrodden' and competed for the endorsement and backing of the subaltern classes. The clerics were not politically homogenous since different sections of them became part of these two fractions of the ruling class. As the supreme leader, Ayatollah Khomeini largely acted as a mediator between the two wings, although he often backed the position of the stratum of government managers in crucial decisions (Valibeigi, 1994: 4).

The revolution strengthened state capitalism and generated two state-linked fractions of the ruling class. Whilst certainly not disputing the importance of a range of measures taken by the revolutionary state to address many of the deprivations that the rural/urban poor and the working class encountered under the Pahlavi state, the provision of food and other subsidies to the poorest layers of the population and job security in SOEs were secondary to the interests of the new ruling class. The provision of welfare programmes, combined with the Islamic revolutionary state's anti-capitalist and anti-imperialist discourse, effectively garnered public backing for the nascent regime despite limited democratic engagement or subaltern-class empowerment resulting from political oppression. Nonetheless, the aforementioned factors contributed to solidifying support for the new state. Recalling the conceptual discussion in Chapter 2 on the notion and different forms of revolution, the 1979 revolution could be conceptualised as a political revolution since it represents the changes in state power without destroying the socioeconomic foundation of the society, i.e., the class power in capitalism. This is because the revolution only replaced the monarcho-bourgeoisie with the new ruling class while neutralising and blocking the initiatives from below that could facilitate the creation of a new foundation for society.

## The crisis of the late 1980s

The revolution did not fundamentally alter the second Pahlavi state's industrialisation policy. As delineated in the previous chapter, Iran's industrial policy during the reign of the Shah was ISI through which import substitution took place in the case of non-durable consumer goods such as food, beverages, tobacco and textiles. Before the revolution, Iran was still massively dependent on imported technology, materials and machinery for the production of intermediate goods and durable and capital goods such as electrical and non-electrical machinery and transport equipment. The revolutionary state continued to pursue the Shah's industrial policies because the manufacturing sector was still dominated by domestic-oriented, consumer-goods-producing industries which relied on imported inputs and technology (Rahnema, 1996: 129–42). The best illustration is the data on industrial imports from 1977 to 1987 which reveal the continuity of the pre-revolutionary and post-revolutionary industrial policies (Ehteshami, 1995: 90).

The continuation of this industrial policy ultimately proved to be disastrous for the economic development of the country by generating a substantial decline in foreign-exchange reserves. The central problem with the ISI was the inability of developing countries to generate adequate foreign exchange to finance the import of intermediate and capital goods, which often escalated the balance of payment deficits. As import controls gave rise to a crisis of accumulation, borrowing from international money markets was the projected solution. In some countries exporting raw materials could partially avoid such an outcome, as in the case of the export of oil in Iran. Nonetheless, the instability of raw materials markets and their price fluctuations ultimately resulted in the 1980s' debt crisis in the Global South (Yaghmaian, 2002: 195–8). In Iran, along with the volatility of the global oil market, the political shock following the 1979 revolution and the war with Iraq substantially affected the foreign-exchange revenues of the country. More precisely, during the 1980s, the unceasing external pressures from the United States in the form of sanctions in response to the revolution made the import of intermediate and capital goods more difficult. Furthermore, the war damaged the oil infrastructures and interrupted its production and price. The setting of production quotas on various branches of industry was the state's solution for the utilisation of the foreign-exchange shortage. As a result, for example, the foreign-exchange quota decreased from $4,000 million in 1983 to $310 million in 1988 for industries under the control of the Ministry of Industry. The Ministry of Heavy Industry faced similar pressure as its foreign-exchange quota declined from $2,400 million in 1983 to only $110 million in 1988 (Rahnema, 1996: 139). This was not a successful strategy since, for instance, the production index of heavy industries fell to 47 per cent of the 1977 level (Rahnema, 1996: 140–1). The financing of the war also significantly diverted the decreasing hard currency from production. On top of that, the purge of 'non-Islamic' managers and skilled technical workers and the continuing exodus of professional personnel added to the acute problems of the production process (Rahnema, 1996: 139). The political uncertainty and ongoing legislative changes, as well as the rise of Islamic banking and the unavailability of credit, also contributed to the reluctance of the private sector to invest (Mazarei, 1996: 302–4). Accordingly, throughout the decade, the rate of investment diminished dramatically and the production index in all branches of industries pointed to a sharp decline. By the end of the decade, the industrial sector realised merely 40 per cent of its potential capacity (Axworthy, 2013: 297; Amirahmadi, 1990). The primary losers in the disruption in productive activities were the medium-sized firms, but, at the same time, the government-owned and publicly owned enterprises only managed to keep their share in the market without increasing their productivity even with monopolistic access to scarce foreign exchange and imported industrial inputs.

The turmoil of the revolution and the unfavourable international conditions eventually resulted in a major crisis in which the gross domestic product (GDP) shrank strikingly, and inflation rose dramatically. In 1986, despite a 47 per cent increase in the population, the non-oil GDP was just 5 per cent more than in 1977. The agricultural output was stagnant, and industrial production was inefficient and underutilised. Moreover, during the same period, while the service sector expanded, its value added had fallen by 9 per cent (Halliday, 1987: 39–40). In 1989, 'real GDP per capita had dropped to only 54 per cent of its peak in 1976' and the per capita income was behind many developing countries. For instance, it was 25 per cent below that of neighbouring Turkey (Esfahani and Pesaran, 2009: 192). The most staggering fact about the economic development of this period is an absolute surge in unemployment. Between 1977/78 and 1990/91, the population grew by around 62 per cent, adding 4.3 million workers to the economically active labour force. The official data indicated that rural and urban unemployment climbed to 15 per cent. Considering that a large number of employed labourers were part-time workers, street vendors, hustlers, panhandlers, or underemployed service personnel, Amuzegar (1997: 64–5) points out that the total number of unemployed and underemployed civilians might have been 'perhaps as high as 30 per cent'. The increase in poverty had thus become a widespread phenomenon, especially from the mid-1980s onwards. Without the government's attempts to provide a safety net to the poorer strata, the impact of poverty on the rural and urban poor could have been even worse (Assadzadeh and Paul, 2004: 652). The severity of the crisis that necessitated a structural change coincided with the expansion of neoliberal restructuring in Eastern and Central Europe and developing countries of the Global South. Accepting the UN ceasefire Resolution 598 in July 1988 paved the way for the initiation of a major shift in the structure of the economy. Under these domestic and global conditions, the first post-Iran–Iraq-war government instigated a series of neoliberal economic reforms to rejuvenate the process of capital accumulation.

## Conclusion

This chapter has analysed the socioeconomic structure and the class character of the Iranian revolutionary state from 1979 to 1989. It has illustrated how the interaction of external and domestic factors led to the Iranian Revolution and the Islamic revolutionary state. Starting with the causes and conditions under which the revolution occurred, we argued that the Shah's agrarian reforms and the rapid industrialisation in line with the ISI strategy put Iran in line with the new direction of the post-WWII global economy, but the White Revolution destabilised the balance of class forces and generated a united front against the second Pahlavi state. Conceptualising the 1979 revolution as a political revolution, we maintained that the post-revolutionary Islamic state more or less retained the state-led ISI strategy despite the fundamental transformation in political power. There were, nevertheless, two key differences between pre- and post-revolutionary capitalism. First, the ISI strategy continued against the backdrop of the unfavourable international environment, in particular the US hostility towards the new revolutionary state. Second, in contrast to the second Pahlavi state that hailed the development of capitalism and the emergence of a modern capitalist class as signs of 'progress', the new revolutionary state framed the top-down state-led development as an act of national liberation of the 'downtrodden', i.e., the victory of workers and the poor against 'exploitative capitalists and landowners' and 'their American masters'. We also revealed that state capitalism augmented in the context of the protracted war with Iraq, which also provided further pretexts for the suppression of political dissent in the first decade of the revolution. As a political revolution, we showed that the significant transformation was the change in the class basis of the state as the stratum of government managers and the bonyad–bazaar nexus emerged as the two main fractions of the ruling class during 1979 and 1989.

The chapter further demonstrated that the first decade of the revolution engendered a major economic crisis. As we argued, at the early stage, a combination of internal and external factors – the widespread confiscation and nationalisation of big industries, banks, mines and real estate, and the trade sanctions and freezing of Iranian assets by the United States following the hostage crisis[15] – jeopardised the security of capital and private property and radically disturbed the accumulation process. Followed by the costly and protracted war with Iraq, the crisis was aggravated by rising inflation, growing rent-seeking activities at the expense of productive enterprise and shrinking of capital stock that ultimately put the country on the verge of bankruptcy by the end of the 1980s (Karshenas, 1995: 89). It thus produced a staggering 58 per cent decline in real national income from the mid- to late 1980s when the population grew at an increasing rate and unemployment rose astronomically (Ehsani, 1994: 17). Faced with this calamity, the Iranian ruling class therefore actively looked for a new developmental model to address the accumulation crisis and neoliberalism emerged as the solution. In the next chapter, we will explore the process of Iranian neoliberalisation and its impacts on the class basis of the state. We will demonstrate that the dynamics of global neoliberal capitalism and the economic structure and ruling class reconfiguration during the first decade of the revolution have played important roles in the trajectory of changes in Iran since the early 1990s.

## Notes

1 Smith (2004: 195–8) provides a detailed account of various stages of the attack on the bazaar from 1975 to 1977.
2 In an interview with *The New York Times*, one shopkeeper revealed the bazaar's level of hostility towards the government: 'If we let him, the Shah will destroy us. The banks are taking over. The big stores are undermining our livelihoods. And the government will flatten our bazaars to make room for state offices' (cited in Abrahamian, 1980: 25).
3 Some have claimed that the opposition of the Sayyid Hossein Ali Tabatabaei Boroujerdi, who had an amicable relationship with the Shah, to the land reform was an important obstacle to the launching of the programme and consequently his death in March 1961 facilitated the Shah's manoeuvre to start the White Revolution (Parsa, 1994: 149).

4 Along with the Khomeinist Islamist discourse, Ali Shariati's radical Islamist discourse was also popular among some sections of society. His discourse camouflaged Marxist concepts in Islamic vocabulary to advocate a utopian classless Muslim community ruled by enlightened thinkers (Matin, 2013a: 130–41). Apart from these two Islamist discourses, small segments of the various classes were inclined towards the liberal-nationalist interpretation of Islam with emphasis on the compatibility of Islam and democracy or the traditional variant that yearned for the past order (Ashraf and Banuazizi, 1985: 30–1).

5 While the situation was ripe for revolution, it is worth pointing out that the new policy of the Carter administration – putting pressure on its allies in the Third World to respect human rights in their fight to combat communism in the Cold War – acted as a catalyst for triggering the outbreak of the revolution. This is because the denunciation of the Rastakhiz Party by numerous political parties and professional associations following the 1977 political opening initiated the first wave of revolutionary protests. It is reported that the Shah reacted negatively to Carter's victory in November 1976 by saying 'it looks like we are not going to be around much longer' (cited in Ashraf and Banuazizi, 1985: 4).

6 Maloney (2015: 114) estimates capital flight during this period was 'in the range of $30 to $40 billion'.

7 In the Persian language, while 'state' is translated to 'dolat', in the Iranian political structure and the public realm 'dolat' generally refers to 'government'. For this reason, a better translation of 'state' is 'hokumat' or 'nezam'. This is crucial in the argument because I consider both government ownership (*bakhsh-e dolati*) and public non-governmental ownership (*bakhsh-e omumi-ye qar-e dolati*) as two forms of state ownership. Accordingly, government-owned enterprises and publicly owned enterprises will be categorised as two types of state-owned enterprises (SOEs).

8 In the Twelver Shi'a Islam, twelve Imams are the leaders of the Islamic community after the Prophet Mohammad. During the Major Occultation of the twelfth Imam (from 940 until now), grand Shi'a jurisconsults (*mojtahehān*) determine the absent Imam's true opinion and establish legal standards. Since the Qajar period, this autonomous judicial authority of the mujtahids has extended to political authority, eventually leading to the doctrine of the guardianship of the jurisconsult (*velāyat-e faqih*). Since the creation of the Islamic Republic of Iran, the title of Imam has been reserved for the supreme leader (*vali-ye faqih*).

9 These industrial complexes were mainly the assets of the country's fifty-one major industrialists. Ehteshami (1995: 85–6) provides the names and business activities of these industrialists before the revolution.

10 Later the name of the foundation was shortened to *bonyād-e mostaz'afān*, and hence we refer to it as the Mostazafan Foundation.

11 The Housing Foundation of the Islamic Revolution (*bonyād-e maskan-e enqlāb-e eslāmi*) and the Reconstruction Crusade (*jahād-e sāzandegi*) were also created to provide housing for the poor and promote grassroots economic development projects in the countryside. These organisations were eventually elevated to full government ministries in the middle of the 1980s (Maloney, 2015: 123–4).

12 The Committee on Guild Affairs was formed in 1979 in order to defend the interests of the bazaar and had a close connection with the Islamic Republic Party (IRP).

13 The Islamic Revolution Guard Corps (IRGC) is the official name of the organisation, but it is also commonly referred to as the Revolutionary Guards by many commentators and outlets. While I mostly use the abbreviation IRGC, I also use the Revolutionary Guards instead of the full official name.

14 The second commander of the IRGC from 1981 to 1997, Mohsen Rezai, also came from the bazaar circles. Although the IRGC was not involved in economic activities at the early stage of the first decade of the revolution, it has become, as I will show in the next chapter, one of the most influential economic actors after the end of the war with Iraq.

15 The Iran hostage crisis was an international crisis in which sixty-six American diplomats were seized at the US embassy in Tehran by a group of revolutionary Iranian students on 4 November 1979. After releasing fourteen of them, the Iranian state held the remaining fifty-two hostages for 444 days until 21 January 1981, which was the inauguration day of Ronald Reagan. The crisis had a profound impact on the Iranian economy and the post-revolutionary political bottle in the society and within the new state, including the resignation of the provisional government after the revolution. It also negatively affected the Carter administration and swallowed up the prospect of Jimmy Carter's second term in the view of some historians. To learn about the basic facts of the crisis, see 'Iran hostage crisis' in *Encyclopaedia Britannica* at: https://www.britannica.com/event/Iran-hostage-crisis (accessed 5 April 2023).

# 4

# Neoliberalisation and the ruling class reconfiguration (1989–2013)

The previous chapter documented how the continual pursuit of ISI in the presence of sanctions and war produced a crisis in Iran. To solve the crisis, some members of the ruling class realised the necessity of embracing an alternative developmental strategy that would generate economic growth and mitigate external geoeconomic and geopolitical pressures. Yet the urgent need for this restructuring was not solely the product of a crisis caused by domestic determinants separated from global dynamics. As expounded in Chapter 1, ISI was at the heart of the global crisis of overaccumulation in the 1970s that hit the Global South in the 1980s. The implemented spatial fix was the internationalisation of production and finance, which has led to the growing influence of GVCs and the instigation of EOI strategy for the developing world. In line with this, the proposed answer of this section of the Iranian ruling class was integration into this new global economy. With hugely unrealised production sites, a large pool of cheap labour power, colossal low-priced inputs such as raw materials and a big market, they viewed the country as a space for the absorption of surpluses in capital globally. For instance, the Economic Affairs and Finance Minister of the first post-Iran–Iraq-war government explicitly expressed 'Iran's need for capital' that necessitated lifting the ownership cap for foreign investors. Likewise, the collapse of central planning in the USSR and Eastern Europe and the adoption of neoliberal economic policies also strengthened the position of these members of the ruling class on the necessity of a fundamental reorganisation of the economy to revive growth. A classified report by the Planning and Budget Organisation a year after the start of the structural adjustment programme in Iran with reference to the 'abortive experience of the Eastern Bloc' illustrates the magnitude of influence of this global neoliberal restructuring:

> Principally, the economies of the countries of the world have inclined to a [new] type of the international division of labour in the present era ... Therefore, developing countries are unable to prescribe another law of development that

can fundamentally overcome their economic problems and achieve development and prosperity but the law of the free market, which is based on economic realities.

Cited in Momeni, 2014: 241

This resulted in the instigation of Iranian neoliberalisation in 1990 which
has proceeded amid a struggle inside the state between different centres of
political and economic power.

By situating Iran within the wider neoliberal process of the global economy, this chapter reveals that, while the uneven development of capitalism,
the movement of international capital and the international rivalries arising
out of the emergence of new global centres of accumulation have drastically
impacted Iranian restructuring, the struggles of the emerging Iranian capital
fractions have equally shaped the process. The chapter shows that the first
phase of neoliberalisation between 1990 and 2005 generated an internationally oriented capital fraction. Emerging as a result of the transformation
of the stratum of government managers, the internationally oriented capital
fraction has been keen to integrate into GVCs with links to non-oil export
sectors and the downstream oil and gas industry. The chapter also documents the bonyad–bazaar nexus transformed into the military–bonyad complex during the second phase of neoliberalisation between 2005 and 2013.
With an inclination towards China and Russia, this capital fraction has
attempted to halt the integration of Iran into the global economy and hampered the entrance of American and European capital despite implementing
neoliberal policies. Finally, the chapter demonstrates that the upshot of this
restructuring has been a particular form of development in Iran by amal-
gamating elements of state capitalism and neoliberalism. Labelled 'hybrid
neoliberalism', it argues that this is the product of the dialectical interaction
of global and local dynamics and international and domestic shaping factors. I should point out that, because the chapter focuses on state policies,
it pays special attention to the competition between capital fractions of the
ruling class inside the state. However, the struggles of subaltern classes and
geopolitical tensions with the West have equally played a meaningful role
in the processes of capitalist restructuring and state reorganisation. While
the struggles of workers and the poor and the impacts of the nuclear programme and international sanctions on the process of Iranian neoliberalisation will be sporadically discussed here, we explore these issues in depth in
Chapters 6 and 7.

The remainder of this chapter is organised as follows. The next section
discusses the quarrel of the late 1980s between the wings of the ruling class
to initiate neoliberal reforms from above. The second section scrutinises
the structural adjustment programme by looking at the development plans

to implement necessary neoliberal policies, followed by the first round of privatisation between 1991 and 2005. This section sheds light on why the neoliberal mechanism of accumulation has been slow despite some changes in social relations and the emergence of a new capital fraction out of the stratum of government managers. As the neoliberal restructuring shifted towards a new direction from 2005 to 2013, the third section examines this second phase of neoliberalisation, which brought about the formation of the military–bonyad complex. The focus of the fourth section is to unpack and reflect upon the differences between the accumulation strategies of these two fractions of capital. As well as summing up the key arguments, the conclusion shows the centrality of these findings for the following chapters.[1]

## Instigation of the post-Iran–Iraq-war reforms from above

The collapsing economy and its potential calamity for the ruling class relatively lessened the intra-class conflict in the final year of the war. This facilitated a dialogue between the stratum of government managers and the bonyad–bazaar nexus around a reconstruction plan for the post-Iran–Iraq-war era. However, the debate regarding the direction and new form of development for the country generated a division among the stratum of government managers. On the one hand, a group of this fraction advocated higher defence spending and reconstruction of productive capacity and infrastructure through a policy of self-reliance. Believing in the necessity of the active role of the state in the economy, they still favoured price control, defended state subsidies and rationing of basic necessities and rejected the benefits of the privatisation of SOEs. On the other hand, a powerful group within this fraction revised their position by arguing that 'the concentration of affairs within the state was a necessity during the war, a necessity which does not exist anymore' (Hashemi-Rafsanjani, 1988 cited in Ehteshami, 1995: 101). They endorsed the idea that a free-market-centred plan acknowledging the importance of the private sector could only stimulate economic growth. Although the debate initially settled around a mixed approach based on a plan drafted by the then Prime Minister Mir-Hossein Mousavi, who was the leading figure of the statist group, the abolition of the post of prime minister in the new draft of the Constitution after the war signalled the marginalisation of those who still adhered to the statist approach and the ISI strategy.[2] The first post-war government drafted a new version of the plan that proposed 'a bolder, flexible, more open and largely market-orientated plan' with a central role for the private sector in economic development (Amirahmadi, 1990: 242–53; Axworthy, 2013: 309). This resulted in the removal of some Islamic leftist militants from the cabinet and the disqualification of others from running for the Majles. Accordingly, neoliberal technocrats occupied key positions in the Ministry of Economic Affairs and Finance, the Ministry of Commerce, the Ministry of Industries, the Ministry of Heavy Industries and the Ministry of Mining and Metals (Siavoshi, 1992: 42–3).

The bonyad–bazaar nexus initially allied with the neoliberal wing of the stratum of government managers and welcomed the new economic plan for two reasons. The First Development Plan explicitly required the banking system to provide funds for 'non-government (public, private and cooperative) sectors' and precluded the privatisation of enterprises under the control of the revolutionary foundations (Law on the First Development Plan, 1990). In addition, the plan could open up fresh economic opportunities and ease the previous constraints. Hence, Mohsen Rafigh-Doust, the then head of the Mostazafan Foundation, hailed the economic policies of the government, in particular, the policy of limiting the government's control over industrial units, arguing that allowing producers to manage their affairs internally would stabilise the sector and increase its productivity (*Hamshahri*, 1996). Similarly, the then head of the Iran Chamber of Commerce, Ali Naqi Khamoushi, who represented the mercantile wing of the bonyad–bazaar nexus, expressed the view that the first five-year development plan would positively encourage the private sector to make more investments (Ehteshami, 1995: 102). As we shall see shortly, this fragile alliance between the neoliberal elites of the state and the bonyad–bazaar nexus was based on short-term gains because promoting foreign investments and some other microeconomic policies of the new administration, which were not clearly specified in the First Development Plan, could target the long-term interests of the bonyad–bazaar nexus. In the following section, after explaining neoliberal reforms introduced through three development plans between 1998 and 2005, we pay particular attention to the first phase of privatisation, with two primary aims: (a) to demonstrate how these reforms from above amid intra-capital fissures reorganised social relations of production in line with the new development trajectory, and (b) to reveal how these changes engendered a new capital fraction.

## Phase I of neoliberalisation and the formation of the internationally oriented capital fraction (1990–2005)

Following the resumption of the Iranian government's communication with the IMF and the World Bank after the end of the war with Iraq (Amirahmadi, 1990: 277), in June 1990 the joint IMF-World Bank mission testified to Iran's determination to move towards economic liberalisation by 'undergoing profound institutional and structural changes' (Nomani and Behdad, 2006: 47). A few days later, *The Economist* reported that 'Iran has voluntarily adopted the principle of IMF's restructuring rules, albeit without asking for IMF loans in return' (cited in Dadkhah, 2003: 98). This is because, unlike heavily indebted developing countries, Iran's foreign debt was virtually nil at the start of the restructuring programme, although a small amount of foreign borrowing was projected for financing part of the First Development Plan (Sadeghi-Brojeni, 2011: 29–30). This therefore casts doubt on the prevailing approaches that portray the materialisation of neoliberalism in the Global South inevitably as the imposition of structural adjustment policies 'from outside' by Western states and international institutions. Here we do not imply that Iranian neoliberalisation can solely be grasped with reference to domestic determinants because, as explained in Chapter 1, most states around the world deployed neoliberalism as the answer for the revival of capital accumulation to counter the economic crisis of the 1970s/1980s. Within this global context, some Iranian state managers/officials similarly viewed this model as an alternative developmental strategy to overcome the crisis, but the intra-capital fissures within the state and class struggles from below produced a unique form of neoliberalism in Iran in the following decades. Let us now examine how this first phase of neoliberalisation between 1990 and 2005 led to the formation of a new capital fraction.

## Microeconomic reforms

In June 1990, the Majles and the Guardian Council approved the first five-year development plan, which intended to promote industrial growth by restraining the role of the state in the economy, providing a favourable climate for domestic and foreign private investment and creating a competitive environment to eliminate corruption. To this end, the government vowed to decontrol most domestic prices, liberalise the foreign-exchange system, remove many non-tariff trade barriers, lower income tax rates, eliminate bank credit ceilings and privatise SOEs (IMF, 1998: 9). In contrast to the rhetoric of the first decade of the revolution that discouraged capital accumulation and profit-making, the government asserted that

> In a healthy economic system, economic actors should be encouraged not prohibited. Indeed, profit is a tool whereby the level of economic performance should be assessed although obviously it might be misused similar to any other means.
>
> Planning and Budget Organisation report,
> 1991 cited in Momeni, 2014: 240

The underlying objective of the plan was a shift in the accumulation strategy from ISI to EOI by boosting non-oil exports in order to reduce the reliance of the country on oil revenues (Nabavi and Malayeri, 1996: 18). The government stressed that a 'non-oil economy' had to become the national development strategy of the country due to the substantial population growth rate, the enormous cost of the extraction of crude oil and probable fluctuations in the global oil market in the future that would make economic planning continually tentative. With an ambitious average annual growth rate of 12.2 per cent as a benchmark, the government thus projected that non-oil exports would reach $48 billion by the year 2016 (Kanovsky, 1998: 57). To encourage non-oil exports, the banking system was obliged to provide the required credits of exporters 'for the importation of raw materials, machinery and spare parts needed for export purposes' (Ghasimi, 1992: 609). Thanks to the increase in the price of oil owing to the first Gulf War, the industrial sector enjoyed a 538 per cent growth in access to banking facilities during this period (Nabavi and Malayeri, 1996: 18). As a result, according to the annual reports of the Trade Promotion Organisation of Iran, while non-oil exports stood at $1 billion in 1989, they reached $4.8 billion in 1994.

The unification of exchange rates was a key policy because the government viewed the unrealistic value of the national currency (rial) as a barrier to the realisation of the new industrialisation strategy. Under the IMF's recommendation, the government adopted a gradual approach by reducing the number of exchange rates from seven to three between January 1991 and March 1993. The three exchange rates included the basic rate at 70 rials/$ applied to oil export receipts, the competitive rate at 600 rials/$ applied to intermediate and capital goods imports, and the floating rate at 1,542 rials/$ applied to remaining transitions in the banking system. However, in March 1993, in a radical move that disregarded the IMF's advice, the government introduced a unified rate of 1,538 rials per US dollar. In practice, however, the government still exempted $3,800 million for imports of necessary goods from the unified rate due to the pressure from the bonyad–bazaar nexus (Farzin, 1995: 987–94). In December 1993, the official rate was finally fixed at 1,750 rials/$, but, faced with a massive foreign-exchange shortage and political lobbying, the government reintroduced new multiple systems a few months later with two rates this time, namely the official rate and the export rate (Celasun, 2003: 3–4). Despite the allocation of the largest amount of funds to the industrial and mining sectors from the $130 billion budget of the first plan, in the final year of the plan the share of the non-oil industrial sector from the total GDP was still a mere 5 per cent while the oil industry, agricultural and service sectors contributed 18.7 per cent, 21.3 per cent and 42.7 per cent respectively. Even more striking, the amount of foreign exchange allocated from the oil revenues to the non-oil exporters was higher than the amount received from the non-oil exports (Delafrouz, 2014: 115–16; Razaghi, 1997: 248–50).

The inability of the government to implement a unified exchange rate regime demonstrated the struggle inside the state since the bonyad–bazaar nexus was highly reluctant to retreat from its privileged position to access the official exchange rate. At the early stage, the bonyad–bazaar nexus supported the technocratic wing of the stratum of government managers mostly because of its liberalisation of the foreign trade policy, which resulted in the upsurge of imports from almost $13 billion in 1989 to approximately $25 billion in 1991. We should also not overlook the promise of limited government interference in the market as part of the first plan that satisfied the bonyad–bazaar nexus. Foreign borrowings with relatively short-term payback periods financed much of the expansion of imports. Whilst $3 billion in borrowing was projected for the first plan, the country was confronted with a gigantic $20 billion short-term debt by early 1994.[3] The lower-than-expected price of oil between 1993 and 1994, which diminished the oil revenues by 30 per cent, exacerbated the debt crisis. Consequently, the value of the rial fell sharply against the dollar in the currency markets despite the official devaluation through the policy of the liberalisation of the exchange rate. Imports and the foreign debt service became expensive and domestic inflation mounted to 35.6 per cent in 1994 and as high as 49.2 per cent in 1995 (IMF DataMapper; Delafrouz, 2014: 115; Razaghi, 1997: 113). Unable to reschedule the payment of the debt, the government imposed restrictions on importing non-essential goods, leading to the fall in imports to around $12 billion in 1994 and 1995 (Trade Promotion Organisation of Iran annual reports). In the midst of the battle regarding foreign trade, the government's attempt to unify the exchange rate further alienated the bonyad–bazaar nexus that benefited from cheap foreign-exchange quotas. Moreover, in the final year of the plan, the government opened a state-funded retail chain Refah (*sherkat-e forushgā-hā-ye zanjirehi-ye refāh*), which directly affected the interests of the mercantile wing of the bonyad–bazaar nexus.[4] The bonyad–bazaar nexus also perceived the privatisation initiative, which we shall explain shortly, as a mechanism through which a new competing class out of the state elites would be created. Therefore, the bonyad–bazaar nexus through the conservative Fourth Majles passed a bill in August 1994 to cripple privatisation by demanding that the government offer an alternative itinerary for denationalisation, whose beneficiaries should be the war veterans and the members of the paramilitary *Basij* (Behdad, 2000: 125–9; Axworthy, 2013: 321).

The policy of the unification of the exchange rate coupled with the devaluation of the rial led to higher prices and hence the exacerbation of the economic conditions of the working class and the urban poor. Unprecedented in the last fifty years of the country, 'the wholesale price index increased by 78 per cent and the consumer price index by 96 per cent' in 1993 and 1994 (Nomani and Behdad, 2006: 51; Razaghi, 1997: 114). The widespread discontent of the urban poor over the calamitous impacts of the economic restructuring on their lives manifested itself in a series of protests and riots between 1991 and 1995 in numerous cities such as Mashhad, Eslamshaher, Qazvin, Shiraz and Arak. The fear of a more general mass resistance was a prominent determinant in the deceleration of the restructuring programme. At the same time, this hostility towards the reforms accommodated a pretext for the bonyad–bazaar nexus to practically halt Hashemi-Rafsanjani's structural adjustment. Although he was re-elected as president, the Majles rejected the Economic Affairs and Finance minister for the second term and forced the head of the powerful Planning and Budget Organisation to resign (Maloney, 2015: 238–9). Furthermore, Hashemi-Rafsanjani handed over several important ministries including the Ministry of Trade and Commerce to the commercial wing of the bonyad–bazaar nexus (Movasaghi, 2006: 334). The Majles also adjourned the approval of the second five-year development plan for more than a year until March 1995 on the grounds of the necessity of a thorough appraisal of the achievements of the first plan (Amuzegar, 2001: 2).

The conflict inside the state produced the mixed second development plan. On the one hand, the plan re-accentuated the importance of the industrial development of the country by giving special attention to the expansion of the non-oil export sector. To this end, it sanctioned the creation of the High Council of Non-Oil Export Promotion and obliged banks, particularly the Export Development Bank, to provide credit facilities with preferential rates to exporters. The programme also demanded that the promotion of FDI be a priority. On the other hand, it prescribed a 'managed floating system of exchange rate' that would abandon a real unification of exchange rate, as a sign of submission to the mounting pressure from the bonyad–bazaar nexus. The plan also only selected all remaining government-owned enterprises under the control of the National Iranian Industrial Organisation and the Iranian Industrial Development and Renovation Organisation for privatisation while excluding firms owned by the bonyads from the programme once again. In fact, the August 1994 Majles bill – demanding the sale of the shares of government-owned companies to war veterans and members of the *Basij* – gave the impression that the bonyad–bazaar nexus was determined to transfer the ownership of these selected enterprises to its direct command. The promised labour market reform and the invigoration of the private sector, albeit with different interpretations, seemed to be in both camps' interests (Law on the Second Development Plan, 1994).

Therefore, the second plan hindered the government's advances in materialising its objectives. In 1996/97, 33.5 per cent of the banking credits were allocated to the industrial and mining sectors whereas the agricultural, construction and service sectors received 25 per cent, 29 per cent and 12.5 per cent of the credit respectively (IMF, 1998: 35).[5] The non-oil export sector was awarded the highest amount of funding with the forecast of an annual growth rate of 8.4 per cent that was never realised. An examination of the composition of the non-oil export commodities during this period reveals that a large chunk of the exports belonged to the energy-consuming industries that were heavily subsidised by the government (Haadi-Zenouz, 2003: 47–8). In other words, industrial non-oil exporters gained access to the international market because of rent rather than the rise in productivity. The IMF thus expressed its dissatisfaction with the government's limited success in creating auspicious conditions for the 'private sector' (Nomani and Behdad, 2006: 54). The third development plan (2000–5) during the Khatami administration – the most radical neoliberal programme due to its globalised orientation and systematic focus on the structural and institutional reforms to deepen liberalisation, deregulation and privatisation – changed this perception (IMF, 2006).

Khatami took office in May 1997 with a landslide victory by promising the promotion of the rule of law and the transformation of the country's 'chronically ill' economy. But these changes seemed to be unfeasible under the second plan and in the presence of the relatively balanced Fifth Majles and a sudden plummet in the crude oil price. Moreover, the disunity in his economic team between the so-called shock therapists led by Nourbakhsh, the Central Bank governor, and the new institutionalists led by Namazi, the Economic Affairs and Finance minister, hampered any meaningful economic reforms (Dinmore, 2000). The government pledged to break down public monopolies and reform the tax system by subjecting the bonyads to tax and transparency (*Neshat*, 1999; Rostami, 1999). A coordinated attack by the government against the Mostazafan Foundation by labelling it 'the biggest cartel of the Middle East' (Afshari, 1999) led to the resignation of its director, Rafigh-Doust, in July 1999. Yet the Guardian Council impeded the government bills to separate the Mostazafan Foundation's charitable and economic activities and lift its tax exemption on the basis that the revolutionary foundations were under the authority of the office of the supreme leader and outside the inspection of the government and the parliament. In line with this, in 2000, the Majles refused to approve government-proposed measures in the final draft of the third development plan regarding the management and taxation of the bonyads. The Majles also rejected the demands for the reduction of subsidies and the elimination of price ceilings for essential commodities to reduce domestic consumption and decrease imports (Amuzegar, 2005b: 47; Maloney, 2015: 289). However, the ratified plan approved sweeping privatisation of SOEs, far-reaching assistance for the private sector and reorganisation of the public administrative system to improve efficiency and competence. The plan also sought to facilitate conditions for restructuring the financial sector, price rationalisation and removal of energy subsidies, greater promotion of non-oil exports, trade liberalisation through replacing non-tariff barriers with tariffs and progressively reducing average tariff rates in line with the WTO rules, deregulation of the process of capital investment and legal reform to precipitate FDI (Law on the Third Development Plan, 2000; see also Khajehpour, 2000: 587–8; Amuzegar, 2005b: 47–8; Delafrouz, 2014: 120).

The plan reiterated the significance of the promotion of non-oil exports and offered a number of government-sponsored incentives to exporters, including an exemption of all exported goods and services from tax and customs duties, an increase in the capital of the Export Development Bank, a provision of low-rate credit and low-cost insurance services, a guarantee of exchange rate and the formation of a new organisation to exclusively deal with exports, which led to the establishment of the Export Promotion Organisation in 2004 (Behkish, 2010: 280–1; Amuzegar, 2005b: 51–2). Accordingly, the non-oil exports witnessed a steady expansion from $3.8 billion in 2000 to $10.5 billion in 2005 (Trade Promotion Organisation of Iran annual reports) of which industrial goods constituted more than two-thirds (Delafrouz, 2014: 121). In 2000, the government instituted the Oil Stabilisation Fund in order to sustain budgetary public expenditures regardless of fluctuations in the oil market, maintain fiscal discipline and prevent the depreciation of the rial. In addition, the November 2000 amendment to the original plan of the Oil Stabilisation Fund 'stipulated that 50% of the Fund reserves should be set aside for lending to domestic private entrepreneurs – in foreign exchange, and at low-interest rates for "productive" investments in the third plan's priority [non-oil export] sectors' (Amuzegar, 2005a: 28). With an average length of eight years and a very low annual interest rate, the government encouraged 'private firms' to borrow from the Oil Stabilisation Fund. Unlike the plan's projection, imports climbed by around three times from $13.2 billion in the first year to $39.2 billion in the final year of the third plan due to the abundance of foreign exchange thanks to the boost in the oil revenues, lowering tariffs and the devaluation of the rial (Trade Promotion Organisation of Iran annual reports).

Despite Khatami's famous claim that his government encountered 'a crisis [created by adversaries] every nine days' (Nikfar, 2001), it accomplished substantial steps towards liberalisation. In July 1997, the government introduced the Tehran Stock Exchange rate alongside the official and export exchange rates. In 2000, it made the Tehran Stock Exchange rate the key market-determined exchange rate except for the imported basic commodities that still used the official rate (Celasun, 2003: 4–5) and, in 2002, it applied the Tehran Stock Exchange rate to all transactions (Dinmore, 2001b). The exchange rate unification that exclusively targeted the vested interests of the bonyad–bazaar nexus was in line with the antitrust law of the third development plan to build a 'competitive economy' (Dinmore, 2001b). Another central neoliberal move was the reform of the financial sector through authorising private banks and introducing changes in the state-owned banks as the then deputy governor of the Central Bank expressed: 'Private banking is part of the reform of the finance system, along with the restructuring of the financial position of the state banks so that we will see more efficiency and competition' (cited in Dinmore, 2001a). Accordingly, over the course of the third plan, the government authorised the licences of four private banks (*Bank-e Eeqtesād-e Novin*, *Bank-e Sāmān*, *Bank-e Kārāfarin* and *Bank-e Pārsiān*), two non-bank credit institutions, and two private insurance companies (Amuzegar, 2005b: 52; Maloney, 2015: 291). In May 2001, to accelerate the process of privatisation, the government established the Iranian Privatisation Organisation. The privatisation of the SOEs was possibly the most substantial legislative act in the emergence of a new capitalist class that generated the most intense battle within the state, which we now turn to survey (see Table 4.1 for a summary of this section).

Table 4.1 Economic indicators (1990–2005)

| Year | 1990 | 1992 | 1994 | 1995 | 1996 | 1998 | 2000 | 2002 | 2004 | 2005 |
|---|---|---|---|---|---|---|---|---|---|---|
| Real GDP (%) | 14.1 | 2.3 | –1.3 | 2.3 | 4.7 | 2.2 | 5.8 | 7.4 | 4.4 | 5.3 |
| Oil exports (in $ bn) | 16.7 | 15.6 | 11.9 | 13.5 | 16.9 | 10.0 | 22.9 | 17.3 | 32.2 | 48.1 |
| Non-oil exports (in $ bn) | 1.3 | 3.0 | 4.8 | 3.3 | 3.2 | 3.1 | 3.8 | 4.6 | 6.9 | 10.5 |
| Imports (in $ bn) | 18.3 | 23.3 | 12.6 | 12.8 | 15.0 | 13.7 | 13.2 | 22.2 | 35.4 | 39.2 |
| Inflation (%) | 9.0 | 23.3 | 35.6 | 49.2 | 23.1 | 18.1 | 10.0 | 15.9 | 15.2 | 12.1 |
| Unemployment (%) | 14.2 | 10.0 | 10.0 | 10.0 | 9.1 | 13.6 | 16.0 | 12.2 | 10.3 | 11.5 |

*Source:* Compiled by the author, based on IMF DataMapper; World Bank, world development indicators; Central Bank of Iran, statistical yearbooks and censuses (various years); Trade Promotion Organisation of Iran, annual reports

*Privatisation scheme and the rise of the internationally oriented capital fraction*

Nearly a year after the approval of the first plan, in May 1991, the process of the privatisation of SOEs began under the supervision of a committee comprised of the ministers of Economic Affairs and Finance, Industries, Heavy Industries and Labour, the governor of the Central Bank and the head of the Planning and Budget Organisation. For the first plan, the government envisaged the sale of 391 poorly performing government-owned enterprises after inspecting 1,875 companies. Although there was a legal constraint on denationalising enterprises involved in 'mother industries' such as steel, banking, insurance, shipping and public utilities, the government reinterpreted Article 138 of the Constitution to pave the way for the privatisation of some companies under the control of the Ministry of Heavy Industries. Among a list of 248 companies in the first stage of the first plan, 173 units belonged to the National Iranian Industrial Organisation under the supervision of the Ministry of Industries and 56 companies managed by the Iranian Industrial Development and Renovation Organisation under the management of the Ministry of Heavy Industry. In the second stage, the government selected 120 enterprises from the former and 17 firms from the latter while the remaining 25 enterprises were controlled by other ministries (Habibi and Khoshpour, 1996: 57–8; Khalatbari, 1994: 188–9).[6] According to a study by the Ministry of Industries, during the First Development Plan, the government sold around 60 per cent of the shares of these companies to the 'private sector' and the rest of the stocks to the banking system and other organisations (Arman, 1994: 35–6).

A quick look at the privatisation process of the first plan reveals the lack of adequate legislation, personal connections and preferential treatment. In 1990, the Central Bank of Iran legalised the creation of investment companies in the banking system to accelerate the process. By reference to Iran's commercial law, the government considered these investment companies 'private' firms despite being run by government managers (Bahmani, 1998: 399, 403). The result was the concentration of some government-owned enterprises in the hands of new financial-industrial groups with dubious connections with the government, such as the National Development Group Investment Company and the Social Security Investment Company, which are currently among the largest corporations in the country. The case of the sale of government-owned enterprises to the 'private sector' requires particular attention. In the name of privatisation and under what is commonly known as the 'management buyout' method, these firms were sold off to the officials and well-placed individuals within the inner circle of the government with nominal prices because the same people calculated their values which bore little or no relation to their market prices (Parkhideh, 2008: 177; Nabavi and Malayeri, 1996: 21). As an example, in an interview, one of the middle-ranking officials of the Hashemi-Rafsanjani administration, with reference to the government-run mines, uncovered that the government offered the new owners highly favourable instalments to purchase the firms due to lack of personal capital (Behdad, 2013). Karbassian (2000: 637) also notes that 'the procurement department of a given ministry would function as a company, selling supplies acquired with the ministry's funds to the ministry, for profit. The profits were then distributed among shareholders, who were mostly the same ministry's personnel.' In the end, because of the under-pricing mechanism and preferential treatment, firm directors and government officials along with some well-connected individuals within the state bureaucracy became new owners.

The government projected the rebuilding of the energy sector as the basis for the revival of the industrial sector. Due to the lack of legal framework and political resistance to reopening the sector to foreign investors, it constructed a new type of contract, known as the buyback contract, with 'the relatively limited time frame and the cap of the rate of return'. Accordingly, the National Iranian Oil Company reached an agreement with a few multinational oil companies for the development of the South Pars field. The government facilitated the creation of the National Iranian Oil Company spin-off firms with public capital that operated as private firms to handle the projects. In addition to Petro Pars, Pedec, IOEC, Pedco, OIEC, and the Naftiran Intertrade Co were among at least 100 spin-off companies that were created during Hashemi-Rafsanjani's tenure and reached their peak throughout Khatami's presidency. These companies were also mostly handed over to officials and their relatives with close ties to the Ministry of Petroleum (Maloney, 2015: 394–6).

The second development plan projected the transfer of the ownership of all remaining companies under the control of the National Iranian Industrial Organisation and the Iranian Industrial Development and Renovation Organisation to the private sector (Parkhideh, 2008: 175). However, due to the August 1994 Majles bill regarding the sale of the shares of government-owned enterprises to war veterans and prisoners of war, families of martyrs and members of the *Basij*, the privatisation was practically halted since the legitimate buyers were not financially able to purchase the shares (Behkish, 2010: 118). Taraghi, the then head of the Imam Khomeini Relief Committee in Khorasan province, sheds light on the perception of the bonyad–bazaar nexus on the privatisation scheme:

In the shadow of the government's economic policies, a 'nouveau riche' stratum was created … [who] made a substantial fortune and controlled almost the heartbeat of the economy. These hand-picked ... technocrat supporters ... seized all government-affiliated enterprises and occupied their board of directors.

*Raja News*, 2015

Hence, during the second plan, the bonyad–bazaar nexus and its media condemned the departure from the idea of justice as the fundamental objective of the revolution in the name of 'economic growth' that glorified 'consumerism' and 'luxurism' (*Resālat*, 1996; *Jomhuri-ye Eslāmi*, 1997a; *Resālat*, 1995). In particular, they prioritised a fight against the 'bonanza phenomenon' and the genesis of *aqazadehha*, which referred to high-ranking government officials and their close relatives who were involved in wealth accumulation and corruption (*Jomhuri-ye Eslāmi*, 1997b; 1997c; 1997d; *Resālat*, 1997a; 1997b; 1997c).

The victory of Khatami altered the balance of power, resulting in the approval of Amendment 35 in the budget law that granted complete authority to the government to determine the ownership of the SOEs in 1998 and 1999 (Behkish, 2010: 118). Khatami was an influential member of the statist wing of the stratum of government managers, whose members were marginalised at the start of the first plan. The intensification of the conflict between the technocratic wing of this fraction and the bonyad–bazaar nexus, as we discussed above, facilitated the links between the government and the members of the ex-statist wing who changed their view on the development model for the country as initially expressed by Mousavi Khoeiniha in 1992:

> Production should be open to the private sector and necessary encouragement given to it ... We are not averse to the argument that growth in productive capacity [policy of reconstruction] of the country is the most important economic solution for the present situation ... and that state monopoly in economic management will not lead to growth in production ... [but] giving total freedom to the private sector and eliminating [the role of] the government [in the economy] is not the solution.
>
> *Salaam*, 23 April 1992, cited in Siavoshi, 1992: 31

The key to their return was the inclusion of its members in huge financial and business projects in oil and petrochemicals as in the case of Petro Pars as well as the privatisation of a dozen newly privatised small and medium-sized government-owned enterprises (Fars News Agency, 2015). Consequently, the statist wing accepted liberalisation and privatisation but still emphasised a pivotal role for institutions in shaping the form, direction and speed of neoliberal restructuring. As clarified earlier, this line of argument initially generated a disagreement between shock therapists and new institutionalists in the economic team of Khatami, but the approval of the third plan settled the issue.

After appointing a committee to identify the potential SOEs, the government published a list of 538 government-owned enterprises for privatisation in April 1999. In addition, for the first time, the government intended to include more than 1,000 publicly owned enterprises under the control of the bonyads on the list, but the resistance from the Guardian Council during the approval of the third plan hindered the government's plot (Khajehpour, 2000: 590; Namazi, 2000: 23). According to the annual data of the Iranian Privatisation Organisation,[7] the government transferred the shares of only 339 government-owned enterprises to the 'private sector' over the period of the third plan, but its proceeds were nearly two and a half times more than the total value of transactions for the first two plans together. Due to the lack of reliable data, the only conclusion we might draw is that the buyers were mostly handpicked from the inner circle of the government and influential individuals. Moreover, during the Khatami administration, the government granted licences for the establishment of private companies in sectors permitted by law, including banking and insurance, power plant, construction, airlines, telecommunications and postal sectors (Harris, 2013: 53).

By exploiting highly non-transparent methods, a new class of government officials-cum-capitalists emerged predominantly through the political nexus and nepotistic networks linked to key ministries. Put differently, during the first period of neoliberalisation from 1990 to 2005, the stratum of government managers transformed itself into what I call the *internationally oriented capital fraction*. While consisting of some private capitalists, this fraction should not be treated as 'private capital' in contrast to 'state capital'. This is because such a dichotomous reading discounts the fact that this fraction comprises many allegedly private firms that are in reality the subsidiaries of various government ministries and is inclusive of some state officials and their relatives. As one of the two dominant wings of power in contemporary Iran (Figure 4.1), in the fourth section, we shall explain its capital circuit and accumulation strategy in detail.

To recap so far, in the wake of the Iranian economic crisis of the 1980s, some state managers facilitated the renovation of capitalism through a set of reforms from above. Subjected to the resistance from the bonyad–bazaar nexus due to the incompatibility of some of the proposed neoliberal reforms to their class interests, as well as some sporadic and incoherent rebelliousness from below by the working class and the urban poor, the neoliberal policies did not integrate the country into the new global division of labour. That said, the reorganisation of the economy, the privatisation of some government-owned enterprises and the formation of new privately owned enterprises led to the emergence of a fraction of the capitalist class from the ranks of the state bureaucracy advocating export-oriented growth and a closer relation with the global economy. In the following section,

| 1979–1989 | The stratum of government managers | The bonyad-bazaar nexus |
|-----------|-----------------------------------|-------------------------|
| 1989–2005 | The internationally-oriented capital fraction | |
| 2005–2013 | | The military-bonyad complex |

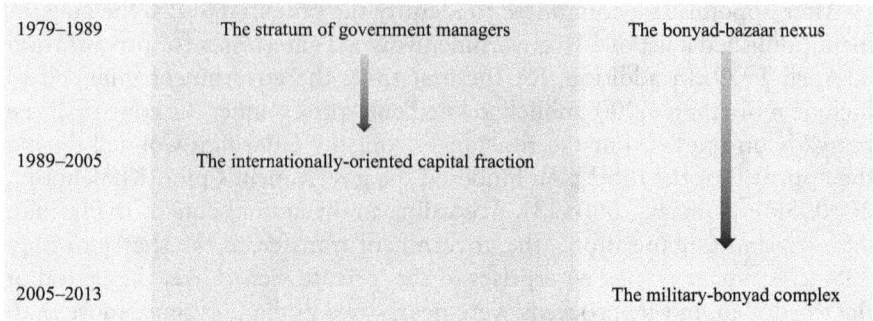

**Figure 4.1** Metamorphosis of the ruling class

we examine how the military forces and the revolutionary foundations exploited the process of neoliberalisation by transferring large government-owned enterprises to their direct control under the name of 'public non-governmental ownership'.

## Phase II of neoliberalisation and the emergence of the military–bonyad complex (2005–13)

In January 2005, the Majles approved the fourth five-year development plan with similar economic goals to the previous plans. It envisioned the stabilisation of a domestic business-friendly climate, improvement of human capital, technology and total-factor productivity, an upsurge in non-oil exports and enhancement in international competitiveness by projecting the growth of the foreign-direct-investment ratio to GDP from 0.6 per cent to 3 per cent by 2010. Other primary objectives included rationalising the price of gasoline, electricity, gas and water, reducing the number of government employees, reforming the budget to reduce the reliance on crude oil exports and increasing revenues from taxes (Amuzegar, 2010: 114–16; see Law on the Fourth Development Plan, 2004). The Khatami government drafted the plan, but the unexpected triumph of Ahmadinejad in the June 2005 presidential election distorted its direction since the new administration merely committed to its goals (Delafrouz, 2014: 125). The reformist government also played an indispensable role in a revision to Article 44 of the Constitution to remove legal obstacles to privatisation, which was ratified by the supreme leader in 2004. According to Article 44 of the 1979 Constitution, the economic system of the country was comprised primarily of the state sector that allowed the government to control all economic activities with a small role for the cooperative and private sectors. The new interpretation downgrades 'the role of government from direct ownership and management to business to a policy-making, supervisory, and advisory role' (Iran Data Portal, no date b). Despite the optimism of the internationally oriented capital fraction that the new interpretation would deepen liberalisation and strengthen their class foothold, it provided leeway for the reorganisation of the bonyad–bazaar nexus following Ahmadinejad's dark horse victory in 2005.

As a former commander, Ahmadinejad had close ties with the IRGC and other revolutionary foundations and loathed the technocrats of the previous administrations. In addition to Ahmadinejad's confidants from the military and security forces that comprised two-thirds of his first cabinet, former IRGC and *Basij* officers replaced a large segment of the technocracy in the government apparatus (Amuzegar, 2010: 126). The administration labelled itself as an anti-corruption government, therefore calling for the upholding of Khomeini's revolutionary principles and demanding more economic support for the poor (*mostaz'afān*). The new government condemned the implementation of the structural adjustment programme of the previous administrations, such as the first round of privatisation and price deregulation, as a symbol of subservience to Western ideologies and a means for rewarding a small group of powerful businessmen, technocrats and politicians. Ahmadinejad also famously pledged to 'bring the oil money to the tablecloth' of each Iranian (Habibi, 2014: 2–3).

His anti-technocratic agenda required an expansionary fiscal policy. An unprecedented hike in the price of oil from around $17 per barrel in 2002 to more than $60 in 2005, which generated more than $700 billion in revenue during his first term (Maloney, 2015: 321, 329), helped to realise some of the administration's programmes, including the Imam Reza Compassion Fund (*sanduq-e mehr-e emām rezā*) and the Compassion Housing Project (*tarh-e maskan-e mehr*). The Imam Reza Compassion Fund with $1.3 billion in funding aimed to provide interest-free loans for youth marriage and education (Ilias, 2010: 7). With $10 billion in funds, the Compassion Housing Project was an affordable housing scheme with the intention of building housing units on unutilised land for deprived people (Maloney, 2015: 329). It covered approximately 30 per cent of housing constructed between 2006 and 2016 since it built altogether around 2 million housing units (Ranjipour, 2017). Some argue that the project increased house prices by 500 per cent in Tehran (nationally 50 per cent) and thus failed to realise its objective because it only helped 5 per cent of the 19 million Iranian poor to get on to the housing ladder (ILNA, 2017; see also Ranjipour, 2017). In addition, the government provided some low-interest loans to farmers and rural residents for the development of agriculture and industry (Ilias, 2010: 7). Perhaps the most significant programme was the justice shares (*sahām-e 'edālat*) that echoed the August 1994 bill. The government stressed that the previous form of privatisation had to be frozen in favour of a new privatisation scheme in which the 'downtrodden' became the primary beneficiaries of ownership rights of former SOEs (Ehteshami and Zweiri, 2007: 88). In reality, the justice shares scheme along with other methods of privatisation during the Ahmadinejad administration was designed to transfer the ownership of large government-owned enterprises to the military forces and revolutionary foundations, which was facilitated by the supreme leader's 2006 executive order in line with the 2004 revision of Article 44 of the Constitution. We now turn to examine privatisation during this period from 2005 to 2013.

### Privatisation in the hands of the military forces and the revolutionary foundations

In 2006, the supreme leader issued a complementary executive decree to the 2004 revision of Article 44 of the Constitution. The decree permitted investment, ownership and management of 'public, non-governmental entities and organs, the cooperative and private sectors' in 80 per cent shares of large mines, large and mother industries, government banks, government insurance companies, airlines and shipping lines, energy companies, post and communications and military and defence industries.[8] It excluded a few sensitive companies and services such as the primary electricity networks and the National Iranian Oil Company and firms involved in the extraction and production of petroleum and gas. In addition, the decree suggested that sufficient measures must be taken to prevent the creation of monopolies and the domination of foreigners over the national economy (Iran Data Portal, no date b). The supreme leader claimed that 'ceding 80 per cent of the shares of large companies will serve to bring about economic development, social justice and elimination of poverty' (*Financial Times*, 2006). Consequently, the government envisaged three methods for offloading the government-owned enterprises for the second phase of privatisation, namely liabilities clearance (*rad-e doyun*), justice shares and 'others'.

The most popular method of privatisation was liabilities clearance in which the government directly transferred its large enterprises to its lenders. To justify the transactions, Ahmadvand, the then head of the Iranian Privatisation Organisation, affirmed that 'since we are obliged by the law to tender all transfers competitively, in some cases, one unit has been offered several times [in the Tehran Stock Exchange]'. Without bids from the private sector, he added, 'we were eventually forced to transfer the ownership of these enterprises to investment funds and other enterprises to pay off government's debts' (Anousheh, 2013). Under the justice shares method, the government insisted on allocating 40 per cent shares of some big industrial government-owned enterprises to low-income deciles of the population at a 50 per cent discount rate (in some cases without charge and as gifts) on the grounds that the legitimate buyers would repay their debts from companies' future profits over the course of ten years. By identifying around 49 million people as appropriate receivers, the government established 30 justice-shares provincial investment companies, but only 33 million people had received stocks and dividends from the programme by 2018 (*Burs*, 2013: 48–9; Ghadimi, 2018). Since the war veterans, the families of martyrs, the members of the *Basij*, and low-income households who received support from various welfare agencies were the primary targets of the programme, the government mainly used the database of the bonyads such as the Imam Khomeini Relief Committee, the Imam Reza Shrine Foundation, the Mostazafan Foundation and the *Basij* for doling out shares. The government kept 20 per cent shares in these firms, but it sanctioned the purchase of the remaining 40 per cent of equities by 'public, non-governmental entities and organs' under the pretext of a lack of demand from the private sector. Although the fate of the people's justice shares is not yet clear, the experience of voucher privatisations in other countries is likely to be the outcome. Similar to the case of the Czech Republic – where investment funds owned by domestic banks with the state majority stake 'ended up owning large or controlling stakes in many firms privatised through vouchers, as citizens sought to limit their risk by transferring their vouchers into these funds' (Nellis, 1999: 11) – the investment companies of the bonyads and the military forces would be well-positioned to own the 'people's stocks'.

During the two terms of Ahmadinejad's presidency, $62 billion (2009 USD rate) worth of shares was transferred through the liabilities clearance and justice shares ($34 and $28 billion respectively). Through the 'others' method, the shares of a few giant companies were sold to 'some big parastatal, public organisation companies' (Sabouniha, 2017: 538) with privatisation proceeds of around $32 billion (Fekri, 2014: 7; *Donyā-ye Eqtesād*, 2017). The figures unveil the unprecedented pace of the privatisation process as the value of offloaded stocks from 2005 to 2013 was nearly fifty times more than during the Khatami government. In short, the heavy involvement of quasi-governmental firms in the bidding for formerly large government-owned enterprises enormously fortified the economic power of the military forces and the bonyads. In addition to facilitating the takeover of the government-owned enterprises, the government protected their interests through other policies such as the supply of their foreign exchanges and the blocking of the entrance of foreign competitors to the domestic market.[9] We now look at the ways in which the economic power of the IRGC and other revolutionary foundations was mostly augmented during the second phase of neoliberalisation.

Based on the class compromise of the early years after the Iran–Iraq war and under Article 147 of the Constitution which encourages the involvement of the military forces in the process of the reconstruction of the country during times of peace, the Hashemi-Rafsanjani government invited the IRGC to participate in the rebuilding of war-torn areas (*Shargh*, 2013). Accordingly, the IRGC formed an engineering firm named Ghorb (Khatam-al Anbiya Construction Headquarters, *qarārgāh-e sāzandegi-ye khātam-ol-ʾnbiā*ʾ) immediately after the end of the war. The Revolutionary Guards' modest participation in economic activities evolved significantly during the Ahmadinejad presidency. In 2012, the US Treasury Department reported that the IRGC was 'the most powerful economic actor, dominating many sectors of the economy, including energy, construction, and banking' through 'a complex web of front companies' that disguise its economic activities. Rather than being directly involved in the privatisation scheme, the IRGC has purchased shares from the Tehran Stock Exchange through its financial arms, most notably the Sepah Cooperative Foundation and the Ansar Financial and Credit Institution. The former owns a dozen companies and investment groups such as Tose'eh E'temād Mobin while the latter has over 600 branches across the country with around 6 million customers. In 'the largest trade in the history of Tehran Stock Exchange, valued around $8 billion', Tose'eh E'temād Mobin became the majority shareholder of the Telecommunications Company of Iran on a no-bid basis by disqualifying the only competitor for security reasons in September 2009 (Alfoneh, 2010: 4–5). Furthermore, an IRGC-affiliated pension fund, the Armed Forces Social Welfare Organisation, which is among the biggest pension funds in the country, secured the ownership of numerous government-owned enterprises as a result of the second stage of privatisation. In 2008, the Armed Forces Social Welfare Organisation secured the ownership of the Ghadir Investment Company (*Irān*, 2016). Today, according to its admission, the Ghadir is 'the largest TSE [Tehran Stock Exchange] listed investment company with a capital of 72,000 billion rials' that operates in various sectors such as oil, gas, petrochemicals, cement, construction, mines and related industries, transportation, power and energy, and financial and commercial activities through its numerous holdings and subsidiaries.[10] Likewise, the financial group of the *Basij*, Mehr Eqtesad Bank, is the largest 'private' bank in Iran with over 700 branches. The main subsidiary of the institution, the Mehr-e Eqtesad-e Iranian Investment Company, has been trading on the Tehran Stock Exchange and is 'one of the largest purchasing entities that owns stakes in a number of major Iranian companies' (Alfoneh, 2010: 4).

Alaeddin Broujerdi, a former prominent member of the Majles, named the Ghorb 'the biggest and the most capable economic and developmental group of the country' (*Resālat*, 2017a). Apart from acquiring control of large government-owned enterprises during the Ahmadinejad presidency such as Iran's biggest marine industrial company, Sadra (Ahmadi, 2012), the

Ghorb was granted lucrative contracts in various projects. After appointing the then commander of the Ghorb to the Ministry of Petroleum in 2011 (*Shargh*, 2017a), the government awarded the firm and its subsidiaries no-bid contracts for the development of several phases of the South Pars field in response to the withdrawal of MNCs such as Shell and Total from Iran due to the nuclear-related international sanctions (*E'temād*, 2014). Some estimated that the oil projects granted to the Ghorb were valued above $25 billion during this period (Omidvar, 2012). In 2017, the Ghorb had 170,000 employees with the completion of over 2,500 projects, mostly after 2005 (*Shargh*, 2017b), including the construction of 4,000 kilometres of oil and gas pipelines, 61 dams, 163 bridges, 2,500 kilometres of highways, 4,000 kilometres of railway, 6 metro lines in Tehran and other cities, 150 kilometres of tunnels, 23,000 fibre-optic networks, over 100 hospitals, and various colossal agricultural projects, among others (*Kayhan*, 2017). As a revolutionary organisation, the economic activities of the IRGC are exempt from tax and excluded from government scrutiny (*Shargh*, 2016) because it claims that Kosar Construction Headquarters, a subsidiary of the Ghorb, uses its revenues for anti-poverty projects across the country (as an example of this claim see *Kayhan*, 2011). There are some claims that the Ghorb alone controlled more than 812 registered companies in 2010 (Borger and Tait, 2010), but, as a multilayered organisation with a complex web of holding companies, front companies, and 'charitable foundations', it is difficult to pin down the exact number of its firms. To illuminate the financial power of the IRGC, in 2015, its annual turnover was reported to be around $12 billion, counting for 'a sixth of Iran's declared GDP' (Hafezi and Charbonneau, 2015).

Another revolutionary foundation known as Setad, the Headquarters for Executing the Order of the Imam (*setād-e ejrāi-ye farmān-e emām*) possesses 38 per cent stocks of Tose'eh E'temād Mobin. Its name refers to a decree by Khomeini before his death to establish an organisation for managing abandoned properties and other assets from the post-revolutionary mayhem (Stecklow, Dehghanpishesh and Torbati, 2013). In the name of supporting 'the families of the martyrs, veterans, the missing, prisoners of war and the downtrodden', Setad generated a substantial amount of funds by confiscating assets during the 1990s. Throughout his presidency, Khatami endeavoured to subject Setad to regular inspections, but the Guardian Council impeded attempts by declaring that the entity is beyond the Majles and government's oversight (Torati, Stecklow and Dehghanpisheh, 2013). In 2000, following the creation of an investment company, Tadbir Investment Co., Setad extended its activities beyond property. Again, the major expansion occurred after the new revision of Article 44 and the executive order of the supreme leader for the privatisation of 80 per cent of shares of large government-owned enterprises in 2006. Setad became the owner of a major bank called Parsian (*bank-e pārsiān*) in 2007, purchased the shares of the Telecommunications of Iran in 2009 and acquired the control of the Rey Investment Company (valued at about $40 billion by the US Treasury Department) in 2010. In the form of two financial arms, the Tadbir Economic Development Group and the Tose-e Eqtesad-e Ayandesazan Company, it is reported that Setad entirely and partially owns the shares of over 150 firms. Its third main unit, the Barakat Foundation (*bonyād-e barekat*), whose prime duty is to eliminate poverty and empower poor communities, now runs the Barakat Pharmaceutical Company with more than 20 subsidiaries. As an economic conglomerate, Setad has invested in everything from banks to ostrich farms, and together with its real-estate empire (the Real Estate and Properties Organisation), it was estimated to have assets worth about $95 billion by 2016 (Dehghanpishesh and Stecklow, 2013; Nowruzi, 2016). Setad justifies its exemption from tax and government inspection by assert- ing that the Barakat Foundation is involved in infrastructure and devel- opment projects in rural areas. For instance, Mehr News Agency (2017) reported that the foundation completed over 25,000 charitable projects, including the construction of more than 1,000 schools, nearly 200 hospitals and health clinics, 1,000 cultural centres (mosques and other religious cen- tres) and 11,000 housing units from its revenues by 2017.

Alongside Ghorb, the Hashemi-Rafsanjani government permitted other bonyads such as the Mostazafan Foundation and the Imam Reza Shrine Foundation to deal with various aspects of the wartime reconstruction as part of the class compromise of the post-Iran–Iraq-war period (Amirahmadi, 1990: 267, 272). Despite pressure from the Khatami administrations through policies such as the unification of the exchange rate, unified social safety net and privatisation of firms owned by bonyads, the revolutionary foundations augmented their grip on the economy (Saeidi, 2004: 489–90). In the case of the Mostazafan Foundation, this only led to the replacement of its head in 1999 without any concrete results. Two years before his forced resignation, Rafigh-Doust claimed that 'the bonyad is the biggest economic entity in Iran and the Middle East and perhaps the biggest in the world in terms of diver- sity [of its activities]' (cited in BBC Persian, 2013). His successor acknowl- edged that 80 per cent of its companies suffered from a lack of financial profitability and pledged to privatise 250 firms, but only 37 out of 400-odd firms were offloaded (*The Economist*, 2001). The foundation comprises three divisions, namely economic, oppressed, and self-sacrificed. During the first phase of neoliberalisation, the expenses of the oppressed and self- sacrificed divisions mainly came from the annual budget while its revenues from economic activities and outstanding taxes were invested in new eco- nomic units (Farzin, 2004: 76–9). In 1997, the Mostazafan Foundation had 'holdings of $12 billion, second only to the state-owned National Iranian Oil Company' (*The Economist*, 1997; see also Maloney, 2000b: 93) and employed 'some 5 per cent of the male workforce' (*Financial Times*, 1997). During the second phase of neoliberalisation, the Mostazafan Foundation offloaded some small and medium-sized firms to the private sector, but it expanded the economic capacity of its large firms and invested in the lucrative oil and finance sectors by founding the Sina Financial and Investment Company and the Sina Bank (Omidvar, 2008). With 11 major holdings and over 200 companies, the foundation is active in all economic sectors, including service, industry and mining, energy, finance and banking, construction and agriculture.[11] Based on the 2016 financial statement of the foundation, its assets were valued at $14 billion, but if we take into consideration the real value rather than nominal value, the value of its assets could be several times more than the stated figure. BBC Persian reported that the net profit of the Mostazafan Foundation was over $700 million in 2016 (Arazmi, 2017).

Similarly, the Imam Reza Shrine Foundation stretched its economic activities following the creation of the Razavi Economic Organisation. This reflected the new policy of massive investment in agriculture and industry which was promised by the management of the bonyad in order to strengthen its power bases and financial independence (Hourcade, 2004: 89). Before 2005, the foundation acquired 90 per cent of the arable land of Khorasan province, where the Shrine is located, and owned fifty-six companies involved in diverse activities from soft drinks to automobile manufacturing (Katzman, 2006), accounting 'for 7.1% of Iran's gross domestic product' (Higgins, 2007). According to Irān Online (2017), the foundation has shares in more than 70 firms, of which 36 are categorised as large companies, but its website claims that the Razavi Economic Organisation currently owns at least 148 firms in various sectors including pharmaceutical, food, textile, construction, agriculture and animal husbandry, oil and gas, information technology and investment (Razavi Economic Organisation website). In addition, as the biggest endowment entity in the Islamic world, BBC Persian (2016a) estimates that the Imam Reza Shrine Foundation possessed approximately 400,000 hectares of agricultural land and orchards all around the country with an approximate value of $20 billion in 2016.

In 1995, the Martyrs' Foundation established the Shahid Investment Company to mobilise the savings of the families of martyrs to invest in diverse economic activities that resulted in the control of numerous firms without any disclosure of the accounts to its shareholders (Rakel, 2007: 125; see also Saeidi, 2004: 88). With a close connection to the Ahmadinejad administration, in addition to firms under the control of the Shahid Group, the foundation set up the Kowsar Economic Organisation that owns more than thirty subsidiaries active in agriculture, industry and mining, finance, engineering, health and transport. In recent years, the foundation launched its own bank, Dey Bank, with over ninety branches throughout the country and fifteen subsidiaries (Sodaie, 2016).[12] Although there are different estimations regarding the economic and financial power of the foundation, one commentator calculates that the Martyrs' Foundation altogether controls the possession of more than 250 enterprises (Sedaghat, 2017: 12). While approximately 3 million people in rural areas received various forms of support under different schemes from the Imam Khomeini Relief Committee in 1995 (Saeidi, 2004: 498), 6 per cent of Iran's population, which constituted nearly 5 million, were directly covered by the organisation in 2017 (*Resālat*, 2017b). The Imam Khomeini Relief Committee generates some of its revenues from religious taxes and endowment properties and receives 'substantial amounts of budgetary transfer ... with no governmental discretion over expenses, as well as massive amounts of resources in the form of implicit and explicit subsidies and transfers for financing other programs' (Saeidi, 2004: 498). Historically, the economic activities of the Committee were relatively few compared to other foundations. Nevertheless, apart from its real-estate unit, the economic arm of the organisation (the Corporate Group of the Relief Committee) has several holding companies and subsidiaries with little information about the value of its companies' shares.

## The formation of the military–bonyad complex

Some estimate that the economic activities of the revolutionary foundations counted for 33 per cent of Iran's total gross national product during the first phase of neoliberal reforms from 1991 to 2005 (Rakel, 2007: 109; Katzman, 2006). Given the significant increase in the economic power of the bonyads and military forces from 2005 to 2013 and considering their exemption from taxation, the total market share of the economic network for military forces and revolutionary foundations could be estimated at around 50 per cent of the country's GDP at current exchange rates.[13] We should treat these figures with some caution due to the unaccountable nature of these institutions, but nevertheless, they are indicative of the profound role of these institutions in the economy.

The emergence of the economic empire of the military forces and the large-scale appropriation of economic assets by revolutionary foundations during the second phase of neoliberalisation strikingly evolved and meaningfully shifted the nature of the bonyad–bazaar nexus. As demonstrated in the previous chapter, the import licences, official foreign-exchange rate and other rent-seeking concessions were granted to merchants with political connections to the revolutionary state in the first decade of the revolution. However, the monopolisation of large-scale commercial activities by the well-positioned merchants and the bonyads resulted in the political disenfranchisement and economic marginalisation of the self-governing traditional network of commerce, wholesale and retail of the bazaar as a whole. Despite this demotion, I opted for the term bonyad–bazaar nexus to describe this fraction of the ruling class that emerged in the first decade of the revolution because of the bazaari social class origins of many important figures of the bonyads, the similarity between the structure and methods of operation of the foundations and the bazaar and the mutuality of economic interests of the post-revolutionary commercial elites and the foundations. The commercial wing of the bonyad–bazaar nexus remained still powerful and played a noticeable role in fostering the post-Iran–Iraq-war development plan, but the neoliberal reforms further dismantled the traditional bazaar as a commercial network and relevant economic actor. During the presidency of Ahmadinejad, the ascendancy of the military forces and revolutionary foundations in the economy with an anti-import rhetoric and policies in favour of national production and consumption alienated the mercantile wing of the bonyad–bazaar nexus. In addition, the use of the IRGC-controlled ports and airports for importing commodities without paying duty fuelled the tension and exacerbated further the relationship between the two wings of the bonyad–bazaar nexus (Rezaei and Moshirabas, 2018: 149). Hence, while the political representative of this mercantile wing, the traditional right, initially supported Ahmadinejad, the new political group linked to the IRGC and bonyads, the Principlists (*Osulgarāyān*), criticised the bazaar-affiliated political organisations and their leading figures (Ehteshami and Zweiri, 2007: 80). Another indication of the disintegration manifested itself in the escalation of the tensions between the Ahmadinejad administration and a powerful faction of the Majles representing the mercantile wing throughout its presidency (Arjomand, 2009: 163). Disillusioned by the economic policies of the Ahmadinejad administration, the marginalised bazaar coordinated an unsuccessful strike in several cities for the first time after the revolution in 2008 to oppose the 3 per cent value-added tax on importers and distributors (Arjomand, 2009: 123). The mercantile wing finally detached itself from the Principlists and officially supported Rouhani's candidacy in the 2013 presidential election. That is to say, after years of gradual metamorphosis, the bonyad–bazaar nexus transformed into the *military–bonyad complex* (Figure 4.1). The military–bonyad complex constitutes the second fraction of the Iranian capitalist class in the neoliberal era because the real economic owners of the enterprises under the control of the military forces and revolutionary foundations are the heads of these institutions and directors of the enterprises, even though the formal and juridical ownership of their businesses allegedly belongs to the 'downtrodden masses'.

Up to now, we demonstrated that Iranian neoliberalisation has engendered two fractions of the capitalist class inside the state with contesting interests since 1990. Because of their different orientations that consequently generated rather different class interests, each fraction has pursued a distinct strategy in relation and response to the advance of the international movement of capital. The next section looks at the conflicting accumulation strategies of these fractions of capital and the manifestation of what I call hybrid neoliberalism as an amalgamation of ISI and EOI strategies.

## The case of hybrid neoliberalism

To unpack the particularity of the form of Iranian neoliberalism, we need to first observe the circuit of capital and accumulation strategy of the internationalist capital fraction and the military–bonyad complex. Let us begin with the internationally oriented capital fraction. From 1991 to 2005, as well as the privatisation of several hundred government-owned medium-sized enterprises and some large firms, many National Iranian Oil Company spin-off companies and export-oriented firms were founded. Issuing licences during Khatami's tenure further led to the creation of more 'private' firms in many sectors of the economy. In this period, the composition of industrial products indicates a shift in favour of intermediate goods and against consumer commodities along the lines of the adopted development strategy of EOI. A closer look at the composition of exported mining and industrial goods illuminates a similar trend (Delafrouz, 2014: 135–6), even though the share of high-value-added goods constituted less than 5 per cent of the total exports (Momeni and Naeb, 2017: 95). In addition, these firms widely employed an administrative and professional division of labour associated with neoliberalism. Government intervention has been central to the emergence of the internationally oriented fraction for two reasons. First, its existence depended on the expropriation of assets either through the privatisation mechanism or appropriation of oil revenues, and second, its export-oriented enterprises heavily relied on various governmental forms of assistance (Nili, Darghagi and Fatemi, 2012: 165–6). Most of the so-called private firms and spin-off companies linked to this fraction have remained attached to various government institutions and ministries to utilise state rents. It is not difficult to understand why capturing the government (the executive body of the state) through presidential elections has always been the main priority and the only realistic hope of this crony-capitalist class to enable their rent-seeking behaviour to survive.[14]

As Table 4.2 shows, Iran's industry is dominated by small and medium-sized firms, but more than 60 per cent of the value added is produced by large firms (Nili, Darghagi and Fatemi, 2012: 147), which are to some degree in the hands of the military–bonyad complex or have not yet been privatised. Besides the manufacturing sector, the military–bonyad complex also has a relative upper hand in the service sector, commerce, banking and agriculture. According to a survey of the top 100 large companies in 2017, at least 44 firms belonged to the military–bonyad complex, 43 companies were still categorised as government-owned enterprises and the rest were controlled by the 'private sector' (*Shargh*, 2017c). Given that some government-owned enterprises in the analysis are subsidiaries of investment groups such as the National Development Group Investment Company and the Social Security Investment Company, the number of large firms in the list under the control of this fraction could potentially increase to twenty. Another study claims that two-thirds of the top twenty corporations that account for 70 per cent of the Tehran Stock Exchange are owned by the military–bonyad complex (Momeni and Naeb 2017: 115–16; see also *Shargh*, 2017c).

Considering these factors, for two reasons I opted for the term 'internationally oriented' to describe this fraction of capital. First, recalling the conceptual discussion in Chapter 1, the circuit of capital of this fraction indicates that, while its outputs to a large extent are aimed to sell internationally, most of its production and reinvestment of the realised capital still occur within Iran. That said, the intended international realisation of products does not mean that all goods are exported because still a large number of products are sold for domestic consumption. Second, in order to compete with the military–bonyad complex and in line with its preferred EOI strategy and integration into the GVCs, this fraction has been the vehement proponent of a conciliatory foreign policy towards the West, particularly the European Union, in pursuit of investments from Western capital, as will be discussed in detail in Chapter 7. To this end, the Hashemi-Rafsanjani

Table 4.2 Number of manufacturing enterprises with ten or more workers

| Year | All | 10–99 employees (small) | 100–499 employees (medium) | 500 employees or more (large) |
|------|-----|-------------------------|----------------------------|-------------------------------|
| 1991 | 4,809 | 3,894 | 630 | 285 |
| 2005 | 16,018 | 14,036 | 1,704 | 278 |
| 2014 | 14,452 | 11,904 | 2,162 | 386 |

*Source:* Compiled by the author, based on Statistical Center of Iran; Islamic Parliament Research Center (2017b: 13) and Razaghi (1997: 312)

and Khatami governments pushed for the pragmatic policy regarding the first Gulf War, full normalisation of relations with European powers, resolving the Rushdie issue, rapprochement with Saudi Arabia, close cooperation with the United States in its fight against the Taliban and post-war political settlement in Afghanistan and a diplomatic resolution of the nuclear crisis (Joyner, 2016: 20; Clawson and Rubin, 2005: 152–3). Along with this foreign policy, the two administrations created six free trade-industrial zones (FTZs) (Hakimian, 2011: 855–62),[15] attempted to become a member of the WTO, reformed the law on foreign investment and reduced corporate tax from 68 per cent to 25 per cent (Dinmore, 2002; Arjomandy, 2014: 939–40). These policies initially eased the inflows of FDI to the country as it climbed more than eighteen-fold from $194 million in 2000 to $3.519 billion in 2002 (Table 4.3). Nevertheless, in the following years, the volume of FDI inflows to Iran remained unchanged (UNCTADStat) due to the coordinated sabotage from the military–bonyad complex, which was initially orchestrated through the conservative-dominated Seventh Majles that hindered successful bids from foreign investors for 'security reservations' and 'incompatibility with the national interests' (*Shargh*, 2010: 4; *Kayhan*, 2016, Prapanchi, 2005).[16] Relatedly, the extensive involvement of the IRGC and security forces in overseas activities largely undermined the reconciliation policy of the internationally oriented capital fraction. The situation later deteriorated because of Ahmadinejad's anti-Western foreign policy and his uncompromising stance regarding the nuclear programme.

On the other hand, the circuit of capital in the military–bonyad complex shows that production, realisation and reproduction mostly occur within

**Table 4.3** FDI inward flows 2000–14 (million US dollars at current prices)

| Year | Iran | Turkey | Saudi Arabia |
| --- | --- | --- | --- |
| 2000 | 194 | 982 | 183 |
| 2002 | 3,519 | 1,082 | 453 |
| 2004 | 3,037 | 2,785 | 1,942 |
| 2006 | 2,318 | 20,185 | 18,293 |
| 2008 | 1,980 | 19,851 | 39,456 |
| 2010 | 3,649 | 9,086 | 29,233 |
| 2012 | 4,662 | 13,631 | 12,182 |
| 2014 | 2,105 | 12,458 | 8,012 |

*Source:* Compiled by the author, based on UNCTADStat

Iran. Inspired by the statist development trajectories in other countries, the military–bonyad complex has embraced the idea of the creation of national corporations similar to those developed in East Asia, as expressed by the chairman of the Setad-affiliated Tadbir Economic Development Group, Afkhami (cited in Dehghanpishesh and Stecklow, 2013):

> In South Korea, companies like Samsung, LG and Hyundai have had an impact on development. In China, Japan, Brazil, Germany and America it is the same … We saw that in Iran we don't have these large corporations. With this in mind, within the Tadbir Investment Company we started slowly, slowly discussing the strategy of entering various arenas.

This strategy is also evident from the IRGC's economic activities because the Ghorb no longer participates in 'small and medium projects' in order to prioritise 'the replacement of foreign corporations' (*Kayhan*, 2011). Moreover, the military has pursued a hostile attitude toward the entrance of Western capital into the Iranian market. There are claims that subsidiaries of the IRGC previously worked with foreign capital, including European companies (Harris, 2013: 64). Furthermore, some bonyads, in particular, the Mostazafan Foundation and the Imam Reza Shrine, appeared to be initially embracing the Hashemi-Rafsanjani agenda and attempted to adjust the direction of their economic activities by utilising both domestic and foreign capital. This resulted in an inconsistent policy because while some bonyad-affiliated firms invested abroad in the 1990s and the 2000s, the head of the Mostazafan Foundation labelled a franchising agreement between Coca-Cola and an Iranian company in 1993 as a sign of the infiltration of Western culture and vowed to 'drive all foreign Coca-Cola plants out of Iran' (cited in Maloney, 2015: 233). This inconsistent policy moved towards a decisive stance during the second phase of neoliberalisation since the economic machine of bonyads and military forces exploited the privatisation mechanism by expanding its control over state monopoly industries and blocking foreign takeovers. Therefore, they emphatically rejected the policy of the incorporation of Western MNCs into these state monopoly industries through privatisation as advocated by the internationally oriented capital fraction. By disputing the idea that Western foreign firms import technology and reduce production costs, the military–bonyad complex framed the pro-FDI argument as the facilitator of foreign domination of the national economy (*E'temād*, 2013).

Several geopolitical and international factors also importantly aided this transformation. We will thoroughly explore the internal relations between neoliberalism and geopolitics in Chapter 7, but for now, it is sufficient to mention that the international sanctions and the rise of China helped to consolidate the power of the military–bonyad complex between 2005 and

2013. This can be seen more than anything else in the foreign policy of Iran throughout Ahmadinejad's tenure. First, the government pursued a nationalist and anti-Western approach to foreign policy with a strong emphasis on the continuation of the development of the nuclear programme in order to further halt the integration of Iran into the Western-centred international system. This policy triggered a round of international sanctions between 2006 and 2009 that in turn justified the unparalleled expansion of the economic activities of the Revolutionary Guards and bonyads in all economic sectors as a response to these sanctions and under the banner of 'economic resistance' and 'self-reliance'. Second, the Ahmadinejad government decisively tightened Iran's economic and political links with China and Russia under the 'Look East' approach in foreign policy in contrast to the Europe-oriented policy of the two previous administrations (Shariatinia and Azizi, 2019: 991) by perceiving the growing economic and geopolitical power of these emerging empires as positive developments that can cement the military–bonyad complex footholds. The rise of China in particular was considered significant. Besides allowing full access to the Chinese market during the sanctions, the military–bonyad complex supposed that the 'Look East' approach would 'open up expanding areas of opportunities' for them due to 'the rivalry between China and the United States, the Westphalian attitude of China toward the concept of sovereignty, its support for Iranian policies in the Middle East, arms trade between the two countries, and economic interactions' (Shariatinia and Azizi, 2019: 992).

The policy towards the working class has been a unifying issue between the internationally oriented capital fraction and the military–bonyad complex since the instigation of the neoliberal reforms.[17] Due to the low level of productivity as a result of the relatively poor and to a large degree outdated technologies in the absence of real cooperation with international capital, both fractions have relied on the imposition of highly exploitative working conditions as the best viable vehicle for capital accumulation. We will return to this issue in Chapter 6, but in the meantime, it is enough to note that the labour force has been under an unceasing onslaught from all administrations for the implementation of a flexible labour market since the early 1990s. This has resulted in the domination of short-term contracts of less than six months, ranging from 80 to 95 per cent of the total labour contracts (Nahvi, 2018: 4). This exploitation of labour is complemented by an absolute increase in the amount of child and forced labour in recent decades. The parliamentary research centre estimated that among the 3.25 million children out of school more than 90 per cent were working in 2012 (cited in Human Rights Watch, 2013). However, the estimation of non-governmental organisations (NGOs) is higher as, for instance, they projected the number of child workers was likely to be as high as 7 million in 2017 (Tasnim News Agency, 2017). According to Global Slavery Index (2018), Iran was also among the top ten countries with the highest prevalence of modern slavery in the world in 2018.

While certainly not disputing the significance of corruption or mismanagement, the explanation of the process based on this analytical framework is highly problematic. The channel of enormous wealth originating in the export of hydrocarbons and the transfer of the ownership of SOEs through policies of privatisation to reconstruct the ruling class cannot be fully grasped through the corruption lens since the same people are more or less in charge of the so-called 'private' and 'publicly owned' enterprises. Nor can this explanatory formula equip us to understand the logic behind the redistribution of wealth from the poor to the rich by implementing labour market deregulation and cutting off state subsidies. To reiterate the conceptual argument in Chapter 1, these policies have emerged out of the necessity of the reorganisation of the system to recover capital accumulation and reconstitute class power.

When we look at the economic model of the post-Iran–Iraq-war era, it is evident that the varieties of assistance provided by the government for the internationally oriented capital fraction point to the fact that the EOI strategy of this wing of power has directly inherited policies of the pre-1989 strategy. Likewise, while the military–bonyad complex has adopted a selection of neoliberal policies including the most exploitative labour practices, they are still heavily influenced by the ISI strategy of the 1970s that continued throughout the first decade of the revolution. Against the pro-FDI policy of the internationally oriented capital fraction, the military–bonyad complex has vehemently opposed the entrance of Western capital to Iran as another sign of the protectionist policies of the first decade of the revolution. In light of this, I argue that the existing general model of development in Iran is the amalgamation of ISI and EOI strategies resulting from the co-existence of different competing class fractions with different interests. This concurrent presence of these two different accumulation strategies in contemporary Iran is a manifestation of hybrid neoliberalism as the product of the recent process of economic restructuring facilitated and influenced by global and local dynamics and international and national shaping factors. While the uneven development of global capitalism acted as a beneficial condition for the neoliberal process of restructuring, the agency of domestic class forces has altered the direction of this trajectory by pursuing different approaches to the economy. As demonstrated in this chapter, the different strategies of the two capital fractions, in turn, can only be explained if we consider their actions in relation and response to the advance of the international movement of capital. Additionally, the emergence of new centres of accumulation and political rivalries, which has to some degree shaken the Western-dominated hierarchical global structure, has equally shaped the nature of capital accumulation and class formation in Iran.

## Conclusion

Against the explanation of the global as a process or force that exists externally to the local and the pervasive approaches that privilege the national space as the ultimate terrain for the interpretation of social phenomena, in this chapter we have reiterated the necessity for moving beyond the analytical distinction between the internal and external in the study of neoliberal restructuring in Iran. Because we view these relations between national and global spaces as internally related to each other, we challenged the framework which views the global economy with an external effect on Iran only through oil revenues and understanding Iran as a confined set of social relations separated from the wider space of global neoliberalism. Given this, the chapter has substantiated that Iranian neoliberalisation must be viewed as part of the global response to the crisis of capital accumulation. We have demonstrated that the post-revolutionary class structure and the agency of local forces have also played indispensable roles in the initiation and destination of neoliberal reforms from above. We thus showed how the process has fundamentally reshuffled the composition of the ruling class by giving rise to the emergence of the internationally oriented class fraction with a focus on the growth of non-oil exports and the opening up of the market for foreign capital, especially European capital, as well as the institution of the powerful anti-Western capital fraction of the military–bonyad complex. Although neoliberal restructuring in Iran has thrown up tensions and contradictions that have been seen throughout the world, the chapter illuminated that it has produced a unique form of development. We conceptualised hybrid neoliberalism as the amalgamation of the ISI state-led development strategy of the post-1960s and the EOI strategy that there has been an attempt to implement since the end of the war with Iraq.

In the next chapter, we will focus on the reorganisation of the institutional setup and the reconfiguration of the ideological base of the state. Focusing on institutions after analysing the changes in process of capital accumulation and the class character of the state does not mean treating institutions as 'derivative, second-order, or in any way unimportant' (Hanieh, 2018: 15). Because institutions are historically determined social forms emerging and reconstituting through the production and reproduction of society itself, my approach prioritises focusing on capitalist social relations to trace 'the

actual dynamics involved in the accumulation of capital and the social relations that form around these' (Hanieh, 2018: 15). In other words, without
analysing the shifting balance between opposing social class forces emanating from regimes of accumulation, it is not possible to analyse institutions.
As we have been equipped with the knowledge of the process of capital
accumulation and the class character of the state in post-1989 Iran in this
chapter, we are thus in a position to look at the institutional and ideological
reorganisation of the Iranian state in light of the process of neoliberalisation
in the next chapter.

## Notes

1 Parts of a previously published article appear throughout this chapter: 'Hybrid neoliberalism: Capitalist development in contemporary Iran' by
  Kayhan Valadbaygi © 2021 The Author, taken from *New Political Economy*
  2021, 26:3, 313–327, © Informa UK Limited, trading as Taylor & Francis
  Group 2021, reprinted by permission of Taylor & Francis Ltd, https://doi.org/
  10.1080/13563467.2020.1729715.
2 The next chapter will thoroughly examine the constitutional reform in 1989
  and its relation with the process of neoliberalisation and transformation in the
  balance of class forces inside the state.
3 The total amount of foreign debt of the country is not entirely clear as various
  figures have been estimated. Keddie (2003: 267) claims that Iran had $37 bil-
  lion in debt in 1993 and Momeni (2014: 315) estimates that the total amount
  of debt was above $40 billion by the end of the First Development Plan.
4 The government-held shares of the Refah stores were later reduced to 35 per
  cent with the remaining shares sold off to the 'private' sector linked to the
  government.
5 It should be noted that 1996/7 is equivalent to 1375 in the Iranian calendar.
6 The full list of the selected government-owned enterprises during the First
  Development Plan is published by the Iranian Privatisation Organisation, available at: http://www.ipo.ir/index.jsp?fkeyid=&siteid=1&pageid=143 (accessed
  5 April 2023).
7 To access the data for the proceeds of privatisation since the start of the
  neoliberal reforms in 1991, check the annual reports of the Iranian Privatisation
  Organisation at: https://ipo.ir/%D8%A2%D9%85%D8%A7%D8%B1-
  %D8%B3%D8%A7%D9%84%DB%8C%D8%A7%D9%86%D9%87
  (accessed 5 April 2023).
8 Non-governmental entities and organs here refer to the state institutions outside the jurisdiction of the government and under the control of the supreme
  leader, i.e. revolutionary foundations and institutions, not non-governmental
  organisations (NGOs) in typical use.
9 Chapter 7 thoroughly investigates the relationship between Ahmadinejad's
  aggressive foreign policy, and the class interests of the military forces and the
  revolutionary foundations.

10  To learn about the history and the subsidiaries of Ghadir Investment Company, see its website: https://ghadir-group.com/about-us (accessed 5 April 2023).

11  To find out more about its activities and affiliated companies, check the Mostazafan Foundation website: https://bonyadnews.ir/ (accessed 5 April 2023).

12  See also the Dey Bank website for information about its subsidiaries: http://www.bank-day.ir/ (accessed 5 April 2023).

13  This figure is also speculated about by some commentators and journalists; see for example Hosseini (2017).

14  In the next chapter, which deals with the form of the state, the institutional setup of the state and the link between various institutions and different fractions of capital will be examined at length.

15  During the first two development plans, the government aimed to attract Western capital and technology mainly for the energy sector by legislating some forms of foreign indirect investment in the framework of buyback and project financing contracts with relative success. In 1992, to attract direct investment from foreign companies, the High Council for Investments at the Finance Ministry lifted the 49 per cent ownership cap for foreign investors, which dated back to the 1955 Law of Attraction and Protection of Foreign Investment (*New York Times*, 1992). Faced with difficulties in attracting foreign investors to the mainland, the government turned to establishing special economic zones with their laws and regulations as envisaged in Article 19 of the First Development Plan. Initially, three coastal FTZs of Kish, Qeshm and Chahbahar were founded in September 1993. This was followed up by the creation of a further three FTZs of Aras, Anzali and Arvand under the auspices of the third development plan to invite FDI as well as domestic investment to boost non-oil manufacturing exports. Operating under the 'Law on the Administration of Free-Industrial Zones', the government offered full protection and guarantees to foreign investors, twenty years of tax exemption, and flexible labour laws for hiring and firing workers (Hakimian, 2011: 855–62). At odds with its intentions, the FTZs had become import rather than export platforms during the 1990s. The total FDI invested in the six FTZs was a mere $2.8 billion between 1993 and 2004 (Hakimian, 2011: 864). Despite the addition of another free trade-industrial zone (Maku), overall inward FDI in all these zones combined remained constant, amounting to a total of $2.6 billion from 2006 to 2015 (Chamber of Commerce, Industries, Mines and Agriculture, 2016: 23).

16  In 2001, the reformist-dominated Majles approved a new legal framework for the promotion of FDI but the Guardian Council vetoed it, arguing that it would 'pave the way for foreign domination of the economy'. The second and third attempts by the Majles met the same fate. Amid objections from the Guardian Council, the bill was sent to the Expediency Discernment Assembly and finally ratified in May 2002 (Dinmore, 2002). The Foreign Investment Promotion and Protection Act (FIPPA) eliminates the ownership restriction, guarantees full protections and rights for foreign investors equal to their Iranian counterparts, and ensures that investments 'shall not be subjected to expropriation or

nationalisation' (full text of the FIPPA here: https://www.fao.org/faolex/results/details/fr/c/LEX-FAOC202448/ (accessed 5 April 2023)). The law was complemented by an enormous reduction in corporate tax 'from a high of 68 per cent to a single rate of 25 per cent' in the tax reforms of 2002/3. As result, a German corporation, Henkel, bought 60 per cent stocks of an Iranian company for the first time in 2002 (*Financial Times*, 2002). However, optimism vanished quickly as the Seventh Majles blocked other successful bids by foreign investors in the following years. To build and operate facilities of the newly constructed Imam Khomeini Airport, a Turkish company, Tape-Akfen Vie (TAV), won the tender among sixteen foreign and fifteen domestic firms including the Ghorb in 2004. A day after its opening by Khatami, the IRGC closed the airport, declaring that it would not be opened until the Turkish company left the Imam Khomeini Airport. After being taken to the Majles for inspection, the contract was cancelled for security reasons and later given to the Ghorb and the NAJA Cooperative Foundation, the economic organisation of the police. Likewise, the agreement with the French Hutchinson Group for the development of Shahid Raja'i Port was revoked. Naming another Turkish firm, Turkcell, the winner of another tender to develop the second operator of a cellular phone network generated a new battle over FDI in September 2004. By signing a \$3 billion contract, the Turkish firm owned 70 per cent stocks of the consortium while another two local Iranian firms controlled the remaining shares. Similar to the previous case, the Majles contested the contract for 'security reservations' and in deliberate disregard of the FIPPA, its shares were reduced to 49 per cent. The following year, the Turkcell share was given to the South African MTN, an Iranian consortium affiliated with the Mostazafan Foundation granted a 51 per cent stake in the project (*Kayhan*, 2016). Whilst security concerns were used as a pretext to repel foreign investors, the then deputy of the Majles, Bahonar, expressed the real intention: 'the foreign management of the Imam Khomeini Airport is an insult to the scientific society and the Iranian nation' and stressed that 'we possess evidence that indicates Iranian companies have the ability to carry out such a project [the development of the cellular phone network]' (Jāme jam Online, 2004). This is lambasted by the proponents of FDI, affirming that the main group against FDI consists of those who 'benefit from the import and production of domestically produced junk products' (*Shargh*, 2010). After all, the Seventh Majles did not revise the new law on foreign direct investment, but it made parliamentary approval mandatory for future deals with foreign firms.

17  In Chapter 6, as well as uncovering the ways in which the process of neoliberalisation has reshaped the working class, urban poor, middle class and petty bourgeoisie, class struggles in contemporary Iran will be analysed.

# 5

# Neoliberalisation and the institutional and ideological reconstitution of the state

By focusing on the role of state policies in the formation of the internationally oriented capital fraction and the military–bonyad complex, the previous chapter touched upon the subject of the state form without providing a detailed account of the form of the state in neoliberal Iran. In this chapter, we explore the extent to which Iranian neoliberalisation and the post-1990 ruling class reconfiguration have rearranged the institutional setup of the state and transformed the state ideology. In other words, the chapter intends to substantiate whether the current form of the Iranian state significantly differs from the revolutionary state of the first decade of the revolution. The prevailing accounts of the post-revolutionary Iranian state either reject a major difference between the 1979–89 period and the post-1989 era or at least do not attribute changes in the state to neoliberalism. This is due to the adherence to the exceptionalist understanding of the 1979 revolution or the key political and economic characteristics of the rentier state theory. In both cases, the dismissal of the analysis of the neoliberalisation process induces the narrative of the unique theocratic form of the post-revolutionary state since 1979. This generates two key problems. First, by largely relying on domestically generated contingent factors such as religion, resource endowment, patronage networks, leadership styles and institutional arrangements to understand the state's form, questions of capital accumulation and class formation are downplayed. Second, because these analytical factors are considered to be the products of the sociopolitical national space, methodological nationalism and exceptionalising frameworks in the analysis of the state are reproduced.

In this chapter, we repudiate the omission of capitalism in the conceptualisation of the Iranian state by giving weight to the specificity of the nature of capital accumulation and its associated class formation. Coming from this angle, the chapter hence defines the Iranian state as a set of institutional forms that reflects social relations which have been generated through the process of capital accumulation and class formation within Iranian society. Yet, as articulated in Chapter 1, this cannot be done with reference to national capital accumulation and domestic class relations alone since this set of social relations has been constituted as a result of the relations between Iran and neoliberal global capitalism. In other words, to understand the institutional form of the Iranian state, we need to first examine the process of neoliberalisation and its impacts on the shifting balance between opposing social class forces, which was the subject of Chapter 4. Building on these findings, the current chapter argues that the Iranian state has undergone a conspicuous institutional reorganisation since the instigation of neoliberalism due to the reconfiguration of the class basis of the state. It thus shows the ways in which the internationally oriented capital fraction and the military–bonyad complex have utilised and modified state apparatuses and institutions in order to realise their interests since the end of the war with Iraq. Understanding it as a contradictory unity of a set of institutions that reflects the fragile and trembling balance of class power within the state between these capital fractions, the chapter contests the conceptualisation of the Iranian state as a government within a government.

With the aim of challenging the treatment of institutional and political relations autonomously from neoliberalism, the chapter is organised as follows. The first section problematises the existing theorisations of the Iranian state and provides a historical materialist framework for conceptualising the state. The second section surveys the effects of neoliberal restructuring on the state apparatuses and institutions by documenting the establishment of new structures and the transformation in the function of the previously existing bodies to reveal that this transformation in the institutional setup is the product of the struggles of the emerging fractions of the ruling class. The third section problematises the strict separation of formal institutions and civil society organisations and unpacks the relationship between Iranian neoliberalisation and the emergence of the post-1990s liberal/reformist interpretation of Islam and the rearticulation of the revolutionary discourse of Islam. The section thus shows how civil society organisations have been either created, attacked, or banned in line with the realisation of the interests of the internationally oriented capital fraction and the military–bonyad complex. After briefly reviewing the arguments of the chapter, the conclusion sets out the direction for the next chapter on class struggles in contemporary Iran in light of the arguments of Chapters 4 and 5.[1]

## Conceptualising the Iranian state

The Iranian theocratic state has for a long time been conceptualised as an 'exceptional' entity. Two sets of theorisations have hugely contributed to this understanding. Because the 1979 revolution is mostly interpreted as an 'exceptional' revolution that cannot be grasped through classical social theories of revolution,[2] its main upshot, the Islamic state, is thus also viewed as a peculiar and unique entity. In addition, the pervasive rentier state theory fuels the exceptionalising explanations of the post-revolutionary Iranian state in numerous ways. The common denominator of the accounts that explain the Iranian state through ideology, Islamic revolutionary elites, personalistic networks of patrons and clients and Islamic revolutionary institutions is the indispensable role that they award to oil revenues in the construction of these factors.

Those who highlight the role of ideas in the makeup of the state can be put into two categories. Some draw our attention to the importance of oil revenues that have aided the state to construct a popular ideology grounded on Shi'a political Islam with flavours of Iranian nationalism and anti-Western sentiments (e.g., Abrahamian, 1993; Ghamari-Tabrizi, 2008; Martin, 2003). Without reference to oil revenue, divergent strains of social constructivism and poststructuralism repeat a similar argument by articulating the Iranian state as a homogenous unit with a singular revolutionary identity that is contested based on several popular discourses (e.g., Moshirzadeh, 2007; Behravesh, 2011; Warnnar, 2013).

In contrast, many researchers challenge this unitary understanding of the state since they detect the multiplicity of power centres within the Iranian state as the key explanatory variable. Within this group of scholars, we can also identify two camps. The first group claims that the emphasis must be on personalistic networks of patrons and clients (e.g., Arjomand, 2009; Sadjadpour, 2008) or a combination of both informal patronage networks and formal institutions (Buchta, 2000; Yeganeh, 2015) for conceptualising the form of the post-revolutionary Iranian state. Again, for them, these personalistic networks and formal and informal institutions cannot be grasped without considering the politics around the allocation of oil revenues in post-revolutionary Iran. The second group that disputes the unitary understanding of the state points to the significance of the multiplicity of 'revolutionary elites' in the formation of the so-called Iranian semi-authoritarian/pseudo-democratic state. These scholars argue that tensions over the share of oil revenues between these elites have been resolved through 'semi-free' elections (Ehteshami, 2017; Morady, 2010; 2011; Boroujerdi and Rahimkhani, 2018). While some of these accounts have a narrower definition of revolutionary elites, others such as Rakel (2008; 2009) attempt to encompass elites who occupy strategic positions in powerful organisations as well as activists in civil society who discursively influence the process of decision-making and policy formation. By deploying the concept of 'politically relevant elites', Rakel thus places elites in 'three concentric centres' – namely, the inner circle which is occupied by political elites responsible for strategic decisions; the second circle which is constituted of administrative elites; and the third circle which includes discursive elites. For these accounts, the conservatives, the pragmatists and the reformists represent the elites in the ideological and political battles over domestic and foreign issues for influence and privileges.

These explanations, as a body of literature, suffer from some noteworthy shortcomings. First, they leave no room for the incorporation of outside interests in their theory of the state by failing to take into account the role and agency of social classes in the explanation of political domination. Since social classes are considered 'aggregates that are overly broad and/or they do not ultimately produce politically important effects' (Codato and Perissinotto, 2011: 7), they insinuate that the Iranian elites/officials act in something of a social void. The assumption that the state enjoys a pronounced degree of autonomy from society invites some criticism, such as that expressed by Harris (2017), who attempts to incorporate the role of social forces in shaping post-revolutionary Iran. Second, these accounts offer an internalist conception of the state whereby the role of intersocietal relations is generally neglected and everything is often reduced to the exceptionality of the nature of the post-revolutionary state, its institutions and its interpersonal networks. As we showed in previous chapters, neoliberal global capitalism has exercised a conclusive role in the constitution and reconfiguration of domestic classes and the state's policies; a significant sway that has consequently imposed itself on the institutional setup and the ideological composition of states around the world. In essence, these accounts are marred by methodological nationalism since the national space is privileged at the expense of global dynamics. Lastly, by putting too much emphasis on the interests of elites, ideology and paternalistic networks, these accounts are in danger of producing a voluntarist account of power, which is incapable of grasping the state as an institutional structure that largely restrains rather than encourages decision-makers from acting according to their whims. Due to this inability, we are left without knowing the place and function of the state apparatuses and institutions and their operators in the process of the reproduction of sociopolitical domination.

An alternative conception of the state should address the links between capital accumulation, class structure, institutions and political relations in a way that transcends methodological nationalism. In Marx's theory of the state, what is crucial is the relationship between political institutions, the power these institutions possess and the privileged position of a ruling class on the one hand, and 'the requirements of the particular social and economic system in which they are situated' on the other. Because in Marx's method 'the procedure moves from the whole inward', understanding the nature of the class society, in our case capitalist class society, is thus prioritised (Ollman, 2003: 201). Consequently, 'class formation – the ways in which classes coalesce around the production, realisation, and appropriation of profit – becomes a central element to understanding social formation and the nature of state power' (Hanieh, 2013: 6–8). As well as a dimension of capitalism, Marx also views the state 'as an aspect of the capitalist class, as something this class does' (Ollman, 2003: 202). Together, this means rather than a separate sphere of politics standing apart from the economic sphere, the state is internally related to the process of capital accumulation and capitalists' class interests. As a *relation*, the state is thus a historically determined social form resulting from contestations over social surplus products, therefore always representing, preserving and defending the class structure of the society (Hanieh, 2013: 8). Accordingly, not only are the actions of the state internally related to the nature of its capitalist class and the requirements of its interests, but so are the specific forms through which these actions occur. The state, in other words, 'is the greatest part of what it means for a ruling class to rule and is an essential feature of the class itself' (Ollman, 2003: 202).

Several points regarding this notion of the state need to be further explained. In the first place, an analysis of capital accumulation and related class formation, which are central to the theorisation of the state, must go beyond the boundaries of nation-states in the context of neoliberal global capitalism. Secondly, the capitalist class as the ruling class cannot be limited to the legal owner of the means of production because many top state bureaucrats and officials can be part of the capitalist class, as we explained theoretically in Chapter 1 and empirically demonstrated in the previous chapter in the case of Iran. Thirdly, by viewing the state apparatuses/institutions as means that provide the capacity for the ruling class to realise their interests, we unravel the objective links between these institutions and the class structure of the society (Codato and Perissinotto, 2011: 2). From this perspective, since the foundation of power is conceived as originating in class relations, these institutions and apparatuses do not thereby possess any power of their own, but rather they materialise and concentrate class relations. Nor can interpersonal relations be seen as the source of power without their links to class relations. This implies that the role of state apparatuses/institutions in the accumulation of capital, reproduction of social relations and representation of class interests heavily depends on the social classes which hold power (Poulantzas, 1978: 26–7; 1973: 115). Put differently, state institutions are political arenas for the exercise of class power by the ruling class in capitalism (Barrow, 2011: 33). Fourthly, although the state as a set of institutional forms is the guardian of the capitalist class structure, this does not imply that subaltern classes cannot take advantage of problems and contradictions of the state by using some part of it to achieve small and temporary wins or to occasionally hamper a capitalist initiative from succeeding (Ollman, 1993: 99–100). Finally, the state comprises two inseparable realms of the 'political society': the state's apparatuses and institutions (government, judiciary, and coercive apparatus); and the 'civil society' that consists of media, education, and non-governmental institutions and organisations (Gramsci, 1971: 263).[3]

## Class power and the institutional setup of the Iranian state

As should be clear by now, the state is a set of institutional forms, which is internally related to the process of capital accumulation as well as capitalists' class interests. Any restructuring of the economic sphere and the subsequent reconfiguration of the capitalist class are thus reflected in state institutions. In Chapter 4, we established that Iranian neoliberalisation as the product of the interaction of global and local dynamics has fundamentally reshuffled the composition of the ruling class, therefore generating two competing capital fractions. In the course of realising their interests, the internationally oriented capital fraction and the military–bonyad complex have been involved in the reorganisation of state institutions, as will be shown shortly. This implies that the post-1990 state form in Iran is reflective of the process of neoliberalisation and its associated class formation rather than the outcome of contingent factors such as patronage networks, resource endowment, leadership styles, etc. Since Iranian neoliberalisation is not an internally generated phenomenon, neither can the change in the form of the state be solely reduced to internal factors and local dynamics.

While the military–bonyad complex is in charge of mostly unelected institutions, the internationally oriented wing is left with the option of the struggle to grab the elected institutions. This conspicuous splitting up of the state's institutions between the two fractions is to some extent rooted in the structure of the state that developed during the first decade of the revolution through which the stratum of government managers controlled the government bureaucracy and most elected institutions, whereas the bonyad–bazaar nexus largely operated through appointed revolutionary institutions and foundations. Considering that the military–bonyad complex was the product of the gradual metamorphosis of the bonyad–bazaar nexus and the internationally oriented capital fraction was to a large degree spawned out of the stratum of government managers, the discernible continuity of this institutional division of power should come as no surprise. That said, the continuation of the preceding structure could explain the present situation up to a certain level since the institutional setup of the state has witnessed meaningful modifications because of the process of neoliberalisation and the reconfiguration of the ruling class.

The military–bonyad complex commands and dominates the most powerful state institution, the office of the supreme leader. Endowed with wide-ranging authority by the Constitution based on the idea of the guardianship of the jurist (*velāyat-e faqih*), the supreme leader delineates general policies of the state, supervises policy execution, declares war and peace, and commands the armed forces. This extensive power puts the supreme leader in a position to appoint and dismiss many key state officials, including the head of the judiciary, the commanders of the IRGC and the regular army (*artesh*), the chief of the law enforcement forces (*niru-ye entezāmi*), the heads of the revolutionary and religious foundations (*bonyād-hā-ye enqelābi va mazhabi*), the head of the Islamic Republic of Iran Broadcasting and the Islamic jurisprudents of the Guardian Council.[4] According to the Constitution, the supreme leader is an elected life tenure, meaning that he must be selected, evaluated and dismissed by another elected body, namely the Assembly of Experts. Because the members of the Assembly are screened before running for their seats by the members of the Guardian Council who are in turn directly and indirectly appointed by the supreme leader, the Assembly of Experts in reality never fulfils its constitutional duty of making the highest office accountable (Alamdari, 2009: 111). In other words, there are no real checks and balances to control the power of the supreme leader. Indeed, by being in charge of appointing the heads of almost all unelected institutions, the supreme leader is the embodiment of the interests of the military–bonyad complex. The Guardian Council executes the electoral preselection procedure which effectively serves to either secure the upper hand of the military–bonyad complex or limit the damage even in the absence of public support. The powerful Guardian Council consists of twelve members – six clergymen chosen by the supreme leader and six non-clerical jurists selected by the Majles at the recommendation of the head of the Judiciary, who is himself carefully chosen by the supreme leader. The Council has consistently been active in the process of the realisation of the interests of the military–bonyad complex through two major functions. The Guardian Council authorises the screening of the qualification of all candidates in presidential, parliamentary and assembly elections and acquires an exclusive power over detecting the compatibility of all the Majles' proposed legislation according to the criteria of Islam and the Constitution (Thaler et al., 2010: 29–30; Yeganeh, 2015: 78). In connection with Islam, the Council has regularly vetted reformist candidates on numerous occasions, most notably disqualifying 3,500 candidates for the Seventh Majles including 80 prominent reformist incumbent members of the Sixth Majles by virtue of 'the lack of practical commitment to Islam' (BBC News,

2004; Rasa, 2016). Concerning its second function, the Guardian Council has repeatedly blocked countless bills in favour of the internationally oriented capital fraction in an attempt to sabotage and disrupt the process of integration into the global economy and foreign capital inflow as documented in the previous chapter.

After the office of the supreme leader, the presidency (in charge of government) and the Majles are the most powerful offices of state. With pivotal roles in economic planning and foreign policy, the presidency and the Majles are subject to general elections every four years. The president oversees the executive and economic matters with the following responsibilities: selecting the government ministers and forming the cabinet, implementing the laws passed by the Majles and supervising foreign policy and international affairs (Yeganeh, 2015: 77). The Majles is responsible for introducing new laws and passing government-proposed legislation, reviewing international treaties and vetting ministerial nominees (Ehteshami, 2017: 27). Since the ultimate objective of the internationally oriented capital fraction is to control these offices, especially the presidency, it has prioritised winning popular votes and become the driving force behind the promotion of fair elections by opposing any form of meddling by the Guardian Council's candidate approval process. Despite difficulties, the internationally oriented capital fraction has managed to control the government (the executive body) for most of the period since 1989, except for the two-term presidency of Ahmadinejad and the recent presidency of Raisi. Winning the majority of Majles seats has persistently been thornier not just because of the vetting process but also because of the role of local, provincial and regional[5] factors in parliamentary elections. Once in power, this fraction has altered the function and character of many ministries and governmental organisations, such as the Ministry of Economic Affairs and Finance, the Central Bank, and the Management and Planning Organisation, by hailing the importance of the so-called non-political technocrats. It also facilitated the creation of new institutions, such as the Trade Promotion Organisation of Iran and the Iranian Privatisation Organisation and reopened the Tehran Stock Exchange. Unsurprisingly, during the Ahmadinejad presidency, the bureaucracy associated with the Hashemi-Rafsanjani and Khatami administrations came under relentless attack. In defiance of the rule of 'independent experts', Ahmadinejad brought the powerful Management and Planning Organisation under the control of the president's office (Harris, 2017: 193). More importantly, throughout the Ahmadinejad presidency, the operation and function of the revolutionary foundations and military forces have changed to ease the entry and expansion of their economic activities (see Figure 5.1).

Considering the unfeasibility of seizing the appointed institutions by the internationally oriented capital fraction and their fragile control over the

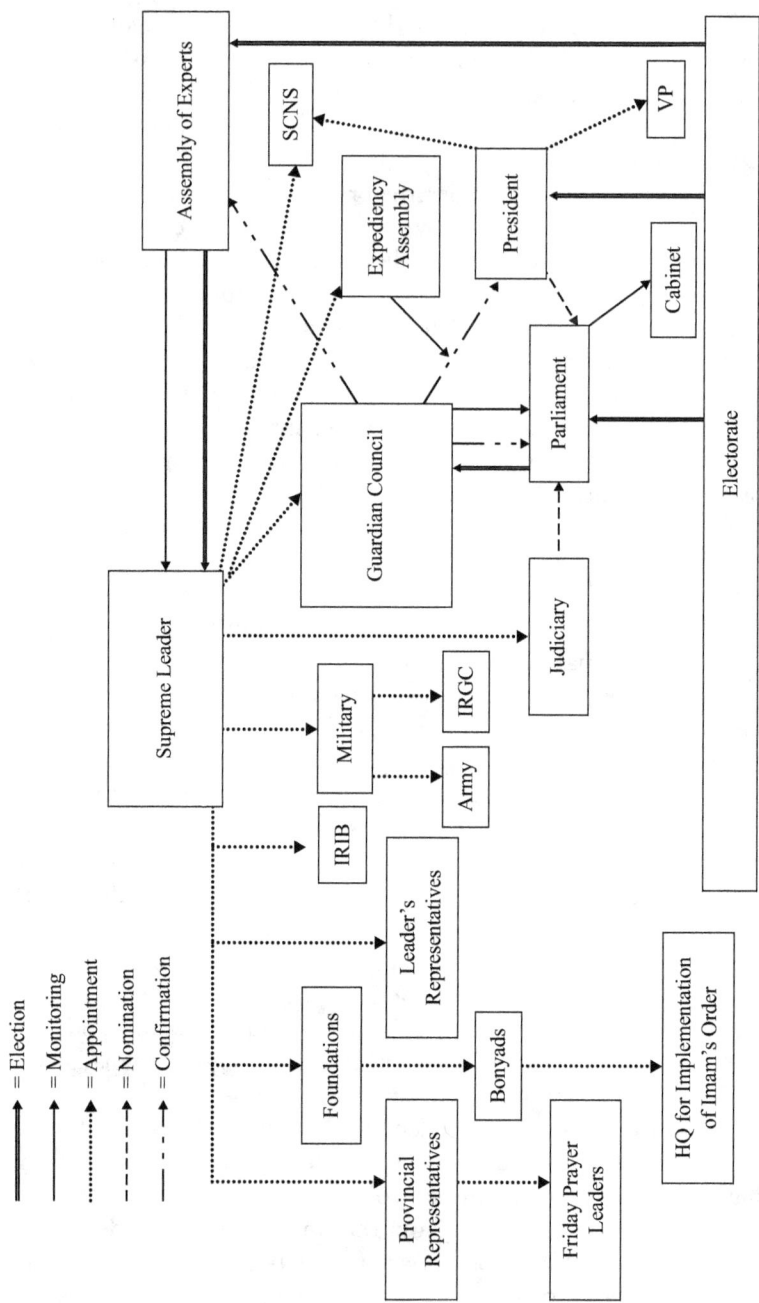

**Figure 5.1** Institutional setup of the state, reproduced with permission from Boroujerdi and Rahimkhani, *Post-Revolutionary Iran* (2018: 37)

elected institutions, it should be easy to comprehend why one of the major political disputes in recent decades has been over free elections, electoral fraud and the legality of the preselection process. This intense political struggle over the electoral system is a clear indication of the difference between the first decade of the revolution and the post-1989 era, illuminating how state institutions are subject to the fractions of the ruling class because of the reorganisation of capital accumulation and not vice versa. The central role of the Guardian Council in elections began to take real shape after the revision of the Constitution in 1989. While the revision of the Constitution reiterates the supervisory responsibility of the Guardian Council on elections (Papan-Matin, 2014: 182), the form of its supervision was still a matter of real contention. In response to a letter from the election commission regarding the issue in 1991, the Guardian Council interpreted that '[t]he supervision stated in article 99 is proactive [*nezārat-e estesvābi*, i.e. with the right to make legally binding interventions] and includes all executive stages of the election, including confirming or rejecting the qualifications of candidates' (Iran Data Portal, no date a). This institutional amendment has to be seen in relation to the short-term class alliance between the neoliberal wing of the stratum of government managers and the bonyad–bazaar nexus which aimed to marginalise the statist wing of the former immediately after the commencement of the First Development Plan in June 1990. Its first outcome was the disqualification of more than a third of the candidates of the parliamentary election of June 1992, including thirty 'Islamist leftist militant' incumbent members of the Majles (Moslem, 2002: 188–9). Likewise, the abolition of the office of prime minister in the new revision of the Constitution was part of the efforts for facilitating the restructuring of the economy to revive capital accumulation. The executive power during the first decade of the revolution was divided between the president and the prime minister, with the former largely possessing ceremonial power despite being elected directly by the electorate, while the latter had the actual administrative power to run the government without popular approval. Although the president recommended the prime minister for the post, the Majles was the real selector of the prime minister through the process of the vote of confidence, which for most of the 1980s was controlled by the stratum of government managers committed to capital accumulation through extensive state intervention in the economy. The collapse of the tactical alliance between the first post-Iran–Iraq-war government and the bonyad–bazaar nexus following the irreconcilability of some of the government neoliberal policies with the nexus interests[6] resulted in the creation of a new political bloc in the fifth parliamentary election of 1996 to represent the interests of the nascent capital fraction (Moslem, 2002: 227–32). However, with the gradual intensification of the struggles between the two fractions of capital over the process of neoliberalisation, the proactive supervision of the Guardian Council has widely been used to justify the disqualification of the political representatives of the internationally oriented capital fraction (BBC News, 2004; Rasa, 2016). The Guardian Council has also obstructed countless bills in favour of the internationally oriented capital fraction. This included blocking foreign capital inflow and the rejection of the privatisation of over 1,000 non-governmental public enterprises in control of the bonyads, which was proposed by the Khatami government (Khajehpour, 2000: 590, Namazi, 2000: 23). Given this, the scope of the authority of the Council has been at the centre of a long-lasting quarrel between the two fractions since the mid-1990s. To curb the power of the Guardian Council, the Ministry of the Interior proposed a bill in 1999 to abolish its 'unconstitutional' supervisory power over elections (Arjomand, 2000: 294–5; see also Kazemian, 1999; Khuzestani, 1999). After the endorsement of the supreme leader, the Majles reconfirmed the supervisory power of the Guardian Council which nullified any legal challenge for some time (*Khordād*, 1999). Yet the issue was at the centre of a political and judicial dispute a decade later (*Āftāb-e Yazd*, 2010; *Resālat*, 2009; *E'temād*, 2010; *E'temād-e Melli*, 2008). This time, the Expediency Discernment Assembly (of the State) (*majma'-e tashkhis-e maslahat-e nezām*) proposed a new bill to reform the electoral law that specified that the national election commission, not the Guardian Council, should be responsible for 'holding elections, reviewing the competence of candidates, controlling and supervising election campaigns and their costs, and scrutinizing electoral complaints'. Likewise, the supreme leader's intervention in defence of the Guardian Council dismissed the bill altogether (*Irān*, 2010). This was part of a broad struggle between the two wings of power since the 1990s regarding the meaning of the revolution, the notion of the Guardianship of the Islamic Jurist and the place of the elected and unelected state institutions among other things, which will be unpacked in depth in the next section (see Figure 5.1).

Two state institutions have been vital for mediating tensions between these fractions in order to preserve the integrity of the state, namely the Expediency Discernment Assembly (of the State) and the Supreme Council for National Security. Both were established after the 1989 revision of the Constitution and took real shape in the following decades with the intensification of intra-class struggles. Before his death, Khomeini (2008: 427) elaborated further on his doctrine about the Islamic State, arguing that the state could and should suspend 'any affair – devotional or else – whose occurrence is against the interests of Islam as long as it is so', i.e., the survival of the system at all costs. The rationale behind the new reading was the fear of the outbreak of an unruly intra-class struggle that would potentially threaten the integrity of the state. This seemed unnecessary during the first decade of the revolution due to the function of the bureau of the supreme leader and the charismatic leadership of Khomeini that ensured the universal hegemony of the ruling class despite his occasional predisposition towards the stratum of government managers. A year before his death, the Expediency Discernment Assembly was founded in February 1988 to institutionalise this function. But the 1989 revision constitutionally formalised it as an institution to resolve the legislative dispute between the Guardian Council and the Majles and support the new supreme leader in the dispensation of his duties. According to the Constitution, the supreme leader appointed the thirty-nine members of the Expediency Discernment Assembly, but the balance of power between the two fractions of the ruling class has been largely well-maintained. Equally important was the establishment of the Supreme Council for National Security in 1989 as part of the revision of the Constitution, which has been populated with representatives of both fractions. With the key mission of drafting strategic-level policies, the Supreme Council for National Security 'plays a crucial role in encouraging collective decision-making and also an unbiased examination of issues of concern to the country' (Ehteshami, 2017: 27).

My explanation would cast serious doubt on the prevalent conceptualisation of the Iranian state as a government within a government, one being the official government under the control of the president and the other being the 'deep' state run by the supreme leader. Whereas if we view the state as a site for the realisation of the interests of the military–bonyad complex and the internationalist fraction, it is possible to comprehend the incoherent and chaotic appearance of state policies since they are embedded in antagonistic class relations and are products of the process of intra-state contradictions. As we established above that civil society should not be viewed as a completely separate domain from the state, we now investigate the involvement of the internationally oriented capital fraction and the military–bonyad complex in the creation, onslaught, or ban of civil society organisations beyond their struggle over formal institutions.

## Class power, civil society organisations and rearticulation of the state ideology

Since the early 1990s, the internationally oriented capital fraction has approved and financed the creation of 'non-state' press, political parties and civil society organisations to advocate the 'democratic/liberal' interpretation of Islam and the compatibility of Islam with liberalism. This interpretation is essential for the realisation of the interests of the internationally oriented capital fraction because it allows them to argue for the affinity

and congruity between the Islamic Republic and the 'international community', i.e., the (Western-centred) world order. On the other hand, the
military–bonyad complex has considered the development of civil society
and the expansion of the press as Western (US) tools for threatening 'Islamic
revolutionary values'. By advocating a nativist, conservative interpretation
of Islam with an emphasis on the importance of independence and cultural
purity in line with its structure and accumulation strategy, the military–
bonyad complex has routinely employed force to shut down civil society
organisations and newspapers, thanks to its monopoly over the coercive
apparatuses of the state. Before examining civil society organisations and
their links to the struggle of these two ruling class fractions, we must look at
the emergence and rearticulation of the democratic/liberal and revolutionary discourses of Islam in relation to Iranian neoliberalisation. For this, the
notion of the material structure of ideology could be instrumental not only
because it helps to foster links between key class agents with the genesis
of dominant ideas, but also because it underlines connections between the
contemporary structure of capitalism and the emergence of new discourses
in Iran.

### Material structure of ideology

The material structure of ideology is an important concept to avoid falling
into the trap of 'crude economism' or 'vulgar reductionism' that considers
ideas as nothing but the reflection of material structure. At the same time,
the concept challenges the position that 'treats ideas as a factor completely
independent from material reality' (Bieler, 2001: 99). From the historical
materialist perspective, Gramsci (1995: 395) notes that 'ideologies are anything but arbitrary; they are real historical facts which must be combated
and their nature as instruments of domination exposed ... precisely for reasons of political struggle'. In other words, ideas and ideologies are the products of ceaseless class struggle throughout the course of history. This does
not suggest that ideas do not have lives of their own but indicates that those
ideas are only realised if they find their justification in the economic reality
at a particular point in time. The relevance and effectiveness of ideas inherently, therefore, depend on their connection to 'a particular constellation of
social forces' in specific periods of history. Put differently, the materialisation of particular ideas in the form of discourses/narratives or ideologies
by various class fractions to a large degree marginalises (not completely
eliminates) other sets of ideas. As Stuart Hall (1986: 44) contends, 'in that
sense, ideological struggle is a part of the general social struggle for mastery and leadership – in short for hegemony'. That is to say, dominant and
relevant ideas have a 'material organisation intended to maintain, defend

and develop the theoretical or ideological "front"' (Gramsci, 1995: 155). A material structure consisting of publishing houses, political newspapers, magazines, periodicals, news agencies and so forth is essential for the dissemination of relevant ideas. Furthermore, by emphasising the dialectical unity of state-civil society, Gramsci argues that the hegemony of class relations is exercised through 'capillary networks' of various organisations of the civil society that give the illusion that individuals govern themselves. In reality, however, this self-governing space is nothing but the normal continuation and organic complement of the political society through which 'organic intellectuals' produce new ideas and articulate strategies of class power beyond the coercive apparatuses of the state. Overall, the concept of the material structure of ideology crucially elucidates why and by whom certain discourses are articulated and how they appear in society. By linking to social relations and class struggle, it is possible to argue that 'discourse does not simply act upon people; people act through discourse, so the world cannot be reduced to discourse alone' (Bieler and Morton, 2018: 72–3; 2008). Building upon this concept, in the next section, we survey the formation of the new discourse of 'democratic Islam' and the rearticulation of the radical interpretation of Islam under the name of 'revolutionary Islam' since the early 1990s by connecting them to the process of Iranian neoliberalisation and the emergence of the internationally oriented capital fraction and the military–bonyad complex.

## Construction of discourses: Which Islam and for whom?

The 'democratic' rendition of Islam is in favour of the diversity of religious truth and calls into question the 'single understanding of Islam, or *fiqh*, the *velayate-e faqih* [the guardianship of the jurist], the Revolution, or the Imam's Path' (Khatami, 2000 cited in Kamrava, 2008: 153). Against this backdrop, it rejects an authoritarian reading of Khomeini's doctrine, the guardianship of the jurist, by advocating that people are the mediator between God and the Islamic ruler in which the consent of subjects is the source of state authority and legitimacy.[7] The former reformist president concisely articulates this point: 'The legitimacy of power relies entirely on the vote of the people [who] have the right to replace this power with another power without recourse to violence' (Khatami, 2006 cited in Harrop, 2009: 116). In contrast to the first decade of the revolution where neither the Islamic nor the republican aspect of the new state was seriously questioned, this post-1990s' democratic interpretation of Islam has accentuated the 'republicanism' of the Islamic Republic (Soltani, 2005: 165). By returning to the meaning of the revolution (see for example *Ettelā'āt*, 1997; 1998a; 1998b; Razavi-Faqih, 2002; *Mosharekat*, 2001), the proponents of this discourse claim that the democratic promises of the revolution have not been fulfilled; the defining aspects that would be achieved only by implementing the neglected sections of the Constitution, respecting civil rights, complying with the rule of law and transpiring economic activities (Ansari, 2014: 318).

This liberal reading of Islam initially appeared in the circle of a few 'religious intellectuals', most notably Abdolkarim Soroush, Mohammad Mojtahed Shabestari and Mohsen Kadivar, in the late 1980s and the early 1990s. Soroush distinguishes between religion *per se* from religious knowledge to argue that, while the essence of religion is divine and hence out of human reach, the latter 'is a sincere and authentic but finite, limited, and fallible form of human knowledge' (Sadri, 2001: 259). By its very nature, his philosophy opens a space for a pluralist rather than a particular interpretation of Islam as the ultimate model, which questioned the office of the clergy (rouhaniat) and the concept of the *velayat-e faqih* for the first time since the consolidation of power by the Khomeinist groups after the revolution.[8] Likewise, by calling for the use of extra-religious sources due to 'the essentially *limited* nature of religious knowledge', Shabestari disputed religious tyranny embedded in the official orthodoxy of the Islamic Republic and contested that a deep understanding of Islam is compatible with democracy and human rights (Sadri, 2001: 261–2). Unlike Soroush and Shabestari, who have been influenced by non-Islamic critical rationalism and hermeneutics, Kadivar's critique of the authoritarian interpretation of Islam is solely articulated within a jurisprudential framework. Kadivar tracks the idea of *faqih* in the history of political thought in Islam to attest that the concept has never been at the centre of Islamic thinking and practice. More importantly, he argues that the idea of the absolute mandate of the jurist (*velāyat-e motlaqeh-e faqih*) has no Islamic scientific basis or rational justification (Kamrava, 2003: 107–8; see also Sadri, 2001: 262–6).[9] In a nutshell, these intellectuals along with a few like-minded thinkers reach a similar conclusion that Islam and popular sovereignty are not essentially in conflict (Ghobadzadeh and Rahim, 2012: 334–51). This statement by Kamrava (2008: 135) concisely summarises their argument on the intimate compatibility of Islam and democracy: 'Islam has not mandated any specific forms of government except those that attend to the material and spiritual needs of the people. The ideal form of government, therefore, is changeable according to the needs and circumstances of the times, which, in the contemporary era, happens to be democracies.' In other words, while stressing the importance of religious ethics in the society, these intellectuals in essence call for the secularisation of the Iranian state.[10]

This post-1990s' reformist interpretation of Islam was not a new and novel intellectual trajectory as its origins could be traced back to the nineteenth century in the work of al-Afghani who supported a rational-ist approach to Islam against the religious authority of ulama (Sukidi, 2005: 401–12). As a source of inspiration for the whole Islamic world, other reformers and intellectuals such as Abduh and Iqbal in the early twentieth century continued al-Afghani's endeavour (Fischer, 2003: xxvii–xxviii). In Iran, the formulation of a modernist account of Islam gathered momen-tum during the 1906–11 Constitutional Revolution when religious lead-ers such as Ayatollah Naini and Ayatollah Khorasani interpreted Islam in favour of a democratic government, elections and parliaments (Kamrava, 2008: 120). Throughout the modernisation reign of Reza Shah, the likes of Shariat Sangilaji and Ali Akbar Hakamizadeh kept alive the flames of this religious reformist tendency with a relatively limited influence on the sociopolitical sphere. In response to the disappointment of the oil nation-alisation movement, some activist-intellectuals called 'religious-nationalist thinkers' put forward the amalgamation of religious ideas with national-ism. In 1961, to realise a formation or reconfiguration of the democratic reading of Islam, this new religious intellectual tradition established the Liberation Movement of Iran (*nehzat-e āzādi-ye irān*) as a political organi-sation. Ayatollah Taliqani (inspired by the work of Ayatollah Naini) and Mehdi Bazargan as the leading figures of the movement argued that Islam is compatible with modernity and inherently democratic since people, not any particular individual or group, are responsible for executing the divine law. Bazargan was appointed as the prime minister of the interim govern-ment after the revolution, but his administration fell apart a few months later due to the onslaught from the radical Islamist forces who labelled his reading of Islam as 'American' (Jahanbakhsh, 2001: 65–112). Hence, in a radically new predicament in the aftermath of the 1979 revolution, the lib-eral democratic version of Islam was marginalised in the battle of ideas with Khomeini's revolutionary reading of religion, and its political organisation was subsequently dismantled. In direct contrast, the revived form of the democratic/liberal reading of Islam has transcended the halls of academia and religious seminars as it has found countless networks, including popular journals, newspapers and publishing houses, since the early 1990s, which has opened up the political scene to debate about freedom, civil rights and the relationship between religion and politics.

The radical revolutionary interpretation of Islam was the dominant discourse in the first decade of the revolution. The discourse claims that Islam offers 'a complete social, political, economic, and moral system' that has answers to all human problems. With the monopolisation of truth at its heart, this discourse is 'exclusionary, monovocal and intolerant to plu-ralism, representing an absolutist and totalitarian ideology that placed a disproportionate emphasis on people's obligations, enforced by draconian social and moral surveillance' (Bayat, 2013: 38). In post-1990 Iran, this understanding of Islam aims to sustain the prevailing political/institutional arrangements of the first decade of the revolution for which the concept of the guardianship of the jurist is central. Similar to the democratic discourse, 'revolutionary Islam' stresses that sovereignty belongs to God, which refers to 'divine sovereignty' in the Islamic sacred texts. However, in contrast to the democratic reading of Islam, it interprets that the Islamic rulers mediate between people and God and, in this context, the political and social leadership, as well as the guidance of individuals, are not determined by the demands, viewpoints, or votes of the people. It thus implies that Islamic rulers possess the divine right to govern Islamic societies since God directly legitimises their appointment. In other words, rather than social contracts or cultural norms, the only source of legitimacy is God, who selects the executors of the law. This right was given to the Prophet Mohammad, then passed to the Imams, and currently, in the absence of the Twelfth Imam, the legitimate holders of power are *vali-ye faqihs*. Moreover, this reading of the religious authority differentiates between legitimacy (*mashrui'yat*) and acceptability (*maqbuliyat*), arguing that the former comes from God while the latter is from the people. Legitimacy and acceptability do not have any relationship with each other because a rightful leader might not have the people's support. Contrary to the democratic discourse of Islam, which either challenges the notion or is in favour of the limited power of the *vali-ye faqih*, the proponents of the radical revolutionary interpretation of Islam declare that the guidance of the jurist is always unconditional due to the inferiority of the consent of the populace (Kamrava, 2008: 101–5).[11] By downgrading the importance of the popularity of the *vali-ye faqih*, the revolutionary discourse accentuates that the electorate can only elect the members of the Assembly of Experts, who select the leader of the revolution.[12] Along with adherence to the orthodox interpretation of the *velāyat-e faqih*, the revolutionary Islamic discourse castigates the redefinition of the Islamic Revolution by the democratic discourse of Islam as a historical distortion. It deploys Khomeini's idea of 'pure Islam' against 'American Islam' to accentuate the centrality of social justice, fight against deprivation and safeguarding of the downtrodden in revolutionary Iran (Darvish-Tavangar, 1997; Mortazavi, 1996). Additionally, the discourse defines true freedom as 'the freedom of human spirit from corruption, lust, temptations, whims, and material bondage' against the 'Western individualistic' notion of freedom. At the societal level, with reference to the main slogan of the revolution (independence, freedom and the Islamic Republic), it emphasises that 'freedom should be defined in terms of national independence' and against 'global arrogance' (Khamenei, 2006 cited in Hovsepian-Bearce, 2015: 327).

My argument here is that merely resorting to holy scriptures or focusing on the role of intellectuals and thinkers does not take us very far in explaining the relevance of these particular interpretations of Islam in Iran since the early 1990s. In contrast, based on the notion of the material structure of ideology, we should pay attention to the socioeconomic conditions generated because of the process of neoliberalisation that have allowed the fractions of the ruling class to render particular interpretations of the sacred texts in their fight for hegemony. In the words of Bayat (2007: 12–13), 'power does not simply lie in words, in the "inner truth" expressed in words, but primarily in those who utter them, those who give truth/power to these words. Discourse is not power, unless it is given material force.' This obviously does not mean that the internationally oriented capital fraction and the military–bonyad complex have constructed the pluralist/democratic and Islamic revolutionary discourses respectively. This simply echoes the Marxist orthodox reductionism according to which the economic base simply generates superstructures. Quite contrary to this proposition, what I am arguing here is that the set of ideas associated with these discourses has had a long history, dating back to the late nineteenth and early twentieth centuries in the case of the former and the 1950s and 1960s in the case of the latter. The reason why the contemporary liberal interpretation of Islam is far more consequential and politically relevant than the antecedent varieties is the emergence of the internationally oriented capital fraction which has rearticulated it and provided the material bases for its realisation. Regarding the revolutionary interpretation of Islam, while the victory of the 1979 revolution made it ubiquitous in the first decade of the revolution, the rise of the military–bonyad complex has been the fundamental determinant in its rejuvenation. Considering the structure and accumulation strategy of each fraction, it should be rather clear why the former is in favour of a liberal, open rendition of Islam while the latter constructs a nativist, conservative interpretation with an emphasis on the importance of independence and cultural purity. In the next section, we show how these discourses have materialised since 1990 through the internationally oriented capital fraction and the military–bonyad complex. At the same time, this investigation links us to the previous claim concerning the battle over the control of civil society organisations as an extension of the state.

## The battle over civil society organisations

Equipped with the democratic/liberal interpretation of Islam and in line with the interests of the internationally oriented capital fraction, the Hashemi-Rafsanjani and Khatami administrations, especially the latter, facilitated the creation of reformist political parties, NGOs and 'non-state' press. Initially, *Kayhan-e Farhangi* provided a space for reformist religious intellectuals, including figures such as Abdolkarim Soroush, who articulated his ideas in article series between 1988 and 1990. Due to the resignation of the editorial board of the journal under pressure, this religious intellectual circle continued their work in the bi-monthly journal *Kian* during the 1990s (Clawson and Rubin, 2005: 128). However, an upsurge in the number of publications due to the liberalisation of the press by the centre-right government of Hashemi-Rafsanjani in the early 1990s precipitated the popularity of the liberal discourse of Islam (Tarock, 2001: 588). Relatedly, the establishment of the Centre for Strategic Research (*markaz-e tahqiqāt-e estrātezhik-e riāsat jomhuri*) under the office of the president was instrumental in the realisation of the reformist version of Islam, which produced policy-oriented analyses inspired by modern social theories (Mohebi, 2014: 71–4). As well as providing space and funding for the dissemination of these ideas, the formation of a new centrist political party in November 1995 – under the name of the Servants of Reconstruction (*kargozārān-e sāzandegi*) with a tight bond to the Hashemi-Rafsanjani government – materialised the real ascendancy of this new narrative. The founding members of the party included a group of sixteen influential state officials, comprising ten ministers, four vice presidents, the head of the Central Bank and the mayor of Tehran. The latter, Karbaschi, was the editor of a then widely read newspaper called *Hamshahri*, which had a circulation of more than a million (Ashraf and Banuazizi, 2001: 251). As a formal political entity, the Servants of Reconstruction appeared in the political arena two months before the fifth parliamentary election in January 1995 to challenge 'the monopoly of power in the hands of a particular group', defend the freedom of thoughts and press, promote free-market ideas and deradicalise/normalise foreign policy (Kulaai and Mazarei, 2016: 416–18).

With the heavy support of the Servants of Reconstruction party and other concurring political groups, Khatami's campaign platform for the presidential election of 1997 demonstrated the total application of the thoughts of the new reformist religious thinkers (*Iran*, 16 March 1997). Moreover, the principles and general policies of the other reformist parties including the newly formed Islamic Iran Participation Front (*jebheh-e moshārekat-e irān-e eslāmi*) and the revived Crusaders of the Islamic Revolution (*mojahedin-e enqlāb-e eslāmi*) revealed the potency of the liberal reading of Islam during this period. The emerging reformist political forces presented the sweeping victory of Khatami in 1997, with more than 70 per cent of popular votes cast,[13] as the repudiation of the non-democratic rendition of Islam. The official weekly magazine of the Crusaders of the Islamic Revolution eloquently expressed this argument:

The people voted for an Islam that not only does not see a contradiction between religion and freedom, democracy, human rights, and civil society, but believes that these [modern] concepts can find their true meaning in Islam. An Islam that recognises the rights of the citizens and discerns the legitimacy of the regime to be based on their consent ... construes the vali-ye faqih to be an elected and lawful leader. One who is the symbol of the country's unity and leads the revolution based on the wishes of people and within the confines of the constitution ... May 23 was a vote for such as a reading of Islam.

*Asr-e Ma*, 16 July 1997, cited in Moslem, 2002: 253

Apart from emphasising the rule of law, protection of civil liberties and moderate foreign policy, the Khatami administration made the building of a 'vibrant civil society' the centrepiece of its political agenda with two main objectives (*Hamshahri*, 1997; 1998). Given the control over the powerful state institutions, including the public broadcasting in the hands of the supreme leader with links to the military forces and revolutionary foundations, the promotion of civil society served as a way to challenge their power. In addition, this promotion of civil society served as an essential instrument for the dissemination of the liberal interpretation of Islam and a source of influence among the electorate. After consolidating their grip on power following two further landslide victories in the municipal elections of 1999 and particularly the Sixth Majles election of February 2000, the reformist government of Khatami fostered the conditions for the rapid growth of political groups and NGOs. While witnessing a gradual increase since the early 1990s, the number of political parties and organisations reached ninety-five in 2000 (Bayat, 2013: 60). There were 1,437 scientific, cultural, artistic and professional organisations in the universities in 2001, which published around 700 student newspapers (Bayat, 2013: 43). At the same time, the number of NGOs relating to women's issues reached 450 in 2004 (only 55 in 1997) thanks to financial support from the government (Mohebi, 2014: 117). More importantly, with the backing of the government through the Ministry of Culture, which issued, for example, more than 799 new presses in the first year of Khatami's presidency alone (Tarock, 2001: 590), the number of newspapers, magazines and literary journals proliferated astronomically, surpassing 1,000 publications in 2000 (Kamrava, 2001: 171; Mohebi, 2014: 89). In particular, as a vital means for the internationally oriented capital fraction, the number of daily newspapers climbed to 34 in 1993, 62 in 1996, and 112 by the end of the 1990s while there had existed only seven newspapers in the 1980s (Mohebi, 2014: 89).

On the other hand, the military–bonyad complex has used two strategies, namely the dissemination of the revolutionary discourse of Islam through official and informal organisations and institutions and the attack on civil society organisations by using the judiciary and violent pressure groups. Apart from controlling national broadcasting with numerous TV channels and radio stations, it has propagated the revolutionary reading of Islam through the supreme leader-appointed Friday prayer imams and several mass-circulation newspapers such as *Kayhan, Resālat, Jām-e Jam*, and *Jomhuri-ye Eslāmi*, among others. Other important tools for the diffusion of this revolutionary discourse have been the *Basij*, which has branches almost everywhere around the country, and traditional community-based organisations such as informal charities that aim to provide services to vulnerable groups (Mohebi, 2014: 127–46).

For the military–bonyad complex, the prevention of the realisation of the rival discourse has probably been more important than the construction of common consent, mostly due to its monopoly over the coercive apparatuses of the state. It has therefore regularly targeted intellectuals, journalists and activists on the grounds that liberal intellectuals are the agents of cultural infiltration of the enemies (the United States and the West in general) who pose an undeniable menace to Islamic values (Taiar, 1996a; 1996b), and that the development of civil society and the expansion of the free press are mechanisms through which this Western cultural assault is materialised (Mohebian, 1998). The supreme leader has unequivocally articulated these arguments:

> If freedom of the press is grounded in driving people to lose religious faith, journalists and newspapers are not free to do so. Such freedom is treachery. If their intent is to conspire [against the system] and spread dissent [throughout the nation], this freedom is a conspiracy [against the state]. This freedom is repulsive.
>
> Khamenei, 2006 cited in Hovsepian-Bearce, 2015: 196

Hence, in viewing the flourishing of the press during the 1990s, especially after Khatami's victory which was welcomed as a step in the right direction by the West, as a real threat, General Safavi, the then commander of the IRGC, remarked that his forces would 'cut the throats and tongues' of liberal journalists (Arjomand, 2000: 289). This was followed by the supreme leader's fiery September 1998 speech declaring that 'I am not going to wait to see what the world is saying or what the global newspapers or global organisations are saying. I am not going to allow international organisations to run this country. I am waiting for the Cultural Council, judiciary and security forces to do their job. Look and see how the press has targeted and attacked the faith of the people. They insult the revolution' (Khamenei, 1998, cited in Hovsepian-Bearce, 2015: 196). The Fifth Majles made the first severe move to curb the influence of the press following the narrow passing of the new press law in July 1999. After being labelled as 'the bases of the enemies' by the supreme leader, the judiciary and the security forces banned forty reformist newspapers and jailed a dozen journalists in April 2000 (Tarock, 2001: 586). The supreme leader also used an obligatory religious decree to block the attempt of the reformist-dominated Sixth Majles to reform the press law as its first agenda in August 2000 (Ghasemi, 2016: 271). In addition to utilising these formal institutions, the military–bonyad complex used the paramilitary *Basij* forces and especially the Ansar-e Hezbollah to violently disrupt rallies and events, beat up individuals and assassinate intellectuals and reformist activists.[14]

## Conclusion

The central argument of this chapter is that the Iranian state should be conceptualised in relation to Iranian neoliberalisation, which is part of the broader process of global neoliberal capitalism. By defining the state as a set of institutional forms reflective of social relations generated as a result of the processes of capital accumulation, it thus argued that the state cannot be understood only with reference to national space. In Chapter 4, after placing the process of capital accumulation in Iran within the broader space of global neoliberal restructuring, we showed how the interaction of both global and local dynamics and external and internal factors has produced hybrid neoliberalism in Iran. We then exhibited that this process has in turn reconfigured the class basis of the state since the early 1990s, leading to the emergence of the internationally oriented capital fraction and the military–bonyad complex with rival accumulation strategies. Building on these findings, in this chapter we subsequently substantiated that the struggles between the internationally oriented capital fraction and the military–bonyad complex have resulted in the reorganisation of state institutions (including some civil society organisations) and the reconstruction of political Islam as the state ideology with the two competing discourses of democratic/liberal Islam and revolutionary Islam. With regard to these discourses of Islam, the claim was not to dismiss the existence of these interpretations before the current era but to attest that these ideas have been realised as they have found their justifications in the socioeconomic reality of contemporary Iran.

In his critique of approaches that are built upon the philosophy of *external* relations, Ollman (2015: 10) contends that 'changes and relations are the basic building materials of the "bigger picture" in every sphere of reality, and reducing them to the role of bit players in a drama whose overall plot is of little concern results in the kind of partial, static and one-sided thinking characteristic of most of bourgeois ideology'. The theorisation of the Iranian state as a relation which was constituted through its relations with global social relations and its interactions with the wider world refutes this one-sided thinking and removes the exceptionalist mantle in the analysis of the state. Grasping the reorganisation of the form of the state by linking it to the process of neoliberalisation is thus radically different and conceptually superior to the rentier state, elite-based and neo-patrimonial analyses of the Iranian state for two reasons. First, it departs from viewing societies/states as self-contained and autonomous objects that affect each other like the way billiard balls bump into one another on a pool table. Second, it challenges the conceptualisation of changes in the form of the Iranian state as a merely elite-driven neo-patrimonial reshuffling of patronage networks as it connects these changes to the imperative of capital accumulation. Having explored the impacts of the process of neoliberalisation on the ruling class and the state, in the next chapter we will turn to the effects of the process on the non-ruling classes, especially the working class and the poor, and their struggle against neoliberalism.

## Notes

1 Parts of a previously published article appear throughout this chapter: 'Neoliberalism and state formation in Iran' by Kayhan Valadbaygi © 2022 The Author, taken from *Globalizations* 2022, First Online, © Informa UK Limited, trading as Taylor & Francis Group 2022, reprinted by permission of Taylor & Francis Ltd, https://doi.org/10.1080/14747731.2021.2024391.

2 Kamran Matin's *Recasting Iranian modernity* (2013a) persuasively reveals and challenges the exceptionalist conceptualisations of the 1979 Iranian revolution.

3 The latter constituent of the definition of the state puts me at odds with another group of scholars who still firmly uphold the dichotomisation of the state and the civil society in their studies of contemporary Iranian society and state (e.g., Jahanbegloo, 2011a; Boroumand and Boroumand, 2000; Adib-Moghaddam, 2006).

4 You can find out about the full roles and responsibilities of the supreme leader in the constitution here: https://www.leader.ir/en/content/14132/Leadership-in-the-Constitution-of-the-Islamic-Republic-of-Iran (accessed 5 April 2023).

5 The term regional here refers to the different regions inside Iran.

6 For a detailed account of this short-lived alliance and struggle surrounding Hashemi-Rafsanjani's first government see Chapter 4.

7 See, for example, Mohammad Khatami's speech at the ceremony of the Office for Strengthening Unity (*daftar-e tahkim-e vahdat*) published in *Salām* (February 1997).

8 Soroush, Sadri and Sadri (2000) and Vakili (1997) provide an essential understanding of Soroush's pluralist interpretation of Islam.

9 Mohsen Kadivar's works, including *Anxieties of Religious Government* (2000) and *Theories of Government in the Shiite Jurisprudence* (1999), are available online: https://kadivar.com/ (accessed 5 April 2023).

10 As Bayat (2013: 54) notes, secularisation is different from secularism at least in the minds of these intellectuals because secularisation refers to the institutional separation of religion and state while secularism implies the diminishment of the significance of religion in society.

11 Kamrava (2008: 85, 105) notes that this 'absolute mandate of the jurist' was enshrined in the 1989 revision of the Constitution because Khomeini initially did not use 'absolute' to describe the scope of the power of the jurist in his seminal work on the concept.

12 As explained earlier, candidates for the Assembly are first screened and approved by the supreme leader's appointed members of the Guardian Council which illuminates the absurdity of the popular indirect election of the vali-e faqih (Amuzegar, 2012: 28).

13 The victory is often referred to as the 2 Khordad Epic (*hamāseh-e dvvm-e khordād*) because the presidential election was held on the second day of the third month (*khordād*) of 1376 in the Iranian calendar, which is equivalent to 23 May 1997.

14 A good example is the assassination of the leading reformist strategist, Saeed Hajjarian, who survived the attack by the Ansar-e Hezbollah outside Tehran's city council in March 2000. Before that, the brutal killing and disappearance of six intellectuals and political activists, which is labelled as the chain murders of Iran, shocked the country and was reminiscent of the violence of the early days of the revolution (see Burns, 2000; Fowler, 2018).

# 6

# Class struggles in neoliberal Iran: From workers' resistance in the 1990s to the post-2017 uprisings

In the previous two chapters, we explored the reconfiguration of the Iranian ruling class and the reorganisation of the Iranian state since the early 1990s. In this chapter, we aim to examine the ways in which neoliberal reforms have reconstituted and transformed the working class and the poor. More importantly, we are eager to find out how the process of neoliberalisation has reshaped the relationship between the ruling class and the subaltern classes and how workers and the poor have reacted to the implementation of neoliberalism from above. The chapter documents that the commodification of every aspect of life and deregulation of the labour market, in particular the expansion of temporary short-term contracts to an unimaginable level, have constituted the precariat as the largest group of the Iranian working class. It also registers the emergence of the new poor as the growing section of the Iranian poor under neoliberalism by identifying unemployed young people, in the age group 15–29 years with a university degree and little prospect for a better life, as the new poor. Despite state repression, the chapter shows that workers and the poor have constantly fought against these neo-liberal reforms that have endeavoured to reconstitute class power in favour of the ruling class and transfer wealth from the poorer to the richer layers of society. While various sections of workers have deployed different means, such as the state-sanctioned labour organisations and the newly established independent unions and networks, to organise labour protests and strikes throughout this period, the poor have angrily revolted against the rising cost of living and the removal of subsidies in the form of impromptu nationwide protests and riots, initially between 1992 and 1995 and later between 2017 and 2019. Workers and the new poor have been equally involved in the Women, Life, Freedom revolt since September 2022.

These arguments unfold as follows. After explaining the impacts of the process of neoliberalisation on the composition of the working class and the poor, the second section sheds light on some major episodes of political turmoil and social upheavals in contemporary Iran. Here we first navigate the struggles of workers during all the post-1989 administrations, displaying that labour protests and strikes have drastically increased since 2015. We then document the apathy of workers and the poor towards the 2009–11 Green Movement by characterising it as the alliance-compromise of the internationally oriented capital fraction and the middle class without mass support against the supremacy of the military–bonyad complex. In the third part of the second section, we zoom in on the spontaneous revolts and rebellions of the poor since the introduction of neoliberal reforms, with a particular focus on the violent protests between 2017 and 2019, known as the Dey and Aban protests. We conclude the second section by examining the latest round of nationwide uprising known as the Women, Life, Freedom revolt. In light of the recent drastic surge in the amount of labour unrest and popular uprisings, the third section explores the possibility of the formation of the Iranian working class, i.e., the conversion from the class as an *economic category* to the class as a *political subject*, and the creation of a broad-based subaltern coalition under its leadership.

## Remaking the working class and the poor: Neoliberal labour market deregulation and the dismantling of the welfare system

As we explained in Chapter 4, the Islamic revolutionary state demolished the independent workers' councils during the violent political struggles for power in the first few years of the revolution. However, as a way to incorporate workers into the new political order, the state authorised three forms of organisations, namely the Islamic labour councils (*shurā-hā-ye eslāmi-e kār*), the Islamic labour associations (*anjoman-hā-ye eslāmi-e kārgari*) and guild associations (*anjoman-hā-ye senfi*) (Jafari, 2021: 145). At the top of these three 'yellow unions', the Workers' House (*khāneh-e kārgar*) was constituted as 'a self-appointed federating "union" with the financial and logistical support of the government' (Nomani and Behdad, 2012: 220–1) to bring together representatives of these newly created 'labour organisations from different workplaces, regardless of their economic sector' (Jafari, 2021: 145). Apart from violence and institutional mechanisms, the new state utilised Islamic populism and nationalist discourses of Khomeinist groups, which significantly augmented after the start of the war with Iraq, to complete the process of the 'sanitisation of labour activism'. Hence, in the first decade of the revolution, 'spontaneous labour mobilisation and independent workers groups had very little space to flourish without being controlled, isolated, and repressed' (Morgana, 2021: 7–8).

Throughout the 1980s, despite agreeing on the destruction of any attempt at the creation of independent labour organisations, the stratum of government managers and the bonyad–bazaar nexus clashed over the formulation of new labour law. The Majles rejected the first draft in 1982, which led to the forced resignation of the Labour Minister, but finally passed a new draft in 1987. However, the Guardian Council specified seventy-four Shari'a law objections to the bill based on a traditional interpretation of Islam regarding workers' rights and state regulations on contractual relations between workers and employers. As the several revisions by the Majles between 1987 and 1990 failed to satisfy the Guardian Council, the Expediency Discernment Assembly's intervention ultimately resolved the issue, leading to the approval of the new labour law in November 1990 (Hesam, 2002: 25). Predictably, the labour law only recognises the Islamic labour councils, the Islamic labour associations and guild associations as the legal organisations for collective bargaining (Article 131). Instead of recognising the right to strike, the new labour law only ambiguously acknowledges the 'stoppage of work while the workers are present in the workplace' (Article 142). Besides outlawing child labour (Article 79), the labour law subjects the termination of employment contracts to the agreement of Islamic labour councils or guild societies. In case of disagreement between two parties, the law mandates the dispute shall be settled by the Board of Inquiry and the Disputes Board (Article 27). The law also stipulates paid maternity leave, feeding time and day-care services at the workplace (Article 76) and requires the provision of housing, sports and training facilities for workers in large enterprises (Labor Law of Iran, 1990).

With the commencement of Iranian neoliberalisation, its proponents labelled the labour law as the product of the political environment of the 1980s that created the greatest obstacle to pro-market restructuring of the economy and the attraction of domestic and international investments. Accordingly, during the first phase of neoliberalisation, the initial attempt to amend the labour law resulted in the exclusion of small-scale enterprises with fewer than five workers from the provision of the law in February 2000. Two years later, the Khatami government legalised the exclusion of enterprises with fewer than ten workers from the provision of the labour law (Jafari, 2009; Morgana, 2021: 11). In both attempts, the government insisted that the labour law allows this exemption on the basis of the approval from the Council of Ministers by referring to its Article 191. During the second phase of neoliberalisation, the Ahmadinejad administration strove to extensively revise the labour law in 2006 to allow 'employers to dismiss permanent workers without penalty by paying sizable severance fees'. The government claimed that 'the amendment would enhance productivity' and improve job security by encouraging job creation (Maloney, 2015: 331–2).

These efforts to entirely redraft the labour law did not materialise for two reasons. First, contrary to the claims of the advocates of neoliberalisation, labour law is not inherently biased in favour of workers as it contains numerous articles in support of employers. Article 7 on employment contracts recognises the recruitment of employees both on 'a definite and an indefinite period', i.e., legitimising both temporary and permanent contracts. Article 11 complements Article 7 by permitting short-term contracts under the name of the 'probationary period of work' with a maximum duration of one month for unskilled and semiskilled workers and three months for skilled and specialised workers during which the contract can be terminated by either party 'without prior notice and without being obliged to pay compensation' (Labour Law of Iran, 1990). Since the early 1990s, these two articles have enabled the creation of state-controlled hiring agencies that serve 'as a tool of recruitment for temporary workers' (Morgana, 2020). Second, and perhaps more importantly, the law has only been partially implemented, if at all, due to the absence of independent trade unions that can effectively defend workers' rights and enforce the law. In addition, with the continuous growth of the Iranian reserve army of labour in recent decades – the unemployed population climbed from 1.5 million in 1996 to 3.3 million in 2016 according to the Statistical Center of Iran – many essential protections envisaged in the law have not been upheld, such as minimum wage, social security, normal working hours and a safe working environment. In other words, the unemployment crisis has lowered upward pressure on wages and decreased the already weak bargaining power of workers, therefore leading to the acceptance of low wages and withdrawal from the social security scheme by many workers. Coupled with the exclusion of small-scale enterprises with fewer than ten workers from the provision of the labour law, the number of precarious and low-paid jobs has significantly increased in recent years. This has also eased the conditions for the expansion of child and forced labour in practice, which is forbidden in the law. In 2017, it was estimated that around 7 million children were child labourers while Iran was among the top ten countries with the highest prevalence of modern slavery in the world in 2018 (Tasnim News Agency, 2017; Global Slavery Index, 2018).

These structural changes have transformed the composition of the Iranian working class since the early 1990s. While the size of the working class was projected to be around 5 million in 1986,[1] according to the Supreme Centre of Islamic Labour Councils (*kānun-e ʿāli-ye shurā-hā-ye eslāmi-e kār*) the number increased to around 13 million in 2018 (Nahvi, 2018: 4). On top of that, it is estimated that currently 'there are three and a half million informal workers who are not covered by the labour law' (Jamārān News, 2022). If we consider our definition of wage labour in Chapter 1 – someone whose labour power is commodified in other ways beyond formal job contracts, including forced labour, semi-free labour, child labour, small artisans, self-employed as well as non-wage activities that workers depend upon, such as unpaid family labour – the figures should, in reality, be higher. In contrast to common perception, public sector workers constitute a small portion of the Iranian working class due to the neoliberal attempts of various governments to reorganise the public administrative system to improve accountability and productivity. However, the most prominent transformation in the composition of the working class has been the constitution of the precariat as the largest group within the Iranian working class. 'Whereas in 1990 only 6% of the labour force worked under temporary contracts, by the end of the 2000s the number climbed to 90%' (Morgana, 2020). According to the Supreme Centre of Islamic Labour Councils, the conditions have further deteriorated in recent years as the number of short-term contracts of less than six months reached 97 per cent in 2021 (ISNA, 2021). Under these conditions, multiple job holding and twelve hours of work a day have unsurprisingly become a norm in the labour market (Khairollahi, 2018: 40–1).

The process of neoliberalisation has also engendered a new group within the poor, that can be called the 'new poor'. Unlike the Iranian traditional poor – who largely reside in rural areas and small cities or are rural migrants in big cities and to a degree are under the support of welfare organisations such as the Imam Khomeini Relief Committee, the Mostazafan Foundation, and the Social Security Organisation – young people, in the age group 15–29 years with a university degree, constitute the new poor. Due to the high fertility rate of the 1980s and the introduction of private universities a decade later, the university graduate population has increased astronomically. For instance, whilst the total number of university students in the 1996/7 academic year was nearly 580,000, less than two decades later there were 4.8 million university students in the 2014/15 academic year (Statistical Center of Iran, 2015/2016: 678). Consequently, the share of the young graduate population within the total unemployed population witnessed a steady growth from 10 per cent in 2001 to 20 per cent in 2005 (535,000) and 41.5 per cent in 2015 (1.13 million), with the expectation that it will be 50 per cent in the near future. Meanwhile, in 2005, 6.32 per cent (2.12 million) of the economically inactive population held a higher education degree. Ten years later, 14.25 per cent (5.7 million) of the economically inactive population had university degrees. Thus, it could be concluded that the population of the new poor in the course of a decade climbed from 2.6 million in 2005 to 6.8 million in 2015.[2] Women have demonstrated exceptional academic achievements, exceeding men in higher education attainment. However, a significant proportion of young female graduates remain inactive due to the low rate of female labour force participation in Iran. As recorded in 2021, Iran's female labour force participation rate stands among the lowest worldwide at approximately 17 per cent (World Bank, World Development Indicators database). Pushed by the harsh realities of the economic conditions, many members of the new poor subsist on family support or live in slums and squatter settlements.

Considering these transformations, it is fair to argue that Iranian neoliberalisation has produced a sharp rise in precarity and absolute poverty, hugely widened inequality and enabled the concentration of wealth in the hands of a few. The international sanctions have played a part in the deteriorating conditions of the working class and the poor, as we shall explore in the next chapter, but the sanctions should also be viewed in the context of their internal relations to the internationalisation of capital, the process of Iranian neoliberalisation and the interests of the internationally oriented capital fraction and the military–bonyad complex. Since 1994, the average income of the richest 10 per cent of the population has been about fifteen times that of the poorest 10 per cent. In the same period, while the top 20 per cent accounted for 48.5 per cent of the income share on average, the lowest 20 per cent held as little as 5.5 per cent.[3] Perhaps the most shocking phenomenon has been the striking upsurge in the number of those who live in extreme poverty. According to the head of the Imam Khomeini Relief Committee, in 2017, 10 to 12 million people lived in absolute poverty, testifying that the number will be between 16 to 20 million (25 per cent of the population) if the extreme poverty line was measured slightly higher (*Resālat*, 2017c). In short, under Iranian neoliberalism that emerged out of the necessity of the reorganisation of the system to recover capital accumulation and reconstitute class power in favour of the ruling class, enormous wealth which originated in the export of hydrocarbons has been channelled to the ruling class, the ownership of SOEs has been transferred to the newly reconstructed fractions of the ruling class through privatisation, and the wealth has been redistributed from the poor to the rich by implementing labour market deregulation and cutting off state subsidies. Despite repressive state measures, the working class and the poor have deployed a myriad action repertoires and different forms of organisation to resist neoliberalism in the last four decades. In the next section, we shall explore these acts of resistance.

## Class struggles in contemporary Iran

### *Labour struggles since 1990*

Since the instigation of neoliberal reforms, workers have used different routes to challenge the deterioration of their working conditions and advance their interests. A section of the working class has found the state-sanctioned labour organisations to be an effective vehicle for voicing their demands and organising protests. In contrast, some workers have struggled to form independent unions and networks. A third but small group of workers has demanded workers' control by calling for the re-establishment of the workers' councils of the early months of the 1979 revolution (Jafari, 2021: 144). In general, in the first phase of neoliberalisation, using state-sanctioned labour organisations was more popular, as indicated by the rise in the total number of these organisations 'from about 2,000 in 1990 to more than 5,000 in 2010' (Jafari, 2021: 145). While the number of state-sanctioned labour organisations continued to grow (to more than 10,000 in 2018), the call for establishing independent unions and networks gained real momentum during the second phase of neoliberalisation. In recent years, with the intensification of working-class mobilisation, the demand for workers' control has been explicitly voiced during protests. The state has routinely used coercive and punitive legal measures as the most effective tools to control workers' militancy. At the same time, the various governments have also constructed discourses that aim at downgrading the role of workers as a tool to increase production (Morgana, 2019: 155). By prioritising the new middle class and the youth, the administrations linked to the internationally oriented capital fractions have refused to address the workers and urban poor. Instead, the governments of Hashemi-Rafsanjani, Khatami and Rouhani endeavoured to shape the mindset of workers as part of their ideal individualised neoliberal subjects with the following characteristics: 'hardworking and dedicated to the production mantra, oriented toward independence and eager to develop specialised skills' (Morgana, 2020: 342). In contrast, while still talking to the masses and the poor, the administrations linked to the military–bonyad complex have encouraged workers 'to resist [against foreign enemies], to wait, to keep struggling for the nation, and to be patient with regard to their own demands' (Morgana, 2021: 1).

The early years of the first phase of neoliberalisation during the Hashemi-Rafsanjani government (1989–97) were dominated by the uprisings of the poor, as we shall explain below. That said, workers gradually became agitated against the economic liberalisation of the administration. In this context, the fear of losing control of workers in the case of independent labour protests, along with the violent urban poor riots, forced the Workers' House to become inclined to organise protests and petitions from the second half of the 1990s onwards. In 1995, factory workers in Khalifeh Abad in the northern province of Gilan organised several rounds of strikes against delayed wage payments and rising unemployment. This was followed by other waves of protests in the form of strikes and sit-ins initiated by oil workers in Tabriz, Tehran, Esfahan and Shiraz between December 1996 and February 1997 (Morgana, 2020).

Many workers supported Khatami in 1997 based on his pledges for reviving the 'chronically ill' economy, weakening the authoritarian structures, enhancing political openness and constructing a vibrant civil society. The hope for change steadily faded away with the intensification of neoliberal reforms during his presidency, most notably the expansion of temporary contracts and the exclusion of enterprises with fewer than ten workers from the labour law. This triggered a series of labour protests during the first reformist government (1997–2001). In 1998, more than ninety cases of labour protests were documented, including strikes reported in large industries such as the oil industry, steel plants, textiles and glass manufacturing (Jafari, 2009). In January 1999, workers in several factories in Kashan organised demonstrations against overdue pay and demanded higher salaries. Between February and June 1999, worker protests in Ahvaz, Abadan, Shiraz, Mahshahr and Bandar Abbas led to the arrests of sixteen labour activists (Morgana, 2021: 11; Morgana, 2020). The number of labour strikes alone reached 266 cases between April 1999 and April 2000 (Jafari, 2009). Further indignation at the neoliberal economic direction of the government amplified collective mobilisation and labour militancy during Khatami's second term in office (2001–5). With the entry of public workers such as teachers and healthcare workers into labour struggles for the first time since the revolution, the number of protests was reported to be 319 between March 2001 and March 2002 (Jafari, 2021: 146). High-profile worker struggles against redundancies and short-term and temporary contracts in 2004 and 2005 gave the resurgent labour movement a national profile. In January 2004, security forces violently suppressed the protest of copper workers in Khatounabad in Kerman province, leading to the killing of several workers and the wounding of more than 300. The second case was the strike of workers in one of the biggest car factories in the Middle East, Iran Khodro, for 'the elimination of temporary contracts from Labor Law, safer working conditions, and higher salaries for night shift jobs' (Morgana, 2021: 12).

A few labour committees, councils, syndicates and unions, such as the Iranian Teachers' Trade Association, emerged during the Khatami presidency (Problematica, 2015).[4] However, the most important development was the formation of the United Bus Company of Tehran and Suburbs as an independent union with 17,000 bus drivers in 2004, which organised protests and called for the replacement of Islamic labour councils with independent trade unions (Morgana, 2021: 13). Given this, one may argue that not only did the minimal opening of the political space during the reign of the reformists encourage independent labour militants to organise meetings and rallies and produce publications, but it also paved the way for the formation of independent trade unions. This is a flawed argument as the neoliberal reformist administration even took several measures to limit the influence of the yellow trade union confederation, Workers' House (Jafari, 2009), let alone tolerating the formation of independent labour unions. In fact, to crush any hope of the recognition of independent labour organisations, the Khatami government consciously refused to ratify the International Labour Organization conventions, including the Freedom of Association and Protection of the Right to Organise Convention, 1948 (No. 87), and the Right to Organise and Collective Bargaining Convention, 1949 (No. 98). With this attitude, it comes as no surprise that the Khatami government legacy on workers' rights was as bad as the previous administration since the security forces brutally suppressed workers' defensive demands and peaceful protests (Nomani and Behdad, 2012: 221–5).

Ahmadinejad's promise to challenge the neoliberal policies of the previous administrations by returning to the social contract of the first decade of the revolution retained the loyalty of the urban poor and some sections of the working class. However, as soon as he took office, the new government adopted necessary measures to tame all forms of activism, including labour struggles. Unshaken by the rise of authoritarianism of the state, workers continued their protests against low wages, temporary contracts, privatisation, corruption and mismanagement during the two terms of the Ahmadinejad administration. Hence, while in the second part of 2005 workers organised around 260 strikes, the number of labour protests was reported to be around 505 between March 2010 and March 2011 despite severe suppression of political activism as a result of the political turmoil caused by the 2009 Green Movement (Jafari, 2021: 146–7). More importantly, between 2006 and 2008, another two independent trade unions, Haft Tapeh Sugar Factory Workers' Union and Free Union of Iranian Workers, emerged after abolishing their Islamic labour councils (Morgana, 2021: 14). Alongside these new 'illegal' independent unions, throughout the Ahmadinejad presidency, independent networks to create national coordination between labour activists appeared. Some of the current (semi-)clandestine organisations (the Committee for the Pursuit of the Creation of Free Labour Organisations, the Coordination Committee for the Creation of Labour Organisations, the Workers' Cultural and Support Organisation, the Union of Labour Committees and the Cooperation Council of Labour Organisations and Activists) were forged during the Ahmadinejad government. To circumvent surveillance and keep labour activists alive, workers also utilised online platforms such as blogs and forums. Among the growing number of workers' bulletins and weblogs with an anti-capitalist outlook, some of them were developed in this period (Jafari, 2021: 147).

During the Rouhani government, several waves of revolts between 2017 and 2019, which will be scrutinised below, overshadowed workers' struggles, but the unprecedented resurgence of labour activism has continued to grow despite the escalation of state repression because of these popular uprisings. In almost all cities where uprisings occurred between December 2017 and January 2018, there had already been some degree of labour unrest by various groups of the working class, including factory workers, teachers, bus and truck drivers, nurses and so forth (Harris and Kalb, 2018). According to a study by BBC Persian (2018a), in nearly 90 per cent of those cities witnessing uprisings, there was at least one labour protest six months before the wave of turmoil. Prior to this, some 400 labour protests in 2015, nearly 350 in 2016, and more than 900 protests in 2017 were documented (Bayat, 2018). Another study based on the coverage of labour activism by the Labour National News Agency (ILNA) estimates that there were '36 protests of all sorts and 21 blue-collar workers' protests per month' between March 2015 and March 2020. The study calculates that 2,183 protests (427 per year) were reported altogether for this period, in which 'blue-collar workers' protests make up 57 per cent of the total'. The analysis of the geographical spread of the protests by the study indicates the nationwide nature of the unrest because during these five years '165 out of a total of 429 counties' had 'at least one reported protest. Out of these 165 counties, 126 (76 per cent) had at least one blue-collar workers' protest' (Kadivar et al., 2021). It is worth pointing out that in ILNA reporting non-blue-collar workers' protests referred to demonstrations organised by groups that were mostly part of the working class in a broader sense, such as nurses, teachers and retirees. One of the key developments has been the conspicuous upsurge in the number of strikes since 2015 as, for instance, 1,169 strikes by labour and trade associations were documented between 2018 and 2022. According to a survey conducted by the Human Rights Activists News Agency (2022), most of these strikes (more than 780 strikes) occurred between May 2021 and May 2022. Of importance is the recent joining of workers in the oil, gas and petrochemical industry to labour discontents. For the first time since the revolution, they organised several rounds of strikes between 2020 and 2021 for higher wages, job security and better health and safety conditions. In August 2020, oil, gas and petrochemical workers organised a two-month strike that spanned forty-two sites in seventeen counties. A year later, more than 10,000 of them joined a larger round of strikes that involved 102 factories and refineries and 39 counties from 19 June to July 2021 (Kadivar et al., 2021).

## Workers, the poor and the Green Movement

Controversy over the presidential election of June 2009 triggered the Green Movement that lasted until early 2011.[5] As we discussed in Chapter 5, disputes over election procedures and results have been one of the key areas of antagonism between the internationally oriented capital fraction and the military–bonyad complex for control of the state since 1989. This time, rather than the supervisory role of the Guardian Council, the dispute was over the results of the election in which the incumbent president, Mahmoud Ahmadinejad, was named victorious. Labelled as unprecedented in the history of the Islamic Republic, opponents questioned the 'dubious manner' of the release of the results. To protest the 'rigged' election, hundreds of thousands took to the streets, mainly in Tehran, claiming their votes had been stolen, and chanting 'where is my vote?' The initial demonstrations were quickly plunged into violence because the IRGC and the *Basij* attacked protesters, resulting in a large number of casualties and a dozen deaths. In addition, authorities closed down newspapers, magazines and websites linked to the movement and arrested several thousand political activists. This extensive use of violence largely prevented mass mobilisations similar to the early days of the Green Movement, but the protesters exploited the permitted public and religious ceremonies, such as the Quds day and Ashura, as platforms to continue their dissent in the following months (Reisinezhad, 2015: 212–14). In the end, the call for a public rally in solidarity with Tunisian and Egyptian protesters in February 2011 acted as the final nail in the coffin of the movement because it led to the brutal repression of small, scattered protests and more importantly the house arrest of the leaders of the movement (Hashemi, 2014: 207–13).

As the dominant conceptualisation, the democratisation thesis characterises the Green Movement as the battle of the 'people' against the authoritarian theocratic state. This narrative contends that 'most Iranians do not feel concerned with the power struggles among the revolutionary elites' (Jahanbegloo, 2011b: 133) because they are ahead of the 'inherited politics, floating ideologies or mismatched theories' (Dabashi, 2011a: 25). Despite viewing it as the representation of a new era in Iran due to its deployment of non-violent tactics, horizontal organisational methods and modern communication techniques (Mahdavi, 2011a: 85), this dominant conceptualisation regards the Green Movement as *only* a new chapter in the long history of 'the popular quest for democratisation of the state and society' (Jahanbegloo, 2011b: 133; Mahdavi, 2011b: 94). In other words, since 'the inherent truth about Iran is that its people desire civil liberties and personal freedoms as much as any other population in the world', the movement should not be seen as 'a singular event in Iranian history' (Sundquist, 2013b: 45) but rather as the continuation of 'an idea [freedom] first instilled in the Iranian mindset in 1906 with the introduction of the first constitution of the people' (Sundquist, 2013a: 33). According to this account that shares many characteristics of modernisation theory, this long-lasting desire for freedom and quest for democracy came back once again to the surface in the form of the Green Movement as a result of several socioeconomic changes in Iran: (1) the high fertility of the first decade of the revolution that has put Iran among the countries with the largest youth population in the world since the early 1990s; (2) the rapid urbanisation in which a 50–50 urban–rural ratio in 1979 has shifted to a 70–30 ratio in recent years; (3) an extraordinary expansion of higher education in Iran, mostly thanks to the post-1990 neoliberal education policies; (4) changes in gender relations; and (5) the availability of new communication technologies (Farhi, 2011: 618; Khosrokhavar, 2012: 176–7; Golkar, 2011). The narrative assumes that these social transformations have engendered a sizeable Iranian middle class with more than 50 per cent of the Iranian population (Hashemi, 2014: 206). This class is portrayed as a class in the possession of *agency* and *subjectivity* that has the burden of confronting the religious despotic state on its shoulders.[6] Farhi (2011: 618–19) neatly summarises the people–state dualism and the celebration of the Iranian 'middle class' as the rightful representation of people's desires and dreams:

> Their demand for political rights, greater cultural openness in the face of a strict Islamic code of conduct, less ideological/religious screening for jobs, better governance and political accountability, negotiated accommodation with the global order, and an end to cliquish corruption are as much a call for democracy as a claim to what they consider their rightful political and socioeconomic power.

Apart from its narrow definition of freedom, which ultimately reduces to 'civil liberties' and 'individual and political freedoms', this notion of the middle class is theoretically and empirically problematic in several respects. First, it does not consider the fact that, due to the 1979 revolution with the promise of providing free education for all, particularly for poor and disadvantaged people, the number of university graduates has dramatically increased in the subsequent decades. As demonstrated above, this eye-catching change has more than anything else contributed to the emergence of the class of the new poor, many of whom subsist on family support or live in slums and squatter settlements, despite having obtained university degrees. Second, urbanisation should not be translated as a sign of the enlargement of the middle class because all historical records across the globe and in Iran illustrate that urbanisation is directly related to industrialisation, which is associated primarily with the growth of the working class and urban poor. With the rise in the number of medium-sized and large firms with complex organisations and skilled workers, Iranian neoliberalisation has indeed moderately enlarged the size of the middle class. However, if we follow the definition of the middle class presented in Chapter 1 – senior officials and high-ranking managers deprived of the ownership of means of production who exercise some forms of authority and possess relative autonomy in the labour process – the size of this class modestly rises from 7 per cent of the workforce population in 1986 to around nearly 13 per cent in 2016 (i.e., less than 3 million of the employed workforce).[7] Third, all members of this small class do not automatically oppose the 'revolutionary conservative elites', who are allegedly in total control of the state.[8] Finally, and relatedly, by assuming the separation of the state and civil society that ignores the intra-class struggle between the two fractions of the ruling class in the realm of civil society, this narrative implicitly (and occasionally explicitly) regards the internationally oriented capital fraction as an integral part of the people against the tyrannical religious state in control of the military–bonyad complex. Given this, the Green Movement is understood as the tale of two Irans: the Islamic state with the support of the minority of conservatives constituting at best 10 to 15 per cent of the population and the rest of the country (Khosrokhavar, 2011: 57–75; Khosrokhavar, 2012: 178).

In contrast to this account, the Green Movement should be comprehended based on the inseparability of the realms of political society and civil society. This allows us to expand the site of social struggles between the internationally oriented capital fraction and the military–bonyad complex for hegemony beyond the state institutions. More crucially, it helps us to navigate the process of alliance-compromise of different fractions of the ruling class with other classes whereby the internationally oriented capital fraction and the military–bonyad complex have endeavoured to forge (short-term) alliances with the middle class, working class, traditional and new poor and petty bourgeoisie to either advance their interests or block the gains of rivals.

While there was some speculation about electoral fraud during the 2005 presidential election, Ahmadinejad managed to narrowly secure a majority in the second round of the election thanks to the support of the traditional poor, some sections of the working class and the petty bourgeoisie. His 2005 election campaign featured two central themes: (i) unmasking the devastating effects of the process of liberalisation of the two previous administrations for the working class and the poor, and (ii) exposing the corrupt nature of the first phase of liberalisation by constructing the notion of what he referred to as *aqazadehha* (high-ranking government officials and their sons who were involved in wealth accumulation). To bring back the revolution to its original track, Ahmadinejad swore to 'bring the oil money to the tables of the people' and transfer the shares of the profitable government-owned enterprises to Iranian families, not the *aqazadehha*, through 'justice shares'. In addition, he appealingly played a nationalist card by representing himself as a national hero who would stand against the 'bullying of the Great Satan' regarding the 'Iranian peaceful nuclear programme' to create a winnable electoral base. As a result, he regained the support of the traditional poor[9] and managed to bring on board the lower strata of the petty bourgeoisie and some sections of the working class who were adversely affected by the previous sixteen-year neoliberalisation process. During the early days of his presidency, Ahmadinejad took several measures to assist these classes through initiatives such as the Imam Reza Compassion Fund and the Compassion Housing Project, but it soon became clear that the whole administration was being run to realise the interests of the military forces and revolutionary foundations with calamitous implications for the labour market and the working conditions of the labouring classes, as explained earlier.

Considering Ahmadinejad's experiment and the previous neoliberal experience of the Hashemi-Rafsanjani and Khatami administrations that alienated workers and magnified the political distance between labour activists and middle-class activists, workers were largely indifferent to the post-2009 election conflicts. A clear indication of this apathy was the failed promise of the leader of the Green Movement, Mir-Hossein Mousavi, to call for a general strike two weeks after the election due to the lack of support from the working class (Kurzman, 2012: 164). Other calls for a universal strike by some young activists similarly failed to generate a response from workers as a cohesive and distinct group. In fact, some labour activists 'dismissed the potential of the Green Movement as speaking for the liberal upper and middle classes and not for the masses' (Morgana, 2021: 15). On the other hand, the internationally oriented capital fraction was passionately backed by a large portion of the middle class that witnessed relatively palpable expansion, especially during the first phase of liberalisation. The internationally oriented capital fraction also enjoyed the relative support of the new poor, who blamed Ahmadinejad's policies for the retrogression of economic conditions and detested the anti-democratic and reactionary social and political policies of the military–bonyad complex. To counter the mobilisation of the internationally oriented capital fraction, the military–bonyad complex contrived a highly securitised political environment by labelling the movement as sedition (*fetneh*) without any national base orchestrated by foreign powers, in particular, the 'criminal United States' and the 'evil England', in the words of the supreme leader. The hostile relations with the West amid the Iranian nuclear controversy, when the United States repeatedly asserted that 'all options including the military action [were] on the table', made the demands of the Green Movement for political reforms more vulnerable to the repression of the military forces (Ritter, 2015: 175–210). Nevertheless, along with the impacts of the crippling post-2010 US and EU sanctions, as we shall explore in the next chapter, the political instability generated as a result of the Green Movement played a key role in the victory of the candidate of the internationally oriented capital fraction, Hassan Rouhani, in the 2013 presidential election with the primary aim of solving the sanctions-related economic crisis through direct negotiations with the P5+1, including the United States (Oveisy and Amini, 2018).

In short, the Green Movement was the attempt of the political represent-atives of the internationally oriented capital fraction to mobilise the middle class and the new poor predominately in Tehran in the aftermath of the 2009 presidential election around its long-standing demands for 'free' elections and dismantling the electoral supervisory role of the Guardian Council. The working class and the large section of the poor showed political indifference towards the 2009–11 mobilisations. Some labour activists even labelled 'the Green Movement's participants as "narrowminded liberals" ' with little care for the demands of the masses (Morgana, 2021: 2). Hence, rather than interpreting it as the battle of the people and the theocratic state, the Green Movement should be viewed as part of the ongoing battle of the internation-ally oriented capital fraction and the military–bonyad complex for control of the state and the exercise of hegemony over the society. In this light, the Green Movement was the manifestation of the impasse of the absolute con-trol of the state by a particular fraction of capital and the representation of minimal hegemony of the ruling class as a whole over the masses.

### The poor against neoliberalisation: From the 1992 riots to the post-2017 uprisings

The urban poor were the first subaltern group to resist neoliberal reforms by taking to the streets. These embryonic forms of resistance against the elimination of subsidies and high inflation resulted in the eruption of several waves of protests and riots throughout the 1990s in Mashhad, Eslamshaher, Qazvin, Tabriz, Shiraz and Arak. The state violently suppressed these 'mostaz'afin' rebellions by labelling the protesters 'agitators' and 'enemies of the revolution' (Morgana, 2020). The Mashhad riot in May 1992 was a clear example of this level of violence against the poor. According to Bayat (1994: 10–11), the riot 'had destroyed over one hundred buildings and stores and left an estimated total damage of 10 billion rials. More than 300 people were arrested, six police officers killed, and four rioters hanged' (see also BBC Persian, 2005; Sharltouki, 2016). In June 2007, once again the poor voiced their anger against the neoliberal policies of the government, more specifically the proposed gasoline rationing scheme. In what became known as the 'Gasoline Riots', protesters in Tehran, Yasouj, Ilam, Shiraz, Isfahan and a few other provincial towns set fire to state buildings, banks and petrol stations. As the main target of these few-day riots, more than 750 petrol stations were estimated to be damaged. The state officials admitted that, during the brutal reaction of the security forces, the Revolutionary Guards and the Basij, several people were killed, but the actual number of casualties was not announced (Amirshahi, 2017; Yeganeh, 2007).

The most significant waves of popular uprisings have occurred in recent years. In 2013, the Iranian people were invited to support Hassan Rouhani's initiative to negotiate with the West regarding the nuclear programme to terminate international isolation, thwart the possibility of war and unshackle Iran's economy from years of sanctions. While Iran reached an agreement with the P5+1 in July 2015, the average purchasing power of ordinary Iranians plunged, unemployment increased significantly and inequality escalated during the Rouhani administration (2013–21). The withdrawal of the United States from the nuclear accord in May 2018 that reactivated the international sanctions was a crucial determinant in the deterioration of the economic conditions, as we will discuss in detail in the next chapter. That said, the aggressive neoliberal policies of the Rouhani government were equally, if not more, responsible for the escalation of the economic crisis. Together, they triggered a series of protests and violent riots, initially between December 2017 and January 2018 and later in November 2019. Prior to these waves of uprisings, some 1,700 social protests by the disenfranchised, including street vendors, farmers, pensioners, the unemployed and other groups of the poor, were reported (Bayat, 2018). Due to their magnitude, a close look at the 2017/18 and 2019 rebellions is necessary.

The Rouhani government rested on two interrelated pillars: resolving the nuclear issue with the West and deepening the deregulation and neoliberalisation to attract foreign investments. As a typical neoliberal administration, the initial attempts to bring inflation below 10 per cent and reduce the budget deficit increased unemployment (Handjani, 2018). The government claimed the problem would be tackled following a nuclear accord with projected growth in the volume of FDI inflows to the country. At the same time, the administration conditioned an increase in the number of people at work on further deregulating the Iranian labour market, considering it a necessary requirement for attracting foreign investment. In his 2010 book, *National Security and Economic System of Iran*, Rouhani labelled Iran's labour law as a major obstacle for businesses to create jobs and prosperity, therefore defending the abolition of the minimum wage and the elimination of restrictions on the laying off of workers. He even viewed the state-sanctioned 'yellow unions' as detrimental for businesses: 'One of the main challenges that employers and our factories face is the existence of labour unions. Workers should be more pliant toward the demands of job-creators' (Rouhani, 2010 cited in Fathollah-Nejad, 2017). To this end, his administration first introduced an internship scheme to facilitate the recruitment of fixed-term interns instead of hiring workers under the stipulation of labour laws and later 'revised and introduced a long-dormant bill that called for further relaxation of Iran's already lax labour laws, proposing to cut the minimum wage by half' (Shaddel, 2018). In addition, the government implemented detrimental austerity measures by cutting social welfare services spending and retreating from public investment in infrastructure in favour of international and domestic private investment (Shaddel, 2018). For instance, in the budget for the 1397 Iranian fiscal year (March 2018–March 2019), the government proposed to limit the cash subsidies system (*yārāneh*) through which almost all poor citizens receive funds every two months. The plan to raise the price of petrol and introduce fees for car registration and departure tax similarly generated massive anxiety among the most disadvantaged groups (New York Times, 2018; BBC News, 2018). In the meantime, the victory of Trump with the promise of unilaterally ending the nuclear deal significantly slowed down the removal of international sanctions. Accordingly, a 40 per cent sudden jump in the price of many basic foodstuffs due to these austerity measures and the prospect of the return of crippling US sanctions triggered a series of violent protests in some 75 to 100 cities and provincial towns from 28 December 2017 through 3 January 2018, known as the Dey protests (referring to the Iranian calendar month).[10]

Alongside the prospect of the return of sanctions and the neoliberal policies of the Rouhani administration, we should also not disregard the escalation of the intra-class struggle between the internationally oriented capital fraction and the military–bonyad complex as a contributing factor at least for the instigation of the unrest. Once having taken office, Rouhani publicly criticised unaccountable centres of power, in particular, the IRGC's economic activities, by describing the privatisation process during the Ahmadinejad presidency as the transference of a part of the economy from 'an unarmed government' to 'a government with arms' (Radio Farda, 2017; Ghadimi, 2017). In the midst of nuclear talks, Rouhani once again criticised the essence of the IRGC, stressing that 'if information, weapons, money, newspapers, news agency, and other aspects of power get together in one entity, Abouzar and Salman [the companions of the prophet Muhammad] become corrupt' (cited in Gharchedaghi, 2017). The government consequently demanded that the military forces and the revolutionary foundations divest from the economy and hand over their enterprises to the so-called 'real private sector'. Despite the Revolutionary Guards' denial (BBC Persian, 2018b), the *Financial Times* reported that government pressure led to the arrests of some members of the IRGC over corruption and forced the organisation to shrink its extensive business empire (Bozorgmehr, 2017). The Rouhani administration also managed to pass a bill through the Majles that repealed the tax exemption of the revolutionary foundations (Radio Farda, 2019). Against this backdrop, conservative political forces with a close tie with the military–bonyad complex encouraged the initial demonstration in Mashhad against rising food prices as a way to put pressure on the government (Bajoghli, 2018). They assumed that it would be a peaceful anti-Rouhani rally, but the protest turned into an anti-Islamic state revolt and rapidly spread to other cities and towns. In response to the protests, all political forces affiliated with the internationally oriented capital fraction and the military–bonyad complex (from the conservatives to the moderates to the reformists) unified against what they called the sedition (*fetneh*). The result was state repression with over 20 deaths, 4,000 jailed and thousands of casualties, according to official figures (Fatollah-Nejad, 2020: 8). Needless to say, the figures were significantly higher in the accounts of activist networks, non-governmental media outlets and independent organisations.

In November 2019, a new wave of protests that first broke out in Khuzestan province in the Southwest quickly spread to more than 100 cities across the country (*The Iran Primer*, 2020). Similar to the Dey protests, the combination of internal and external pressures as a result of the reimposition of devastating US sanctions and the continuation of the aggressive liberalisation measures of the Rouhani government caused this new round of nationwide protests known as the Aban protests (referring to the Iranian calendar month). The falling of oil exports and the departure of many MNCs in an attempt to escape Washington's punitive measures, coupled with the government's radical neoliberal reforms of the labour market and the welfare system, pushed the Iranian economy into a deep recession. Accordingly, the national currency (rial) lost about 70 per cent of its value, the economy experienced a 6 per cent contraction, and inflation rose at an average annual rate of 40 per cent (Kerr, England and Bozorgmehr, 2019; Hafezi and Barbuscia, 2020). Whilst ordinary Iranians encountered one of the biggest economic crises of recent history, the announcement of a sudden surge in fuel prices by the government acted as a catalyst for triggering the Aban protests. As Ali Fatollah-Nejad observes (2020: 4), this wave of demonstrations, blockades and clashes with security forces was more significant than the Dey protests in several ways:

> (1) there was an almost five-fold increase in the number of protesters (200,000 compared to 42,000, according to interior ministry figures), making the Aban Protests the largest anti-regime demonstration since the 1979 revolution; (2) people's resolve was much more ferocious and they expressed their anger more openly; and (3) the state response was unprecedented, with a bloody crackdown resulting in the deaths of up to 1,500 protesters (plus at least 2,000 wounded and 7,000 arrested). The state crackdown was carried out during a near-total internet shutdown and thus hidden from national and international scrutiny.[11]

It has been claimed that workers in the informal sector were engaged in the organisation of these waves of protests in 2017/18 and 2019 (Jafari, 2021: 148). However, considering the geographical locations of the protests and the age groups of those arrested, it can be concluded that the new poor were the main social group involved in the Dey and Aban protests. For instance, according to official figures, more than 90 per cent of those arrested during the Dey protests were under 25 years old and often educated (Eltagouri, 2018). The frustration of young, educated Iranians against the entirety of the system throughout these protests indicated a clear breakdown of the relationship between the new poor and the political representatives of the internationally oriented capital fraction since they largely backed the Green Movement and the election of Rouhani. Following the violent suppression of the Aban protest, a new round of uprisings known as the Women, Life, Freedom revolt emerged in 2022 that went beyond the economic demands of the poor and working class. In the next section, we will delve into this development.

### The 'Women, Life, Freedom' revolt

In September 2022, the death of Jîna (Mahsa) Amini, a 22-year-old Kurdish woman, in the custody of the notorious Morality Police on the charge of violating the dress code for women (hijab), sparked a series of demonstrations in her hometown region under the banner of 'Women, Life, Freedom'.[12] The outrage over the circumstances surrounding her death rapidly went beyond Iranian Kurdistan, leading to a wave of discontent across the country.[13] Although the aforementioned structural causes (neoliberal policies of the state and international sanctions) have been integral to its development, it is notable that the Women, Life, Freedom uprising has achieved greater success in galvanising a varied range of societal groups when compared to the post-2017 uprisings. The common denominator of the previous unrests and rebellions was a heavy focus on immediate economic demands with a narrow understanding of class oppression separated from gender and ethnic repression. The reason for the Women, Life, Freedom revolt's relative success is its simultaneous rejection of all manifestations of class, gender, and ethnic oppression that serve as the foundation of the theocratic neoliberal regime in Iran. After having shed light on class exploitation as a result of the process of neoliberalisation in the preceding sections, we now briefly look at gender and ethnic discrimination in contemporary Iran to contextualise the Women, Life, Freedom revolt.

With the establishment of the Islamic Republic, the new state gradually imposed mandatory hijab and repealed the top-down reforms in family law of the Second Pahlavi era (e.g., tougher conditions for polygamy, raising the age of marriage for girls to 18, putting divorce under the authority of family courts, giving women custody rights, and easing penalties against abortion). The state offensive against these rights invited hostility, most notably the demonstration on 8 March 1979. That said, in the first decade of the revolution, these demands were pushed aside or at best considered 'secondary issues' by subaltern-class women, who prioritised health, sanitation, education and welfare needs (Mahdi, 2004). Following the end of the war with Iraq and the instigation of neoliberal policies, the situation changed. The reform project ignited optimism among the rising number of young women who sought to overturn the state's exclusionary gender policies and bolster female involvement in both political and economic spheres. Accordingly, women in large numbers cast their vote for Khatami as the emerging rights-oriented Islamic feminism after the war with Iraq viewed the reformist movement as a viable vehicle for pushing back many discriminatory laws against women. However, the consequence of the failure of the reformist movement has been the enduring infringement of fundamental rights concerning the female body. Furthermore, as explained above, a substantial portion of the inactive workforce is comprised of women. Accordingly, young educated women have emerged as a noteworthy segment of the new poor as a result of the process of Iranian neoliberalisation. The exacerbation of the economic crisis since 2012 has resulted in a greater decline in opportunities for labour market participation among numerous ambitious young women who aspire to nothing but a life of dignity and independence. To put it differently, the profound predicament that ensued after 2012 has spurred a radical transformation within the women's movement. Therefore, as the Women, Life, Freedom revolt embodies many of these demands and frustrations, the heightened participation of young women in the uprising does not come as a surprise.

The recent crisis in Iran has also led to a questioning of the Persian and Shi'i-centric nationalist foundation upon which the post-revolutionary state is built. The expensive nuclear programme and support for regional allies, including the Syrian regime and Shi'i militia groups in Iraq, Lebanon and Yemen (see Chapter 7), have come at great cost to ordinary Iranians who are struggling through one of the worst economic crises in modern history. This has caused many people within the country's centre to doubt the validity of the new version of Iranian nationalism as a central tenet of the state's ideology after the revolution. Such doubts have cast light on ongoing ethnic minority oppression that is seen by some as being sustained under this same framework. As expounded in Chapter 3, Khomeini's declaration of 'jihad' against Kurdistan in 1979 triggered a prolonged conflict with the military forces of Kurdish political parties (known as the Peshmerga), and along with the war with Iraq, resulted in an increasing militarisation of the region. These factors, coupled with continued post-war militarisation, have led to dire economic consequences and further underdevelopment of Kurdistan. Consequently, it is justifiable to assert that, since the revolution of 1979, there has been a persistent state of exception in Kurdistan as evidenced by systemic militarisation employed by the central state seeking to maintain control over this territory. Any pro-Kurdish political activity is regarded as a national security issue even during the reformist project which had gained noticeable support from Kurds. The state has pursued similar policies in some other peripheral regions, most notably Baluchestan. The Women, Life, Freedom revolt represents the sole instance of a nationwide mobilisation in Iran since the 1979 revolution that addresses this ethnic oppression. Accordingly, the recent protests throughout Iran have demonstrated newfound solidarity with traditionally marginalised regions such as Kurdistan and Baluchestan and their uprisings – despite government attempts to paint them as threats to national integrity. This represents a shift since Khomeini's 'jihad' against Kurdistan when the Kurdish movement for regional autonomy was met with little sympathy or support from other parts of the country.

Notwithstanding this relative accomplishment, the Women, Life, Freedom movement has encountered significant obstacles both domestically and internationally. Ever since the onset of the uprising, the state has employed disproportionate force to suppress the insurrections in Kurdistan and Baluchestan. However, in the later stage of the revolt, the severity of the state's actions also escalated to an unprecedented degree in the rest of the country. This is exemplified by the execution and sentencing of protesters to death or charging them with capital offences following brief trials devoid of due process. Moreover, in conjunction with this mounting inhumane violence, the state has vigorously intensified its propaganda campaign against the movement, characterising its continuation as a trigger for Iran to become a second Syria. Externally, both global and regional powers have striven to deflect the Women, Life, Freedom movement from a radical critique of the neoliberal order, in a manner akin to how they subdued the 'Arab Spring' revolutionary rupture from below, to reassert counter-revolutionary neoliberal restoration in the region. In this regard, their media outlets have disentangled social and political liberties from economic emancipation, thereby limiting the scope of the Women, Life, Freedom movement to either narrow social freedoms or at best depicting the revolt as a clash between the 'autocratic state' and 'true political and economic liberalisation' (read pro-Western neoliberalisation). Furthermore, a number of these global and regional powers have heavily invested in extremist right-wing political groups (including the former Shah's son and chauvinist forces affiliated with him) as a viable alternative. In addition to being more assertive neoliberals than the existing ruling elites, these Iranian right-wing factions are staunch advocates of a centralised state based on discriminatory Iranian nationalism. Moreover, their highly misogynistic political stance hinders any fundamental attempts at dismantling patriarchy in Iran.

As shown so far, one significant accomplishment of the Women, Life, Freedom movement has been its emphasis on forging connections between the poor and working-class opposition to neoliberalism with women's and ethnic minorities'/oppressed nations' struggles against patriarchy and exclusionary Iranian nationalism. This approach provides a glimmer of hope and a ray of optimism for the future and underscores a crucial aspect of progressive politics that could pave the way towards a fairer tomorrow. However, it is essential to note that merely rejecting all forms of class, gender and ethnic repression by fracturing entrenched patriarchal norms, a century-old Iranian nationalism and unequal economic relations do not ensure the establishment of an inclusive popular coalition capable of transcending the current system and existing deeply ingrained unequal societal structures. To effectively attain this objective, it is imperative to broaden one's perspective beyond the mere identification of grievances, and instead focus on formulating an actionable programme that comprehensively addresses the aforementioned concerns. One fundamental reason for the absence of the emergence of this cohesive sociopolitical programme based on principles of social justice, decentralised democracy and gender equality can be attributed to disagreements among various constituent movements involved in this struggle. Despite having the potential to lead such a coalition, the Iranian working class has failed to do so thus far. In light of this, in the last section of this chapter, we will investigate the obstacles pertaining to the formation of working-class identity and the development of a broad-based coalition spearheaded by the Iranian working class that can bring together and unite all subaltern groups and offer a viable but fundamental solution beyond neoliberalism with sensitivity to interrelated class, gender, and ethnic oppression.

### The challenge of the formation of working-class identity and subaltern broad-based coalition

The instigation of the process of Iranian neoliberalisation in the early 1990s gradually dismantled the post-revolutionary populist relationship between the state and lower classes and made a fertile breeding ground for popular discontent. The two phases of neoliberalisation, coupled with the post-2012 crippling international sanctions, have further alienated the subaltern classes, leading to the unprecedented level of labour militancy and the eruption of protests across the country against the totality of the Islamic Republic, especially after 2015.[14] However, the labour unrests and the eruptions of poor anger during the two rounds of uprisings between 2017 and 2019 seemed to be occurring in parallel without clear connections between them. Moreover, during these popular revolts, 'workers did not emerge as a distinct organised group, nor did cross-class alliances have the chance to develop in the street' (Morgana, 2020). While the Women, Life, Freedom revolt has linked the grievances of women and ethnic minority movements with those based on class, it has not yet been able to establish a cohesive cross-class coalition. Nor has the working class played a prominent role in spearheading the formation of this subaltern coalition amidst the Women, Life, Freedom revolt. In other words, the formation of a working-class identity and the construction of a subaltern broad-based coalition under the leadership of the Iranian working class has remained a major obstacle to the advancement of progressive politics in Iran. To unlock this puzzle, a quick look at the notion of class formation might be beneficial.

From the historical materialist perspective, while relations of production distribute individuals into class positions, this does not imply that class simply equals relation to the means of production. This is merely 'objective class situations' or what is often referred to in Marxist terminology as a 'class-in-itself'. At the same time, 'these situations entail essential antagonisms and conflicts of interest, and they therefore create conditions of struggle. Class *formations* and the discovery of class consciousness thus grow out of the process of struggle, as people "experience" and "handle" their class situations' (Wood, 2016: 80). In other words, the breakdown of the objective relations of production should be the point of departure for any class analysis, 'but this is the beginning, not the end, of class formation' (Wood, 2016: 81). Moreover, sharing common experiences and identifying common interests for people in class ways is always a complex and often contradictory historical process whereby their class situation may give rise to a fully fledged class formation. Relatedly, the formation of classes is not a permanent phenomenon because in the course of history 'every class is always caught up in a process of reconstitution and deconstitution, variation and transformation, emergence or disappearance' (Mohandesi, 2013: 75). Given that resurrection, reanimation and reorientation of their cultural heritage, common experiences and shared traditions in a strategic manner are necessary elements of the process of class formation, the working class makes itself as much as it was made (Thompson, 1963: 194). Two further points need to be highlighted concerning the notion of class formation. First, class as a relationship is not restricted to a relationship between classes but also involves 'an *internal* relationship' among members of the same class (Wood, 2016: 93–4). Second, 'while the structural basis of class formation is to be found in the antagonistic relations of production, the particular ways in which the structural pressures exerted by these relations actually operate in the formation of classes remains an open question to be resolved empirically by historical and sociological analysis' (Wood, 2016: 98).

As documented above, since the early 1990s, Iranian neoliberal restructuring has fundamentally reconfigured the working class and the poor. The central transformation of the working class has been the gradual dominance of casualisation and temporary contracts in the labour market, which made the structural pressures more striking and the exploitative class relation more conspicuous. However, this asymmetrical, antagonistic relationship has not appeared in the same way and with the same intensity throughout this period. During the Hashemi-Rafsanjani, Khatami and Ahmadinejad presidencies, workers protested over pay, casualisation and redundancies and demanded independent unions. Aside from carrying out these protests in the heavy presence of police and security forces, labour activists and trade union leaders were subjected to arbitrary arrests and violence. In recent years, the deterioration of work conditions and the unparalleled vulnerability of workers to the demands of employers alongside the general exacerbation of economic conditions have crystallised in a noticeable surge in the amount of labour unrest. The main demands of workers have largely continued to be better working conditions, wage increases and the reversal of the privatisation of SOEs, but some have pursued radical proposals to bring privatised enterprises under workers' control. Moreover, in solidarity with protesters and as a part of the Women, Life, Freedom movement, workers have persisted in their strikes and other forms of dissent in recent months. These conflicts, struggles and collective organisations have shaped the social experience of some workers in class ways, enhanced their class consciousness and relatively transcended working-class divisive particularities. That said, this is far from the formation of an Iranian working class capable of establishing a working-class hegemony that, in turn, unifies the popular masses against the ruling class and the state. This is because the transformation to a class-for-itself requires the interaction of the naked experience of exploitation with a range of other processes and possibilities that currently seem to be absent.

One key impediment is the enduring difficulty of creating independent labour organisations due to the authoritarian nature of the state. As workers' agitations for the formation of independent unions have amplified, repression of workers has intensified, leading to long-term prison sentences for many trade union leaders and activists[15] on the grounds of 'national security charges such as "gathering and colluding to commit crimes against national security", "spreading propaganda against the system", "disrupting public order" and "forming a group [i.e. independent labour unions] with the purpose of disturbing national security" ' (Amnesty International, 2017).[16] The political repression has not only crucially hindered the creation of political strategies at the national level, which is typically possible in the presence of workers' parties, unions and other organisations, but it has also made the collaboration between workers and other subaltern groups more difficult.

In addition to state repression, another two key obstacles to the formation of an Iranian working class and the creation of a subaltern alliance can be identified. Both impediments are derived from the inability to consider that a vast variety of practices and actions could be perceived as acts of class resistance because capitalist social relations are *not* confined to the immediate relations between capitalists and workers but encompass 'the whole world of production, exchange and distribution, of power and culture' (Barker et al., 2013: 13). First, in contrast to this broader notion of class struggle, the universality of the confinement of capitalist social relations to the immediate relations between capitalists and workers among Iranian labour activists has reduced working-class politics to the fights of blue-collar workers, often in large factories, against the process of neoliberalisation. The immediate upshot of this narrow understanding of social relations in capitalism is the separation of the fights of blue-collar workers from white-collar workers in sectors such as education and healthcare. More importantly, it blocks the possibility of recognising the struggles of farmers, self-employed and informal workers as part of working-class struggles, let alone incorporating the needs and demands of workers whose labour has been commodified in other different ways such as child and unpaid domestic female labourers. In other words, large segments of Iranian informal and informalised labour, similar to many places around the world, 'are not so much engaged in class struggle, as they are still trapped in "struggles over class". They are still fighting to be recognised as a labouring class and develop their own consciousness' (Mezzadri, 2019: 39). This in turn has drastically limited the political horizons of workers and inhibited the effectiveness of their struggles.

Second, the prevalent narrow conception of capitalist social relations has failed to grasp that capitalist rule advances through a process of differentiation and hierarchal re-ordering of the working class along the lines of gender, race, nationality and ethnicity (Virdee, 2019). In other words, the pervasive 'workerist' understanding of struggle among Iranian labour activists has had difficulty with the view that opposition against gender and ethnic oppression is 'not distinct from or opposed to class struggle', but that these are mutually independent parts of the class politics (Barker, 2013: 53). Accordingly, labour activists have done little to form a broad-based coalition that includes the demands of ethnic minorities and women who have been actively involved in the creation of their movements. While the inconsistent rebellion of the poor has been conceived more positively, there is also little evidence that the current Iranian workers' movement has an appetite to organise the poor even if we remove state repression from the equation. Neglecting the demands of the ethnic minorities/oppressed nations is not just problematic for the creation of a subaltern coalition/alliance, but it could also be troublesome for the formation of Iranian working-class identity. In a country that is constituted by several nations in a hierarchical structure, the current crisis has made the already existing acute ethnic tensions more prominent as much as increased labour activism. By inflaming the religious and national sentiments of the dominant nation in the context of external pressure, the ruling class can thus divide the masses to continue to repress the radical politics of oppressed ethnic groups.

## Conclusion

The objective of this chapter was twofold: to reveal the effects of Iranian neoliberalisation on the composition of the subaltern classes and to show the struggles of the working class and the poor against neoliberal reforms. We demonstrated that this process has made the precariat the largest working-class group and engendered the new poor, comprised of unemployed educated young people. We illustrated that workers and the poor have tenaciously resisted privatisation, casualisation, redundancies, overdue pay, the rising cost of living and the elimination of state subsidies since the very early stage of Iranian neoliberalisation, despite lethal coercive practices and unjust legal measures by the security forces and the judiciary. Concerning the workers' movement, we underscored that the creation of independent labour unions and networks and the calls for bringing privatised enterprises under workers' control are of particular importance. Regarding the resistance of the poor against neoliberal reforms, we observed that the severity of the recent economic crisis has fostered total opposition to the existing political order during the latest wave of protests. Although the revival of the workers' movement and the mounting antagonism of the poor were perceived as welcome developments for the formation of a subaltern-class consciousness, we argued that the Iranian working class is not yet in possession of agency and subjectivity to forge a comprehensive subaltern coalition and lead a popular struggle that could challenge the current system to realise a more just new sociopolitical order.

As highlighted throughout the chapter, one key determinant for fuelling the frustration of workers and the poor and augmenting their resentment against the Islamic Republic has been the imposition of devastating international sanctions, particularly US sanctions during the Obama and Trump administrations. In the next chapter, we will survey the internal links between Iranian neoliberalisation, the nuclear programme and the international sanctions.

## Notes

1  This number is calculated based on the 1986 census by combining state employees (including political functionaries), private sector employees and unpaid family workers. For more information about these different groups of the working class, see Nomani and Behdad (2006, 88–106).
2  To calculate the size of the new poor, I used three parliamentary reports of the Islamic Parliament Research Center (2016: 13; 2017a: 18–19; 2017b).
3  Data generated from the World Development Indicators of the World Bank:  https://databank.worldbank.org/source/world-development-indicators (accessed 5 April 2023).
4  The source is no longer available because the security forces closed down the radical left *Problematica* website in 2022.
5  The choice of colour for the movement has nothing to do with environmentalism. Green was initially chosen by Mir-Hossein Musavi for his 2009 election campaign and later became the symbol for protesters as it is the colour of Islam.
6  The civil rights movement account (Dabashi, 2011b; Tahmasebi-Birgani, 2010: 78–86; Rostami-Povey, 2010; Vahdat, 2011) is different from the democratisation thesis in many respects but it is safe to say that in both accounts the middle class is perceived as an avant-garde social class.
7  Author calculations based on the Statistical Center of Iran Censuses for 1886 and 2016.
8  Except for Farhi (2011: 619) who notes that 'the Islamic Republic has given birth to an ideologically differentiated middle class', all the above-mentioned studies conceptualise the middle class as a homogeneous class with one voice.
9  It could be argued that, since the revolution in 1979, the traditional poor, both in rural and urban areas, ideologically and materially have been tied to the bazaar–bonyad nexus and later the military–bonyad complex through charities and revolutionary foundations.
10  The number of cities and towns that witnessed the demonstration is not clear as different sources refer to different numbers. The lowest number is 75 while another estimated 100 cities (Jafari, 2021: 147) and some cases reported 'over 140 cities in every province' (*The Iran Primer*, 2020).
11  It is worth pointing out that Amnesty International (2022) can only document the deaths of 321 protesters during the November 2019 uprisings while the US State Department estimated that the security forces 'killed more than 1,000 people' (*The Iran Primer*, 2020).
12  This section was rewritten in the beginning of 2023, during the ongoing Women, Life, Freedom revolt, despite a decrease in street protests.

13 For an in-depth analysis of the lineages of the Women, Life, Freedom revolt see Sadeghi-Boroujerdi (2023).

14 The anti-regime slogans during the labour protests and the uprisings of the poor are clear indications of this political radicalism since they attacked the economic structure ('Iran, France, Lebanon, Chile ... The same struggle. Down with neoliberalism'), questioned the ability of the ruling class to incorporate the demands of subaltern classes in their various political projects to limit their political horizons in the current conjuncture ('Principlists! Reformists! The game is over!') and targeted the integrity of the state ('Death to the Islamic Republic'). The tone of the slogans has become increasingly radicalised during the Women, Life, Freedom revolt.

15 The list includes the leaders of the Teachers' Trade Association, the Committee to Pursue the Establishment of Workers, the Syndicate of Workers of Tehran and Suburbs Bus Company and the Haft Tapeh Sugar Factory Workers' Union.

16 To highlight the current level of repression against workers, the remark from the supreme leader in February 2018 is illuminating. Labelling the recent labour discords as unsubstantial and having been fomented by enemies of the Islamic Republic inside the country and foreign powers, Khamenei claimed that the anti-Islamic Revolution forces have always attempted to agitate workers against the system, adding that 'one of the major activities of our enemies [the United States and Israel] has been to create a recession and obstacles in our factories and among our groups of labourers – particularly the big ones – so they can provoke the workers' (Radio Farda, 2018). In the Iranian political context, this remark means nothing but a green light for the intensification of repression against labour activists.

# 7

# Neoliberalism and geopolitics: The Iranian nuclear programme, international sanctions and regional policy

In Chapter 4, we briefly touched upon the impacts of geopolitical factors on the process of Iranian neoliberalisation and the emergence of the internationally oriented capital fraction and the military–bonyad complex. This chapter surveys these effects in depth by exploring the links between Iran's nuclear programme, international sanctions and regional policy with the processes of neoliberalism in Iran, the Middle East and globally. This investigation will be advanced based on the theoretical framework developed in Chapter 1 regarding the relations between the internationalisation of capital, imperialism and geopolitics with several main conceptual propositions/claims. To begin with, we argued that because imperialism is the tendency of leading capitals to dominate the world market, and geopolitical confrontations and capitalist development are internally related to each other, we disputed the idea that geopolitical competitions/conflicts do not pertain to the neoliberal processes of capital accumulation at the national, regional and global levels. Moreover, due to the internationalisation of capital that has generated the dialectic of competition and unity of interests between states, we stressed that the relationship between the global centres of power should not be viewed as either continuous rivalry or amicable cooperation. Third, due to the hierarchal structure of contemporary capitalism that permits the global centres of power to deploy geopolitics in order to (re)shape neoliberalism in regions and states for the consolidation of their power, we maintained that the dual tendency of imperial rivalry and consensus provides space for sub-imperial states or peripheral powers to exercise agency in relation to geopolitical tensions.

This chapter situates Iran as a regional power within the dual tendency of rivalry and cooperation between the United States, the European Union, China and Russia in two different periods since the instigation of Iranian neoliberalism: (a) the US triumphalist era between the collapse of the Soviet Union and 2007, and (b) the post-2008 neoliberal global crisis. In each phase, we explore how these global centres of power have utilised the Iranian nuclear programme and economic sanctions to shape neoliberalism in the

Middle East and in Iran. In addition, we document the ways in which the Iranian internationally oriented capital fraction has endeavoured to reach a comprehensive nuclear deal and facilitate rapprochement with the West and the pro-Western regional powers to further integrate into the global chains of American and European international capitals whereas the military–bonyad complex has deployed the nuclear programme, international sanctions and an interventionist regional policy to fully put Iran in line with China and Russia. While this reveals the active agency of the Iranian ruling class fractions in these geopolitical conflicts, the chapter at the same time argues that the lack of total political cohesion of the Iranian ruling class resulting from the tensions between these two capital fractions has to some extent limited the decisiveness of Iran's actions as a regional power.

The remainder of the chapter proceeds accordingly. Drawing on the dialectic of rivalry and unity of interests between the United States, the European Union, China and Russia, the first section navigates the geoeconomic and geopolitical strategies of these global centres of power in the Middle East in the neoliberal era. The following two sections scrutinise the place of Iran in the neoliberal world order and within the context of the complex relations between these core and emerging centres of capital accumulation in order to explore the internal links between the Iranian nuclear programme, international sanctions and regional policy with the internationalisation of capital and neoliberalism during the two different historical periods, namely 1990–2007 and 2008–21. The final section concludes with a discussion of the broader implications of the chapter.

## Post-1990 geoeconomic/geopolitical strategies of the global centres of power in the Middle East

As we discussed in Chapter 3, due to the growing importance of oil for the global economy, the major imperialist powers spearheaded by the United States have attempted to control the Middle East and neutralise any regional challenges since the end of WWII. While this policy continued, in the 1990s and 2000s, the United States strove to reshape national neoliberal programmes and integrate the regional accumulation into GVCs dominated by its MNCs. Through a series of trade and financial initiatives, most notably free trade agreements with the Gulf states, Israel, Egypt and Jordan, Washington aimed at tightening the linkages of regional capital with Western capital, and reconstructing hierarchies within the Middle East in favour of the Gulf monarchies and Israel to consolidate its power (Hanieh, 2013: 33–9). At the same time, to punish regional challenges to its neoliberal economic order, the United States operated military interventions and deployed economic sanctions coupled with the threats of using military force against 'rogue' states in the region, namely Iraq, Iran, Syria and Libya under the name of 'fighting terrorism', 'defending human rights' and 'preventing the spread of weapons of mass destruction'.

The European Union similarly endeavoured to augment its influence by integrating the Middle East and North Africa into European production and trade networks. Accordingly, Brussels initially through the EU–Mediterranean Partnership (EMP) and after 2003 through the European Neighbourhood Policy (ENP) negotiated free trade agreements with Middle Eastern and North African countries such as Egypt, Israel, Jordan, Tunisia, Algeria, Lebanon, Palestine, Syria and Libya (Hanieh, 2013: 39–42). The European Union also endeavoured to facilitate the infiltration of European capital into Iran by entering a series of trade and investment negotiations. In contrast to the United States, the European Union thus viewed Iran, Syria and Libya as part of its strategy of restructuring the region in line with the needs of its MNCs, therefore occasionally contesting US geopolitical measures against these countries. The powerful Franco–German axis within the union that stood up against the US invasion of Iraq despite the support of some other EU members for the military operation was the epitome of this transatlantic rift (Fakiolas and Fakiolas, 2006).

From the early 1990s to 2007, China and Russia's geoeconomic and geopolitical policies in the region revolved around forming linkages with countries outside the US orbit such as Iran, Syria, Libya and Iraq (until the fall of Saddam Hussein in 2003). Russia mostly focused on the sale of military equipment and hardware and security collaboration with these states. For instance, in addition to the commitment to build the Iranian Bushehr nuclear plant, Russia resumed arms sales to Iran in 2000 and 'agreed significant arms deals with Syria in 2005 and Libya in 2007' (Dannreuther, 2012: 550). On the other hand, due to the expansion of its export industries, China predominately regarded the Middle East as the key region to meet its growing energy demands, leading to the surge of China's crude oil imports from the region including the Gulf states (Yetiv and Lu, 2007: 203). Moreover, China's investment in the energy sector of the Middle East gradually became noticeable. As the key site for oil exploration and production, China's oil-related trade and investment in the Middle East thus climbed between 2000 and 2007. Furthermore, alongside purchasing equity stakes in other development projects, China's exports to the Middle East rose exponentially. Against this backdrop, Iran for Beijing was one of the untapped markets in the Middle East and Southeast Asia 'where it did not have to compete for contracts with Western nations, thanks to US sanctions and intimidation (Yacoubian, 2021).

By diversifying its oil and gas imports, the Chinese strategy for the region moved beyond its immediate energy needs after 2008, even though five

Middle Eastern countries were still among the top ten oil exporters to China in 2018 (Saudi Arabia 10.7 per cent, Iraq 10.5 per cent, Iran 7.8 per cent, Oman 7.4 per cent and Kuwait 5.8 per cent) (Wu, 2021: 450). With an increasing economic presence, China has thus striven to meaningfully reorientate the trade and financial flows in the Middle East in its favour. By 2021, as well as being 'the largest trade partner with Iran' and 'the largest source of imported goods for Turkey', China was 'the second largest trading partner of the Arab world as a whole, and the largest trade partner of 10 Arab countries, including Egypt, Saudi Arabia, the UAE, Oman, Iraq, Lebanon, and Sudan' (Wu, 2021: 451). More crucially, through the promotion of the BRI in the Middle East, which strategically connects Central Asia with Europe, 'China stands to achieve several objectives, including energy security, transport connectivity, redefined global supply chains, deepened trade and investment relations with ME [Middle Eastern] countries and promotion of the use of the RMB [renminbi] by the world's largest oil producers' (Kamel, 2018: 78). In particular, because Iran is a major country along the China–Central Asia–West Asia Economic Corridor of the BRI and second largest economy in the region, it is central for the initiative. Being a link between the region and Central and South Asia, Iran is thus a strategic hub for the Chinese land-based Silk Road Economic Belt and the Maritime Silk Road. Furthermore, as the eighteenth largest economy in the world with a robust infrastructure and industrial and diversified economy compared to the Gulf states, Iran is an ideal place for the absorption of China's capital surplus (Kamel, 2018: 85–6). That said, China has pursued a 'strategic ambiguity' and 'hedging' in the region rather than taking a clear position in favour of Iran or other countries outside the Western orbit. A clear indication of this policy is the signing of partnership agreements with most Middle Eastern states (fifteen out of twenty-five), including 'comprehensive strategic partnerships' with Iran, Saudi Arabia and Egypt (Niblock, 2020: 500–1). In addition, the Chinese post-2008 proactive policy in the Middle East has been cautiously framed around trade and investment to prevent becoming publicly mired in regional tensions and rivalries (Burton, 2021: 203).

Since 2008, Russian trade and investment in the Middle East have remained behind the United States, the European Union and China, even though the presence of Russian key sectors such as the agricultural and military-industrial complexes and oil and gas industries in the region has considerably increased (Stepanova, 2018: 51). The whole Middle East has been the main destination for exports of Russian grain with Egypt, Israel and Saudi Arabia among the largest buyers, but Russia's arms sales and gas and oil exploration projects have often centred around 'anti-Western' Middle Eastern states. Concerning the former, the demands from these states have been an indispensable factor for substantial growth in the sale of Russian arms in the Middle East in recent years, ranging from around 10 to 35 per cent of its total arms exports. Following the write-off of the Libyan $4.5 billion debt to the Soviet Union in 2008, Russian gas and oil companies invested in its energy sector, and a major Russian company (Rosneft) and Libya's National Oil Corporation signed a cooperation agreement in 2017. Similarly, as a result of the restructuring of Syria's $14 billion debt to the Soviet Union, Russian energy and infrastructure investments in the country reached $20 billion by 2008. In 2011, a Russian gas firm (Soyuzneftegaz) signed an agreement with Syria for the exploration of its oil and gas fields, and other Kremlin-linked firms have gained lucrative oil profits in Syria since the direct military involvement of Russia in the Syrian war. Russian firms have equally increased their presence in the hydrocarbon exploration projects in Iran, especially following Iran's nuclear deal. Gazprom has intended to assist in the construction of the Iran–Pakistan–India gas pipeline and help Iran to build its first liquefied natural gas plant. In addition to these countries, Russia has also attempted to invest in the energy sectors of some other Middle Eastern countries, such as a $1.5 billion deal for the development of Egypt's oil and gas sector between 2015 and 2017. It has also tried to cooperate with the Gulf states to shape the global flow of hydrocarbons (Kozhanov, 2018: 11–21).

This Russian desire to actively intervene in the energy sectors of these Middle Eastern countries is based on an overarching strategy that aims at preventing Europe from diversifying its heavy reliance on Russian gas and at the same time substantially increasing Russia's gas exports to the Asian markets particularly China (Kozhanov, 2018: 11–21). Accordingly, Russia's interests have been largely limited to its energy sector and arms exports. As this has enlarged its threshold for regional instability, Russia has favoured a more aggressive policy in the region (e.g., the military intervention in Syria, closer relationship with Iran and involvement in the Libyan conflict, among others) despite Moscow's claim of pursuing a policy built around dialogue with all Middle Eastern countries without offering unique guarantees to any regional state or coalition (Burton, 2021: 192). The increasing Russian political and military presence in the Middle East, along with the growth of the economic role of China, has encouraged the confidence of Iran as a sub-imperial power to intervene in regional crises. The Russian assertiveness in the region in the last decade should also be viewed in the context of America's strategy of the 'pivot to Asia' and the so-called 'retrenchment from the Middle East'.

In the post-2008 global economy, the containment of China has made the Asia-Pacific region a key priority for the United States. Moreover, the preservation of European security and stability has become vital for the European Union and to some degree the United States following the

Russian annexation of Crimea and the invasion of Ukraine (Karlin and Wittes, 2019). Yet the United States and the European Union have maintained their upper-hand position in the Middle East despite these extra-regional challenges and the growing influence of China and Russia in the region. We should also bear in mind that Chinese and Russian ambitions have not brought about total unity between the two sides of the Atlantic in the Middle East as Washington and Brussels' occasional strong disagreements and rivalries can be witnessed for instance in their divergent views/positions on the Iranian nuclear programme. Washington has continued the policy of deepening the connections between regional capital and American capital and the maintenance of the regional hierarchy in favour of its allies, namely Israel, the oil-producing Gulf regimes and other Arab states such as Egypt and Jordan. The pronounced EU presence in the region has equally been sustained since 2008 and the flows of investment between Europe and Middle Eastern countries have remained above the flows between China and the Middle East thanks to the EMP and the ENP (Niblock, 2020: 498).

Although there are similarities with past policies, the shock and severity of the 2008 financial crisis on the US and EU economies, coupled with the Chinese economic and Russian military challenges, have forced Washington and Brussels to amend the means to achieve their objectives in the Middle East. Concerned with China gaining too much economic ground in the region, the United States has 'sought to prevent ties between Beijing and its regional allies and partners from advancing past a point where they may adversely affect American regional interests'; this has included pressurising Israel and the UAE to limit their cooperation with China in recent years (Burton, 2021: 191). By the same token, the Europeans have striven to minimise the impact of Chinese involvement in the Middle East, but their level of influence to exert pressure on the regional allies is still behind that of the United States (Burton, 2021: 191).

One major change in US policy in the region since 2008 is the replacement of direct military engagement and large-scale deployment of boots on the ground with (i) wide-ranging economic sanctions with devastating impacts and (ii) a 'leading from behind' strategy. With regard to the former, as we explained in Chapter 1, the United States and the European Union have increasingly and with different magnitudes deployed economic sanctions to counter the economic rise of China and the return of the military power of Russia. Besides directly targeting these emerging empires, the United States and the European Union have used economic sanctions to block the entire world from trading with targeted 'rogue' states to destabilise and overthrow them or force them to accept policies in favour of American and European capitals. Iran and Syria have been the main targets of these sanctions in the region, but aggressive US sanctions have had more debilitating effects due to the centrality of the dollar in the global economy.

Through the leading from behind strategy, the United States has encouraged regional allies and European partners to deal with their challenges and share the burden of regional military and security costs (Ahmadian and Mohseni, 2021: 786–7). While some read this as indicative of US retrenchment – if not abdication – in the Middle East, which has created anxieties and uncertainties among the Gulf states (Niblock, 2020: 497), there is little evidence that the United States has abandoned its commitments as the security guarantor of these regimes/states. Rather, all post-2008 US administrations have cautiously avoided taking the lead in dealing with the post-Arab Spring crises in Libya, Syria, Yemen, Bahrain, Egypt and elsewhere by calling their allies to take initiatives and shoulder their responsibilities (Gerges, 2013: 322). Trump was strikingly similar to his predecessor despite utilising different rhetoric about the Middle East and having a different preference for regional powers (Karlin and Wittes, 2019). Whereas the Obama administration was critical of the Gulf monarchies for ' "free-riding" on US security guarantees and regional policies' and often viewed Turkey as a suitable regional power to fill this role (Ahmadian and Mohseni, 2021: 786–7; Gerges, 2013: 318), the Trump government heavily favoured the traditional allies, i.e., Saudi Arabia and Israel. Accordingly, the Trump administration was a pivotal force behind the Abraham Accords to deepen economic and diplomatic relations between Israel and the Gulf states and other pro-American Arab countries. For the administration, not only would the Abraham Accords further normalise relations between Israel and the Arab world but they were also viewed as a tool to contain China and Iran (Burton, 2021: 196). Trump's support for the creation of an 'Arab NATO' as a security alliance among six Gulf states, Egypt and Jordan should be viewed as part of this attempt (Karlin and Wittes, 2019).

Against this backdrop, Turkey and Saudi Arabia have become proactive and risk-taking players, embarking on more activist foreign policies in the Middle East and North Africa region. The autonomous actions of these regional powers have largely been in coordination with the United States, but at times they have defied Washington, which reflects the reality of 'regional powers' or 'sub-imperial' states as we explained in Chapter 1. This has manifested itself more than anything else in the Gulf Cooperation Council (GCC) and Israel's open opposition against the so-called US tilt towards Iran during the Obama administration and their active endeavours to undermine and revoke the 2015 nuclear deal (Ahmadian and Mohseni, 2021: 787). Nevertheless, the intervention of the bloc of the Gulf capital led by Saudi Arabia has been a decisive factor in taming the Arab Spring revolutionary rupture from below and reimposing the counter-revolutionary neoliberal restoration in the region in favour of the United States and the European Union.

Whilst the post-2008 transformations in the global economy – the relative decline of the United States and the European Union, the economic rise of China and the military retrieval of Russia – have affected the economic and political dynamics in the Middle East, the patterns of rivalry and tacit/explicit cooperation between the global centres of power to deal with the region have continued. Because 'China's interests in the Middle East are more multidimensional and multifaceted, owing to economic exchange that is both widening and deepening across a range of different sectors', Beijing has recognised the vitality of stability. Given this, China has shown more diligence in its relations with the United States, the European Union and the regional powers to expand its influence and realise its interests in the Middle East. In contrast to these Chinese multidimensional and multifaceted economic interests in the region, Russia's limited economic interests in the Middle East have enabled Moscow to take more risks with regional instability in order to challenge the United States and the European Union (Burton, 2021: 192). Again, this should not be characterised as an incessant enmity since Russia has cooperated with the United States and the European Union in the region whenever their interests have aligned. In the next two sections, by situating Iran within these policies of the great powers and the dialectic of rivalry and cooperation between them in the Middle East during these two periods (1990–2007 and 2008–21), I shall explain the links between Iranian foreign policy, its nuclear programme and interrelated sanctions with the internationalisation of capital and neoliberalism.

## Geopolitics and Iranian neoliberalism during the US triumphalist era (1990–2007)

In line with the newly initiated process of neoliberalisation, the government of Hashemi-Rafsanjani (1989–97) embarked upon a new foreign policy that defied the 1980s' isolationist approach and hostile attitude towards the West. In a radically different interpretation, the new government thus declared that integration into the world community is the prerequisite of Iran's sovereign independence (Ramazani, 2012: 9). To this end, as a result of the compromise between the bonyad–bazaar nexus and the neoliberal wing of the stratum of government managers at the early stage of neoliberal restructuring, the government attempted to diminish the Islamist leftists' propaganda in favour of the export of the revolution in the region and controlling the IRGC's overseas activities. In addition, it took a pragmatist policy regarding the first Gulf War despite Saddam's unilateral offer to restore the 1975 border agreement and to give Iran everything they wanted 'in return for its support against the common enemy' (Sick, 2011: 362). Furthermore, the government reinstated ties with regional powers and made serious efforts to restore relations with Europe and downgrade hostility towards the United States. As an instance of sending positive gestures to open channels with Washington, President Hashemi-Rafsanjani remarked that 'I have always been opposed to completely breaking our ties with the United States. They provide us with much needed spare parts and we sell them petrol. Therefore, our economic ties have never been completely halted and some kind of dialogue must always exist' (cited in Forozan, 2015: 175).

As explained in Chapter 4, the compromise between the government and the bonyad–bazaar nexus broke down after 1992 and the internal fight exacerbated during Hashemi-Rafsanjani's second term in office from 1993 to 1997, resulting in the resurgence of terrorist activities that sabotaged the government's rapprochement with the West. The IRGC and the security forces assassinated a Kurdish opposition group leader in the Mykonos restaurant in Berlin in September 1992, attempted to assassinate Salman Rushdie's Norwegian translator in October 1993, and allegedly planned the bombing of the Jewish centre in Buenos Aires in July 1994 and of US installations at the Khobar Towers in Saudi Arabia in June 1996 (Arjomand, 2009: 164; Forozan, 2015: 176). While Hashemi-Rafsanjani and his close associates endorsed similar actions before the start of neoliberal reforms, the government considered them damaging in the context of the new direction of foreign policy after 1990. To make the situation worse, the Fifteen Khordad Foundation declared in February 1997 that the bonyad would increase the blood money for the assassination of Salman Rushdie from US$2 million to US$2.5 million. Although the government reaffirmed that the bonyad had no bearing on official foreign policy, the foundation's statement prompted an international outcry (Buchta, 2000: 6).

During this period, the Hashemi-Rafsanjani government exploited the frictions between the European Union and the United States on Iran. Encouraged by Iran's stance about the Iraqi invasion of Kuwait, the European Union advocated the normalisation of relations with Tehran as an essential step for the stability of the region. Therefore, under the framework of the 'critical dialogue', the Union entered talks with Iran in 1992 to enhance economic relations conditioned upon the improvement in human rights, finding a resolution for the Rushdie issue and ceasing terrorism (Dryburgh, 2008: 257–8). By the mid-1990s, the European Union had become Iran's main trading partner, counting for 36 per cent of its exports and 40 per cent of its imports (Ehteshami, 2017: 199). With major disagreements regarding trade, geostrategy and the position of the Iranian moderates in the state, the United States pursued the policy of dual containment[1] contrary to the

European Union's critical dialogue. By viewing the initiation of neoliberal reforms and the rise of moderate forces in the country as constructive developments, the European Union challenged US efforts to punish the Iranian state collectively, labelling it as an 'unhealthy obsession with Tehran'. The United States justified its policy by insisting on the inability of the Iranian government to control the overseas terrorist actions of the radicals inside the state and the allegation of acquiring nuclear weapons (Sabet-Sadie, 2012: 60–1; Drenou, 2012: 79). To put pressure and isolate Iran, in addition to its long-standing embargo, the Clinton administration passed unilateral extraterritorial sanctions in 1996, known as the Iran-Libya Sanctions Act, with the aim of penalising any international firm that would invest more than \$40 million in the energy industries of Iran and Libya. Alienated by the US action, the European Union then openly opposed the imposition of these sanctions and threatened to take the United States to the WTO (Arms Control Association, 2013: 76). The European Union withdrew the complaint after ultimately resolving the matter diplomatically, but subsequently 'the United States did not declare a foreign company to be in violation of the U.S. sanctions against Iran for more than a decade' (Gordon, 2013: 982).

While the Mykonos verdict in April 1997 seemed to put the European Union and the United States on the same side following the suspension of the critical dialogue and recalling of European Member States' ambassadors to Tehran, Khatami's victory in May 1997 under the platform of a liberal project at home and détente in foreign relations changed the situation. In harmony with the interests of the emerging internationally oriented capital fraction, the Khatami government (1997–2005) intended to align with the post-Cold War order by advocating the 'dialogue of civilisations' and calling for breaking the wall of distrust between Tehran and Washington (Ehteshami, 2017: 200–1). Beyond the rhetoric, the new administration found a diplomatic resolution for the Rushdie issue that led to the resumption of full diplomatic relations between Iran and the United Kingdom for the first time after the revolution (Rundle, 2012: 97). This was followed by the rapprochement with Saudi Arabia, cooperation with the United States in its fight against the Taliban, a post-war political settlement in Afghanistan (Joyner, 2016: 20; Clawson and Rubin, 2005: 152–3) and endorsement of King Abdullah's peace plans by stating that Iran would not stand against a two-state solution if it was acceptable to Israelis and Palestinians (Arjomand, 2009: 123; Rundle, 2012: 100). Against these efforts, the IRGC, security forces and revolutionary foundations actively undermined the reconciliation policy of the government. The assassination of several prominent writers and dissidents in 1998 and the detention of a few Iranian Jews on espionage charges caused vocal international condemnation (Axworthy, 2012: 110–11). Whereas Iran officially supported King Abdullah's peace plans, the IRGC sent arms to the Palestinian groups without the knowledge of the government. In contrast to the government approval of the American-led coalition attack on the Taliban, a number of al-Qaeda leaders fleeing Afghanistan were sheltered at IRGC bases (Arjomand, 2009: 165–6). While the government searched for common ground to take part in the political process of post-invasion Iraq, the IRGC, through its Quds Force that is responsible for its extraterritorial operations, orchestrated 'guerrilla warfare against invasion modelled on a decentralised-defensive doctrine known as the Mosaic doctrine' (Forozan, 2015: 183).

Notwithstanding its concerns over the negative role of the 'hardliners' inside the Iranian state,[2] the European Union welcomed the new direction of Iran's foreign policy by resuming talks under the name of the 'comprehensive dialogue'. The central part of the negotiations was a discussion over the expansion of trade and investment, framed as the Trade and Cooperation Agreement (Kaussler, 2008: 269–72). By promising to support Iran's accession to the WTO, the European Union viewed the negotiations as an essential means for a deeper liberalisation of the Iranian economy that could further facilitate the entrance of European capital (Kaussler, 2013: 22). In contrast, the new Iranian government's détente policy only led to a few US conciliatory statements about the 'regrettable' American role in the 1953 coup d'état against Musaddiq and its 'imprudent' Iraq–Iran war policy. The remarks by the Secretary of State Madeleine Albright on the necessity of bringing down the walls of mistrust between the two states also accomplished nothing (Clawson and Rubin, 2005: 151–2, Sick, 2011: 368). In fact, despite promising to waive sanctions against foreign firms investing in the Iranian oil industry and lift restrictions on the sale of agricultural and medical goods and civilian passenger aircraft parts (Sick, 2011: 367–8), the Clinton administration 'did not take any meaningful steps to lift the sanctions' (Sahimi, 2021: 179).

The tensions between the United States and the European Union over Iran intensified after George W. Bush took office in 2001. The new American administration soon named Iran a member of the 'axis of evil' under the charge of pursuing weapons of mass destruction, exporting terror and denying its people's hope for freedom (Joyner, 2016: 21). This was part of the Bush Doctrine that emphasised pre-emption and reliance on military power and unilateralism to reshape the Middle East in line with the US neoliberal economic and political order (Simpson, 2016: 25–34). Under the auspices of this doctrine, 'the United States arrogated to itself the right to employ pre-emptive military intervention as a tool of counter-proliferation and to effect regime change as a means of ensuring disarmament' (Takeyh, 2004: 54) which resulted in the invasion of Afghanistan and Iraq. Against this backdrop, the revelation of the scale of the Iranian clandestine nuclear programme in June 2002 provided the pretext for the intensification of aggressive US rhetoric and threats to use military force against Iran (Ehteshami, 2017: 166–7, 209–11).

Iran resumed work on its pre-revolutionary nuclear programme after the end of the war with Iraq.[3] The IRGC was put in charge of the nuclear and missile programmes as part of the post-war compromise to ensure the compliance of military forces with the government. Throughout the 1990s, the IRGC's intelligence units 'were reportedly involved in the acquisition of military materials and nuclear weapons' from abroad and built 'ties with a wide range of organisations, such as defence industry organisations, university laboratories and companies engaged in Iran's nuclear research' (Forozan, 2015: 189, 181–2). With a strong hold over Iran's national defence policy that bypassed the government, the IRGC publicly reprimanded Khatami's rapprochement policy, dialogue of civilisations and signing of chemical and nuclear non-proliferation because of their failure to withstand the threats from 'America and international Zionism' (Forozan, 2015: 182). While the secret nuclear programme and its allegedly military aspects (Fitzpatrick, 2006: 8–11) profoundly weakened the government's détente policy, the Khatami administration allegedly offered the United States a 'grand bargain' initiative to deal with all unresolved issues between them, including the nuclear programme, regional insurgent groups such as Hamas, Hezbollah and al-Qaeda, the Arab–Israeli peace process and the post-war Iraq and Afghanistan political settlements in May 2003 (Kaussler, 2013: 23–4). Since the violation of the Nuclear Non-Proliferation Treaty obligations provided a desirable basis for the neoconservatives within the United States to tighten the military pressure on Iran (Arjomand, 2009: 127), Washington rejected the offer. Hence, the Iranian government turned to the European Union for a diplomatic approach to the crisis given the escalation of tensions between Europe and the United States following the invasion of Iraq. The European Union warmly received the call for talks by the Iranian government on the grounds of avoiding another war.

In this context, the Foreign Ministers of Germany, France and the United Kingdom jointly visited Tehran in October 2003 while the Bush administration aggressively pursued the referral of Iran's dossier to the Security Council (Kaussler, 2013: 29). As a confirmation of its good intentions, the reformist government of Khatami agreed to completely suspend uranium-enrichment activities, implement the Additional Protocols of the International Atomic Energy Agency (IAEA) and provide a wide-ranging account of its nuclear activities (Clawson and Rubin, 2005: 142). This was followed by the November 2004 Paris agreement through which Tehran voluntarily decided to extend its suspension of all nuclear enrichment-related and reprocessing activities in return for the resumption of the Trade and Cooperation

Agreement negotiations with the European Union for the deepening of economic ties, support of its application to join the WTO and placing the Iranian dissident group (the People's Mojahedin Organisation of Iran) on the list of terrorist organisations (Drenou, 2012: 81; Simpson, 2016: 46). The coinciding of the deal with the re-election of Bush with the promise of completing his 'mission' in the Middle East led to the swift rejection of the Paris agreement by the United States in February 2005 (Arjomand, 2009: 168). Frustrated with the Bush administration, the European Union blamed the United States for the failure to construct a workable nuclear accord, as Jack Straw, the then British foreign secretary, explicitly voiced in 2013: 'had it not been for major problems within the U.S. administration under President Bush, we could have actually settled the whole Iran nuclear dossier back in 2005, and we probably wouldn't have had President Ahmadinejad as a consequence of the failure as well' (cited in Oborne and Morrison, 2013; see also IRNA, 2017). In a visible indication of using the nuclear programme for their advantage, the internationally oriented capital fraction encouraged the European Union to intensify its efforts because, according to a top Iranian diplomat, the Iranian government desired to 'move closer to the West and wants European business, especially in the energy sector, to invest' but the way Iran was being treated by the United States 'was playing into the hands of the fundamentalists in Tehran'. The Iranian Embassy in London similarly portrayed the coercive foreign policy of Bush as a dangerous strategy that would move Iran 'to go down the same path as North Korea rather than towards "Westernisation"' (cited in Kaussler, 2013: 28).

The EU position decisively changed during the second phase of Iranian neoliberalisation under the Ahmadinejad presidency. In the first phase of neoliberalisation from 1989 to 2005, Europe's policy was geared towards the normalisation of relations with Iran and backing of the moderate and pragmatist political forces within the Iranian state who pursued the détente policy. Moreover, Europe lambasted the US sanctions and criticised the flip-flopping of the Clinton government and the hardline stance of the Bush administration against Tehran. Given the high level of trade between Iran and the European Union in the 1990s and the early 2000s, this position should come as no surprise. Besides this growing commercial relationship, Iran was also viewed as one of the best potential destinations for European foreign investment due to the availability of a large pool of cheap skilled labour power and access to cheap inputs such as land and raw materials, most notably oil and gas, as well as intermediate goods thanks to the presence of a large number of domestic small and medium-sized enterprises. The Ahmadinejad victory amended the EU normalisation policy towards Iran because, as far as Brussels was concerned, in the words of a European diplomat, 'Iran had entered a tricky phase following the [2005 presidential] elections. It could no longer be said there was a range of views within Iran's ruling elite – all institutions are now in the hands of the hard-line/radical camp' (cited in Kaussler, 2013: 42). According to the European Union, this transformation inside the Iranian state dictated a new tougher policy towards Iran in the form of international sanctions. While still publicly asserting the likelihood of military action against Iran, the Bush administration was also practically left with the imposition of international sanctions as the best realistic option following the publication of the United States National Intelligence Estimate report regarding Iran's nuclear weapons programme in 2007.[4] Hence, the European Union's push for tougher non-military measures against Tehran in the control of 'anti-Western hardliners' brought Brussels and Washington closer on Iran.

As explained in Chapter 4, Ahmadinejad came to power on a platform of anti-corruption that depicted the liberalisation policies of the two previous administrations and Khatami's compromise over the Iranian enrichment rights as indications of a treacherous retreat from the pledges of the 1979 revolution. In the context of US intimidation and constant threats of regime change and invasion, by portraying the 'indigenously' developed nuclear programme to be as historically important as the nationalisation of the Iranian oil industry, the new government effectively provoked 'popular indignation and demands for the assertion of Iran's national rights and dignity' (Arjomand, 2009: 169). Predictably, throughout Ahmadinejad's tenure, a security-oriented approach to foreign policy that intended to halt further integration of Iran into the global economy was implemented, in line with the rising power of the military–bonyad complex. With strong nationalist and Islamic revolutionary themes, the new administration pursued public diplomacy that aimed to conquer the hearts of Muslims in the region who loathe the US military interventions and dispute the legitimacy and actions of the Israeli state. Accordingly, in a series of deliberately antagonistic remarks against Israel, Ahmadinejad dismissed the two-state solution. He also challenged the authenticity of the Holocaust by depicting it as a myth fabricated for the creation of an illegal and illegitimate state and questioned the right of the existence of Israel by stating that 'it must be wiped off the map' (Axworthy, 2016: 140–1; Ehteshami, 2017: 220–1). These comments generated strong opposition and outrage in the West. Regarding the nuclear issue, the new government immediately abandoned the Paris agreement and declared that it was resuming the uranium-enrichment programme in August 2005 (Simpson, 2016: 47). Another significant element of their strategy was to extend challenges against the US military and its political agendas in the Middle East. In so doing, with the IRGC's increasing role in defence and foreign policy following the replacement of the bureaucrats of the previous administrations with its veterans' personnel, the Quds

Force intensified its support and links with Iraqi and Afghani militia and insurgent groups, encouraged and heavily sponsored Hezbollah's military campaign against Israel in summer 2006 and signed military and strategic treaties with Syria two years later (Forozan, 2015: 185–6).

This position triggered the referral of Iran's case to the United Nations Security Council (UNSC) in February 2006. Subsequently, three Security Council resolutions were unanimously passed during Ahmadinejad's first presidential term. The first round of the UNSC sanctions targeted certain entities and individuals related to the nuclear and ballistic missile programmes such as the Iranian Atomic Energy Organisation (UN Security Council Resolution 1737, 2006). The central targets of the second resolution passed in March 2007 were the IRGC-affiliated entities and key individuals connected to the nuclear programme (UN Security Council Resolution 1747, 2007). Iran's rigid stance invited the third Security Council Resolution in early 2008 that extended sanctions on a few Iranian banks with alleged links to the nuclear programme and instructed an asset freeze on various state officials (UN Security Council Resolution 1803, 2008). Ahmadinejad disdainfully labelled the first round of UNSC sanctions as a 'worthless piece of paper' and the supreme leader described it as 'an opportunity' for the development of an independent national economy (Borszikp, 2014: 10). This is because these sanctions were in line with the rising power of the military–bonyad complex as they facilitated the halting of Iran's integration into the Western-centred international system. Consequently, the Revolutionary Guards and bonyads justified the unparalleled expansion of their economic activities in all economic sectors as a response to the international sanctions and facilitation of 'economic resistance' and 'self-reliance'.

Contrary to the internationally oriented capital fraction that viewed the European Union as a potential partner against the aggressive Bush policy, the Ahmadinejad administration conceived the emergence of new centres of accumulation and political rivalries as significant developments, therefore decisively turning to Russia and especially China after distancing itself from the European Union and lambasting the United States (Sabet-Saeidi, 2012: 57). The military–bonyad complex perceived Beijing as a potential strategic partner by recognising the rise of China as a real phenomenon. More precisely, due to the prominence of maintaining the free flow of oil and natural gas for the economic development of China, the Ahmadinejad government insisted that Iran's energy reserves would be more important than ever for Beijing. In the possible conflict between China and the United States in the future, there was a belief that, because the entire Middle East apart from Iran is under the control of the United States, the only 'independent and secure' country in the region that could provide the energy demands of China without the influence of Washington would be Iran (Ghafouri,

2015). As explained above, since this was in line with China's policy towards the Middle East during this period, Beijing attempted to maximise these opportunities offered by the international sanctions. The alignment of China and Iran under the role of the military–bonyad complex resulted in a sharp hike in the imports of Iranian crude oil and major Chinese investments in the exploration and production of several critical gas and oil fields in Iran (Yetiv and Lu, 2007: 203–4). In particular, after the gradual withdrawal of European companies, the China National Petroleum Corporation dominated the Iranian oil and gas industry and dictated the rules of the game in the absence of competition from Western energy corporations. As a result, Iran was among China's top three sources of oil imports, while China was the leading destination for Iranian oil exports (around 25 per cent of its oil exports) (Calabrese, 2018: 175; Yacoubian, 2021). Coupled with an unparalleled export boost of Chinese industrial products to Iran, China had thus replaced the European Union as Iran's top trading partner by the end of the 2000s (Aizhu, 2012).

## Geopolitics and Iranian neoliberalism since the 2008 global financial crisis

### *Crippling sanctions and the nuclear deal (2008–16)*

As outlined above, in the post-2008 global economy, the United States and the European Union have used extensive crippling economic sanctions as a new method for imposing their will. To deal with the Iranian nuclear programme, the Obama administration set in motion the so-called 'dual-track approach' of direct engagement coupled with harsher sanctions (Joyner, 2016: 44–9). In the first step, this resulted in the UNSC Resolution 1929 in June 2010 that further prohibited Iran's access to proliferation-sensitive items, technical assistance and technology (Arms Control Association, 2013: 13). While all post-2006 UN Security Council resolutions on Iran, for the most part, used explicit and binding language to target its ballistic missiles and nuclear weapons proliferation, they contain 'other non-binding terms, terms that are not part of the operative provisions at all, or terms that sound innocuous and vague' such as 'exercising vigilance' (Gordon, 2013: 991). In the second step and more crucially, by invoking the use of this vague and ambiguous language in these resolutions, the United States introduced extremely broad and damaging unilateral sanctions after 2010 to debilitate the Iranian economy (Gordon, 2013: 991–6). To target Iran's key sectors, namely the oil and financial and banking sectors, the Obama administration and Congress passed a series of sanctions between 2010 and 2012 whereby the various US extraterritorial sanctions were extended. Besides subjecting foreign firms involved in the Iranian oil industry to serious restrictions that limit their access to the US market or services, these sanctions imposed financial sanctions on foreign banks that would conduct transactions with all Iranian banks. The objective was to 'cripple Iran's energy sector, its access to global banking, its ability to generate revenue from oil sales, and its capacity to ship goods of any sort' (Gordon, 2013: 982). Likewise, the European Council passed several devastating sanctions, most notably the sanctioning of all Iranian banks, including the Central Bank, and denying Iran access to SWIFT in 2012, which to a large degree cut off the country from the international economic system (Arms Control Association, 2013: 13–19; Davenport, Himball and Thielmann, 2015: 38–9).

After the revolution, Iran was constantly under the US sanctions regimes, but the banking and financial sector was not targeted and oil exports continued without many restrictions. In fact, not only was Iran able to sell its oil during the war with Iraq, but the United States also never ceased its oil imports from Iran. For instance, 'the United States was the largest purchaser of Iranian oil in the early 1990s, taking around 30 per cent of Iran's oil exports' (Ahmadian and Mohseni, 2019: 348). The new harsh restrictions on Iran's key sectors compelled the state to actively look for novel ways to circumvent the sanctions. Accordingly, Iran devised numerous 'illegal' methods, including smuggling routes via Turkey and the United Arab Emirates that also involved other countries such as China. To this end, Iran used Dubai's free trade zones to repackage, reprocess, or modify goods that provided cover for firms evading sanctions (Bridenthal, 2021: 324). As a result, 'contraband goods accounted for a quarter of Iran's total imports, including 83 per cent of mobile phones, 47 per cent of toys, 27 per cent of clothing and apparel, and 21 per cent of house appliances' by late 2012 (Yıldız, 2021: 605). Moreover, to sell its oil, 'Iran discreetly transported shipments to China and other Asian countries by renaming and reflagging its vessels. By July 2012, Iran was using more than 60 tankers – roughly two-thirds of its tanker fleet – to store up to 40 million barrels of crude oil at sea while it located buyers' (Yacoubian, 2021). Relatedly, many high-level Iranian state officials and businessmen engaged in smuggling gold and dollars through Dubai and Istanbul to free up the payments of its oil from buyers (Yıldız, 2021: 615–18).

Alongside the circumvention of the sanctions, the Ahmadinejad government intensified its attempts to strengthen what they refer to as the 'axis of resistance' in the region to further challenge the military and political agenda of the United States and its regional allies. Following the 2003 Iraq War, the military–bonyad complex was actively involved in the construction of the 'axis of resistance' as a geopolitical bloc that included Syria, Iraq, Hezbollah and some Palestinian resistance groups (Mohseni and Kalout, 2017). Given that the initial regional uprisings in 2011 mostly occurred in the pro-US secular dictatorships, the military–bonyad complex viewed the Arab Spring as an opportunity, therefore hailing it as an 'Islamic awakening' modelled on the Iranian revolutionary success (Ahmadian and Mohseni, 2019: 249). This led to the support of the transition of power in Egypt, Tunisia and Yemen to the Islamist groups and the heavy backing of Shi'a uprisings in Bahrain. However, during the Arab Spring, among these states, only Yemen provided a space for Iran to extend the sphere of the 'axis of resistance' by supporting Ansar Allah – a majority Shi'a Islamist political and armed movement informally known as the Houthis. In contrast to recognising the revolts elsewhere as Islamic awakenings, the military–bonyad complex framed the Syrian uprisings as a foreign plan that aimed to alter the regional balance of power against Iran. Contrary to the political forces linked to the internationally oriented capital fraction who publicly denounced the Syrian regime and highlighted the atrocities committed against its people, the military–bonyad complex vehemently defended Bashar al-Assad as the key figure of the 'axis of resistance'. The IRGC Quds Force thus intervened in the Syrian civil war to change the balance of force in favour of the Ba'ath regime. During the Ahmadinejad government, the IRGC initially deployed the strategy of establishing local militias and later incorporated transnational fighters in the war effort in Syria (Ahmadian and Mohseni, 2019: 355–8).

Neither the regional interventions to solidify the 'axis of resistance' nor the use of the black and grey markets and other circumvention methods with the help of China alleviated the impacts of the crippling sanctions, which promptly aggravated the economic conditions to the point of a catastrophic crisis. With an over 50 per cent reduction in Iran's oil exports to less than a million barrels a day in 2012, which cost the country more than $5 billion in lost revenue every month (Arms Control Association, 2013: 17), inflation and unemployment had exponentially surged. Coupled with the plunge of the value of the national currency against the dollar by more than half, 'purchasing power had dropped by 72 per cent', 'prices rose by over 40 to 50 per cent on average after 2010' and 'the country's GDP contracted by over 5 per cent a year in 2012 and 2013' (Ehteshami, 2017: 232). Hence, in a complete U-turn on the previous comments that described the 2006–07 sanctions as worthless pieces of paper, Ahmadinejad admitted in the parliament in 2013 that this new set of US and EU sanctions were 'the most extensive … sanctions ever' and 'the heaviest economic onslaught on a nation in history' because 'every day, all our banking and trade activities and our agreements are being monitored and blocked' (cited in Gerges, 2013: 319).

The imposition of these devastating sanctions called into question the foreign policy of the Ahmadinejad government, especially its nuclear stance. The policy intended to facilitate control of the military–bonyad complex over a large segment of the Iranian economy by hampering the entrance of Western capital and linking Iran's economy to China. While the approach practically functioned until 2010, the international pressure ultimately turned it on its head even though the Revolutionary Guards benefited from the circumvention of the sanctions in the short term due to its control over the maritime and territorial borders (Yıldız, 2021: 611–13). In the long term, not only did the sanctions curb the economic interests of the military–bonyad complex as they directly targeted its major entities such as Khatam-al Anbiya, but they also threatened the integrity of the state and jeopardised the survival of the Islamic Republic system. In addition, the international sanctions considerably altered the balance of power in the society in favour of the internationally oriented capital fraction by opening up spaces for moderate political forces to promote yet again the necessity of direct negotiations with the major powers, even the United States, to dismantle the nuclear-related sanctions and reverse Iran's economic and diplomatic isolation. Along with the political ramifications of the Green Movement that discreetly improved the position of the internationally oriented capital fraction inside the state, as examined in the previous chapter, this international pressure set the stage for the sweeping victory of Hassan Rouhani in the 2013 presidential election.

The new administration used the power of the ballot box as a political card to enter negotiations with the major powers, including the United States, as the newly appointed Foreign Minister Javad Zarif highlighted: 'In our recent presidential election, which was a proud manifestation of the ability of an Islamic model of democracy to bring about change through the ballot box, my government received a strong popular mandate to engage in constructive interaction with the world, and particularly with our neighbours. We are dedicated to making use of this mandate to instigate change for the better' (cited in Ehteshami, 2017: 237). Accordingly, just a few months after the inauguration, the new Iranian nuclear negotiation team entered talks with the P5+1 (the five permanent members of the Security Council plus Germany) in Geneva, reaching a provisional agreement named the Joint Plan of Action in November 2013. As part of this interim agreement, Iran suspended uranium enrichment above the 5 per cent level, halted working on its heavy-water reactor and building new centrifuges and agreed to allow UN inspectors daily access to its facilities in exchange for US$6–7 billion in sanctions relief from the United States (Joyner, 2016: 60). This successful first round of negotiations, which facilitated a direct dialogue between Washington and Tehran for the first time since the revolution, put in place a mechanism that precipitated a definitive agreement. Subsequently, Iran and the P5+1 signed the Joint Comprehensive Plan of Action (JCPOA) in Vienna in July 2015 (Simpson, 2016: 132). Under the JCPOA, Iran committed to putting significant limits on the development and expansion capacity of its nuclear programme, which practically diminished the possibility of building nuclear bombs. This included reducing the uranium-enrichment level to less than 3.67 per cent, decreasing the number of operational centrifuges from 20,000 down to under 6,000 and accepting the continuous supervision of existing sites and unrestricted access to other facilities on request, among others (Axworthy, 2016: 172; Simpson, 2016: 133; Joyner, 2016: 62–3). In return, the P5+1 and the European Union vowed to coordinate the lifting of the post-2006 economic and financial sanctions on a gradual basis depending on the fulfilment of Iran's obligations.[5] Less than a week later, on 20 July 2015, UNSC unanimously endorsed the JCPOA by adopting Resolution 2231.

Described as the best enforcement mechanism for the nuclear deal, the Iranian government advocated intertwined economic ties with the world, particularly Western countries, in the shortest possible time (BBC Persian, 2015b). In line with this, even before the IAEA approval of Iran's commitments, during a business opportunities event in Austria a few days after the deal, the Iranian Minister of Industries and Mines presented a pro-market package to 400 potential investors from Europe, the United States and Asia to encourage foreign investors. By referring to Iran's remarkably liberal Foreign Investment Promotion and Protection Act of 2002, Namatzadeh 'promised his audience that basically everything except the country's national oil company theoretically was for sale' (Erdbrink, 2015). In the same meeting, to ensure the trust and confidence of foreign investors, he reiterated the determination of his government to restrict the economic activities of the military forces and revolutionary foundations (BBC Persian, 2015a). This enthusiasm for greater economic integration was shared by European counterparts more than by other parties as several ministers accompanied by numerous economic delegations from Germany, France, the United Kingdom and Italy visited Tehran shortly after the accord, declaring their strong interest in the rejuvenation of commercial relationships with Iran. China seemed to be another major beneficiary as the deal would facilitate Chinese investments in Iran under the BRI framework. With the announcement of the IAEA in January 2016 that Tehran met the necessary conditions for the implementation of sanctions relief, the influx of international firms to Iran was precipitated (Axworthy, 2016: 173, 180). Accordingly, until the American withdrawal from the nuclear agreement in May 2018, hundreds of lucrative deals were signed with Iran in almost all sectors of the economy, including oil and energy, finance and banking, insurance, aviation, automobile and infrastructure.[6] It is useful to recall that Iran's economy is 'surprisingly diverse' since 'the oil and gas industry made up only 10 per cent of GDP in 2014' with 'around 30 other sectors listed on the stock exchange'

(Webb, 2016). While European firms led the race, China's direct investment in many sectors of the Iranian economy also increased by 20 per cent from March 2014 to late January 2018 (Kamel, 2018: 84). Russian oil and gas firms were also 'among the first companies to return to Iran in 2015–16' (Kozhanov, 2018: 17).

By interpreting the JCPOA as a move that could reshape the Middle East against the long-term US strategy in the region in favour of the GCC, Israel and other Arab allies, Riyadh and Tel Aviv reacted negatively to the accord on the ground that it only temporarily postponed Iran's desire to build nuclear weapons. Inside Iran, some political forces affiliated with the military–bonyad complex also condemned the Rouhani government for giving too much ground to the United States and the European Union that would expose the country to Western influences (Ehteshami, 2017: 241). Three key elements of the JCPOA included: (a) the cessation of the application of economic sanctions against Iran's oil industry; (b) the termination of sanctions against the banking sector to allow Iranian banks and firms to reconnect with international financial systems such as SWIFT; and (c) the complete opening up of the Iranian market for the entry of MNCs. The military–bonyad complex supported the first two elements because the integrity of the state was in jeopardy without oil exports and access to the global financial system. Although the military–bonyad complex considered that the deal would help to realise the potential of the Chinese BRI and augment the role of Russia in Iran to unleash its national and regional ambitions, the infiltration of American and European capitals was viewed as a threat. At the very least, they considered it as the means for the consolidation of the power of the internationally oriented capital fraction inside the Iranian state at their expense. Given this, besides attempts to hinder the entrance of Western capital following the signing of the JCPOA, the military–bonyad complex 'sought to balance the successful outreach to the West under the administration of the moderate President Rouhani by engaging more closely with Russia against the United States and EU' in Syria and Yemen 'to prevent Iran from moving too close to a western orbit' (Ahmadian and Mohseni, 2019: 359). With the direct military involvement of Russia, the IRGC thus drastically enlarged its operation in Syria after 2015. Equally, the IRGC's support for the Ansar Allah evolved into a partnership following the post-2015 Saudi Arabian-led intervention in Yemen. Hence, the provision of political support and military assistance of the IRGC Quds Force has gradually strengthened Ansar Allah to achieve military and political dominance in Yemen in recent years (Ahmadian and Mohseni, 2021: 792–6).

The Iranian nuclear deal has been considered the epitome of international cooperation among the global centres of power, but it can only be fully grasped in the context of the dialectic of rivalry and cooperation in the post-2008 global political economy. The Obama administration's response to the rise of China was the 'pivot to the East'. Accordingly, in order to divert the focus from the Middle East to the Asia-Pacific region, Washington encouraged Europe and its regional allies to take a more active role to manage the post-Arab Spring crises. Another significant aspect of this strategy was the intensification of US efforts to solve the Iranian nuclear crisis by deploying unprecedented sanctions and building an extensive coalition under the name of multilateralism. Since the United States and European sanctions impeded China's investments in Iran and indirectly hampered the realisation of the BRI in West Asia due to the importance of Iran to the Silk Road Economic Belt and the Maritime Silk Road, Beijing was compelled to cooperate with other great powers to advance its economic and strategic interests. The sanctions also made it difficult for Russia to expand its influence in Iran. In light of this, China and Russia were deeply involved in the talks on the Iranian nuclear issue, and were key parties in the JCPOA (Wu, 2021: 453). In addition, the post-2008 global financial crisis necessitated the finding of new, fresh avenues for capital accumulation of American, European and Chinese firms.[7] Of less significance, the appetite of Russian companies to enter Iran was also evident as Moscow made it clear during the negotiations that Russia only 'agreed to hold the US$1 billion project at the Bushehr nuclear facility [Iran's oldest nuclear site]' in exchange for 'a substantial stake in Iran's economy' after the sanctions (Kaussler, 2013: 31). Against this backdrop, the opening of the Iranian market through resolving the nuclear programme was considered to be 'an economic game-changer, providing global investors' access to one of the most promising markets in the developing world' (Heydarian, 2015). The then UK Secretary of State for Business, Sajid Javid, explicitly articulated the desire of European capital to enter the country by arguing that post-sanctions Iran would be 'the biggest opportunity among the emerging markets in the last quarter century' (Pickard and Mance, 2016; see also BBC Persian, 2016b). Due to their traditional trade links that made their return easier and quicker, European and Chinese companies anticipated that they would be the main winners of the nuclear accord. In particular, Europeans were sanguine because of their close ties with the Rouhani government.

### Building closer ties with China and Russia amid the reimposition of US sanctions (2017–21)

The Obama and Trump administrations shared the necessity of the pivot to the East to curb the influence of China and preserve US supremacy. However, in contrast to Obama's return to multilateralism in international affairs dictated by 'the costly "war on terror"', the shock of the global financial crisis and the growing problem of the massive federal debt' (Gerges, 2013: 302), Trump embraced militant unilateralism, especially in the form of economic sanctions. In regard to the Middle East, like the Obama government, Trump refrained from taking a lead and demanded collective responsibilities for dealing with ongoing grave regional crises. Nevertheless, in a completely different approach to the Obama administration, Trump depicted the JCPOA as 'the worst deal ever negotiated' that harmed US regional allies and emboldened Iran and China. To the delight of Israel and the GCC, particularly the Saudis, who perceived the nuclear deal as 'a larger shift in U.S. strategy on Iran' and feared marginalisation 'in consideration of the future order in the Middle East' (Ahmadian and Mohseni, 2021: 787), Trump promised to dismantle the JCPOA as his priority.

Once in power, the Trump administration used all opportunities to portray Iran as an existential threat to Israel and the Gulf States. In the first place, this led to the authorisation of an arms deal worth $110 billion between the United States and Saudi Arabia in 2017 that hugely advanced the interests of the US military and defence industries. As part of a series of deals between the two countries with a total value of US$380 billion within ten years, the then US Secretary of State, Rex Tillerson, claimed that the arms agreements would ensure the long-term security of the entire Gulf region 'in the face of malign Iranian influence and Iranian-related threats which exist on Saudi Arabia's borders on all sides' (cited in Aljazeera, 2017). In the second step, to force Iran to accept its proposed 'grand bargain' that included the nuclear and ballistic missile programmes and its regional role, the United States pulled out of the nuclear accord and reimposed sanctions in May 2018 (Fleming and Manson, 2018). The administration demanded twelve tough conditions for the renegotiation of the nuclear deal (Aljazeera, 2018), which, according to a European diplomat, 'If the Shah was in power, he wouldn't [agree to] all these things [either]' (England and Bozorgmehr, 2019). Under a maximum pressure campaign that aimed to fully isolate Iran and cut its oil exports to zero, the reimposed US sanctions went even further than the previous ones. While initially offering short-term exemptions for some countries including Japan, South Korea, China and India to still import Iranian oil, the Trump administration ended sanctions waivers in April 2019 following negotiations with Saudi Arabia and the UAE to minimise the impact of the elimination of Iranian oil in the market (Sevastopulo et al., 2019). The United States also amplified its efforts to prevent Iran from circumventing the sanctions, including pressure on the UAE government to crack down on Iran's sanctions-busting (Bridenthal, 2021: 324). Moreover, the United States designated the IRGC, including its Quds Force, as a foreign terrorist organisation and sanctioned the supreme leader and the then Foreign Minister. As a result of the reimposition of sanctions – that were not even relaxed at the height of the COVID-19 pandemic – 'Iran's economy that had grown by about 13.4 per cent in 2016, contracted by about 6 per cent in 2018 and another 6.7 per cent in 2019. The rate of inflation that was 7.2 per cent in 2016, jumped to 18 per cent in 2018 and 40 per cent in 2019' (Sahimi, 2021: 183). The crisis played a crucial role in triggering the post-2017 series of uprisings, as discussed in the previous chapter.

To deal with the new US administration, the Rouhani government initially utilised Trump's threats to secure his victory in the 2017 presidential election. The political representatives of the internationally oriented capital fraction constructed the duality of 'Rouhani or war' that convinced the public that voting for the rival candidate Ebrahim Raisi (the then head of the powerful Imam Reza Shrine Foundation) would precipitate the prospect of war (Hamshahri Online, 2017; Shariatmadari, 2017). Internationally, in early May 2019, the Rouhani government gave Europe, Russia and China a sixty-day ultimatum to develop a mechanism for Iran to sell oil and conduct banking transactions before leaving the deal (*Financial Times*, 2019b). More than other parties, the Iranian government tried to use the European Union's dissatisfaction with the US withdrawal to save the JCPOA due to Brussels' repeated references to the nuclear deal as a key tool for the stability of the region that pledged to rescue it (see for example *Financial Times*, 2019a). The tension between Brussels and Washington over the nuclear deal resulted in the setting up of a trading mechanism INSTEX (Instrument in Support of Trade Exchanges) by the European Union to bypass US sanctions and continue trade with Iran under the JCPOA (Bridenthal, 2021: 323). However, the attempt largely failed because the continued importance of the dollar and the US market forced almost all European firms to leave Iran – including 'France's Total, Airbus, and PSA/Peugeot; Germany's Allianz, and Siemens; Denmark's Maersk, Italy's Eni; Japan's Mazda and Mitsubishi UFJ Financial Group; and the UK's BP'[8] – to escape Washington's punitive measures.

In contrast to the European Union's timid moves, this time China and Russia have more actively helped Iran to circumvent US sanctions. In recent years, Russia launched 'its "oil-for-goods" programme that exchanges Iranian oil for Russian machinery and investments'. Under this scheme, acquiring several million tonnes of Iranian oil annually to be sold by Russia internationally would allow Moscow to supply Iran with billions-worth of goods (Kozhanov, 2018: 17–18). Apart from adopting the Russian-made alternative to Visa, Mir bank cards (Reuters, 2022), Iran is expected to be an important part of the System for Transfer of Financial Messages that Russia has been developing to replace SWIFT (Beal, 2021: 40). The reluctance of Chinese firms to leave Iran after the reimposition of the sanctions has made them a US target. Consequently, 'two major Chinese telecommunication companies ZTE and Huawei have faced severe penalties from the U.S. over their trade ties with Iran' (Shariatinia and Azizi, 2019: 993) and the Zhuhai Zhenrong Co., a state-run energy company, along with other five Chinese companies and six Chinese nationals were sanctioned by the US Treasury in 2019 for having 'knowingly engaged in a significant transaction for the purchase or acquisition of crude oil from Iran' (Yacoubian, 2021). China has also facilitated Iran's resumed subterfuge and financial trickery to sell its oil, including keeping Iranian oil in bonded storage to allow 'Tehran time to find a buyer in Asia without payment of tariffs or other duties' (Yacoubian, 2021). As part of the efforts to circumvent the sanctions, Iran has deployed other methods such as turning off identification systems, changing the names and identification numbers and stopping reporting the positions and their tankers. Iran has also offered discounts to Asian buyers; for instance, it cut the price of its light crude 'by $1 per barrel, approximately 30 cents a barrel lower than Saudi Arabia's light crude' in 2019. As a result, 'Iran's oil shipments to China had returned to pre-sanctions levels' by 2021, accounting for 'five per cent of China's oil imports' (Yacoubian, 2021).

The return of crippling economic sanctions and designating the Revolutionary Guards a foreign terrorist organisation has put the military–bonyad complex in a strong position within the Iranian state. The new US policy put the IRGC in a better position in terms of public opinion 'by saying they are directly targeted by the enemy', according to an IRGC-affiliated business executive (cited in Williams and Bozorgmehr, 2019). It has also offered opportunities for the military forces and the revolutionary foundations to expand their grip on the economy in a more favourable international environment. For instance, the development of phase 11 of the South Pars gas field was handed to the Ghorb to replace French Total despite enormous previous efforts of the Rouhani administration to curb its economic influence, which led to the arrest of some senior members and business associates of the IRGC (Khalaj, 2019). More crucially, the return of US sanctions profoundly invigorated the 'axis of resistance' strategy and the 'Look East' foreign policy approach of the military–bonyad complex. By pointing to the reimposition of sanctions, the IRGC has found valid justifications for the appropriateness of its involvement in Syria, Yemen, Iraq and Lebanon to sabotage the interests of the United States and its allies in the region, which has meaningfully increased in recent years thanks to the assertiveness of Russian policy in the Middle East. The sanctions also called into question the 'Europe-oriented' foreign policy approach of the internationally oriented capital fraction that emphasised 'the necessity of balancing Chinese influence through expansion of relations with the European Union and the United States' and argued that 'the EU has a key role in preserving the JCPOA and its subsequent economic Benefits' (Shariatinia and Azizi,

2019: 992). The signing of the 25-year Iran–China agreement in March 2021 and the victory of Ebrahim Raisi in the June 2021 presidential election were the major outcomes of this power shift. Under the 25-year agreement, Iran and China signed a $400 billion trade and military partnership for tighter economic relations in oil, infrastructure, telecommunications and banking (Bridenthal, 2021: 325).

The US departure from the JCPOA put Washington against Brussels and triggered more active Chinese and Russian roles in the circumvention of the Iranian sanctions, but this should not be interpreted beyond the dialectic of rivalry and cooperation between the global centres of power in the Middle East. Despite their attempts to undermine the US decision, the European Union, China and Russia have always called for the return of the United States to the deal. The European Union still views the JCPOA as the best mechanism for acquiring the Iranian market for its international capital. As far as China is concerned, the return to the full implementation of the nuclear accord is the safest mechanism for the fruition of its interests in the Middle East. China signed the 25-year agreement with Iran and the pro-Sino military–bonyad complex is currently in control of the Iranian state institutions, but so far only Chinese companies without ties with the global financial system and the Western markets have shown interest in investing in Iran. Given this, some commentators have raised well-placed scepticism about the feasibility of the 25-year Iran–China agreement due to its negative implications for China's larger strategy of global engagement and economic development, including the strategic ambiguity or hedging in the Middle East. Under this strategy, China has built 'substantial relations with Saudi Arabia, Israel, and a number of other Iranian neighbours and regional rivals'. Even though Iran is an important component of this larger strategy, China is reluctant to put 'all of its eggs into one basket' (Figueroa, 2022). Perhaps, Russia has more than other global centres of power endeavoured to build closer relations with Iran, but one could equally argue in favour of the benefits of the revival of the JCPOA for Russia, at least until the invasion of Ukraine in February 2022. As some powerful forces within the US state, including the new Biden administration, have viewed the withdrawal from the Iran nuclear deal as a major deviation from the pivot to the East strategy, the resumption of talks between the P5+1 and Iran to revive the JCPOA since April 2021 should not come as a surprise.

## Conclusion

This chapter has navigated the relationship between Iranian neoliberalism and geopolitical tensions with the West. We have shown that the history of the last few decades of Iran's nuclear programme and related economic sanctions, along with other geopolitically related issues such as the charge of terrorism and regional instability, is the clear manifestation of the interiority of relations between geopolitics and the internationalisation of capital/ neoliberalism. After revealing that the internationalisation of capital dictates the dialectic of rivalry and unity of interests between major centres of capital accumulation, we explained the geoeconomic and geopolitical strategies of the United States, the European Union, China and Russia in the Middle East since 1990. Under the strategy of reshaping the hierarchy of the Middle East in line with the interests of its international capital, we argued that the United States has pursued aggressive policies to marginalise Iran. In the post-2008 era, there have been some major differences to curb the Iranian 'threat', such as solely concentrating on the nuclear programme or constructing a more comprehensive deal that also includes Iran's regional interventions and missile programme. But ultimately, the various US administrations have similarly deployed the imposition of crippling sanctions to solve the Iranian dilemma, which can be read as part of attempts to enable the 'pivot to the East' strategy. We documented that the European Union has from time to time contested these US geopolitical measures as they have fettered Europe's attempts to deepen economic ties with Tehran. Perceiving the internationally oriented capital fraction as a strategic ally and Iran as an ideal place for the investment of European capital, Brussels has unwaveringly utilised all geopolitical tensions to open up the Iranian market. On the other hand, we illuminated that Russia and China's economic and political influences in Iran have significantly enlarged since 2008 because Iran is an important location for the realisation of the Chinese BRI project and Russia views the involvement in the Iranian gas and oil industry as crucial for its overarching strategy of dominating the global gas market. However, both countries have so far resisted the temptation of building real partnerships with Tehran given their strategically ambiguous policy in the Middle East that has simultaneously enhanced relations with Iran's regional rivals such as Saudi Arabia and Israel. That said, Russia's higher thresholds for confrontation with the United States and the European Union resulting from its relatively limited integration into the flows of trade and investment in the Middle East have, in turn, enabled the military–bonyad complex to extend its regional interference. In the end, this has resulted in a complex geopolitical game of rivalry and cooperation between the global centres of power to influence the processes of neoliberalism in Iran and the region in favour of the interests of their international capital.

The chapter has also substantiated that Iran, as a regional power, has endeavoured to use the dual tendency of imperial rivalry and consensus over geoeconomic and geopolitical tensions. More specifically, due to the lack of political cohesion within the Iranian state, we demonstrated that the internationally oriented capital fraction and the military–bonyad complex have often differently deployed the nuclear programme, international sanctions and regional policy. The internationally oriented capital fraction has taken advantage of the nuclear programme by disseminating the danger of a short-sighted glorification of the programme as a national achievement without considering the impacts of devastating economic sanctions and the possibility of devastating war. At the same time, it has used the nuclear programme to bargain with the European Union and the United States for further economic integration into Western-dominated GVCs. Under the 'Europe-centred' foreign policy, the internationally oriented capital fraction has thus tried to reduce the influence of Chinese capital in Iran. On the other hand, the military–bonyad complex has been the major force behind the development of the nuclear programme, the construction of the 'axis of resistance' strategy and the 'Look East' approach to foreign policy. These policies have aimed to challenge the interests of the United States and the European Union in the region, curb the inclusion of Iran into the circuit of European and American capital and put Iran in the orbit of China and Russia. It is important to note that both capital fractions have ditched their disagreements whenever the integrity of the whole state was under threat, such as during the crippling Obama sanctions and Trump's maximum pressure campaign.

## Notes

1  The dual containment strategy was the US official foreign policy to curb the threats of Ba'athist Iraq and revolutionary Iran in the 1990s.
2  The Head of the Iran Section of the Foreign and Commonwealth Office of the United Kingdom between 1998 and 2000 sums up this battle inside the Iranian state: 'through this period, we felt as though we had been invited to dinner by a warring couple. As we tried to enter the door, one of them was trying to open it and welcome us in, while the other was trying to jam it shut again' (Axworthy, 2012: 109).
3  The nuclear programme was instigated by the Shah in the 1970s but halted in the aftermath of the revolution. Saddam's use of unconventional weapons during the Iran–Iraq war led to speculations over its restoration in the mid-1980s, but this never materialised (Bowen and Kidd, 2004: 263–4).
4  The US National Intelligence Estimate report in 2007 on Iran's nuclear weapons programme radically mitigated the credentials of claims for a military intervention against Tehran. The report specified that 'we judge with high confidence that in fall 2003, Tehran halted its nuclear program', while adding that 'Iran has the scientific, technical and industrial capacity eventually to produce nuclear weapons if it decides to do so' (cited in Simpson, 2016: 58–9).

5 For a detailed account of the key requirements and actions mandated by the JCPOA for involved parties, see Davenport, Himball and Thielmann (2015: 35–6).

6 For a detailed account of foreign investments in Iran after the nuclear deal see Reuters (2017) and BBC Persian (2018c; 2018d).

7 It is worth reiterating that Chinese capital, especially through its state-owned enterprises, has become increasingly integrated into international circuits of capital, including global networks of production, finance, trade and infrastructure. For instance, three Chinese state-owned enterprises are in the top five companies in 2022 (Fortune Global 500: http://fortune.com/global500/list/ (accessed 5 April 2023)).

8 For a comprehensive study of the impacts of the return of US sanctions on foreign investment in Iran, see Adesnik and Ghasseminejad (2018: 1–47).

# 8

# Conclusion: Future paths under the crisis of neoliberalism, the changing global order and revolts from below

This book has set out to explore the political economy of Iran in the era of neoliberal global capitalism. To this end, it embarked on the critique of existing methodological nationalist studies that ignore the questions of capital accumulation and class formation. To overcome internalism and offer an original account of the development of capitalism in contemporary Iran, the book adopted the radical social ontology of the philosophy of internal relations. Conceptually, therefore, the dominant thread of argument throughout this work has been built upon a global perspective with a focus on a dialectical method that problematises the dualism of internal/external and local/global. This social ontology provided a ground for the construction of the historical materialist approach of the study that called for the inter-related conceptualisation of the production and reproduction processes, class modality, state formation and geopolitics. The perspective allowed us to trace the neoliberal transformation of the country since the early 1990s, but rather than focusing merely on the documentation of neoliberal policies, it advanced a scrutiny of the ways in which the process has underpinned the patterns of class and state formation. Accordingly, it demonstrated how the implementation of neoliberalism has brought about new contested class dynamics that have fundamentally reconstructed the ruling class and aggressively shaped/reshaped other social classes, particularly the working class and the poor. The framework also offered an opportunity to analyse how the same process has generated a fresh, pivotal impetus that has altered the state apparatuses and institutions and directly contributed to Iran's volatile foreign policy, in particular opposing approaches regarding the nuclear programme, relations with the global centres of power (the United States, the European Union, China and Russia) and regional policy.

After examining the longue durée of the emergence and consolidation of capitalism in Iran, we showed that the second Pahlavi capitalist restructuring based on ISI strategy continued during the first decade of the revolution from 1979 to 1989 despite the formation of the new Islamic state and the major transformation in the composition of the ruling class with two wings (the stratum of government managers and the bonyad–bazaar nexus). We then contended that the crisis of the late 1980s, which resulted from the impasse of the ISI strategy and the direct and indirect geoeconomic and geopolitical pressures from the United States, jeopardised the integrity of the state. Against the background of the global neoliberal revolution, some state officials propagated a radical renovation of the economic structure that challenged ISI and the inward direction of the economy, thereby leading to the instigation of Iranian neoliberalism. Empirically, we substantiated that the dialectics of the external and internal and continuity and change gave rise to the formation of the internationally oriented capital fraction (between 1989 and 2005) and the reconstruction of the bonyad–bazaar nexus into the military–bonyad complex (between 2005 and 2013). Their competing approaches to the economic development of the country and the international movements of capital have produced a peculiar form of development characterised as 'hybrid neoliberalism'. In addition to the recomposition of the ruling class, we also found out that the reconstitution of the working class and the poor as a result of the process of neoliberalisation has gradually dismantled the 1980s' populist relationship between the state and the lower classes. This has resulted in continuous struggles of workers and the poor against neoliberal policies that have exponentially grown in number and geographical spread in recent years. In the first place, besides problematising a clear boundary between state capital and private capital, our tracing of the construction of different fractions of the ruling class and their accumulation strategies challenges the prevailing accounts of power in contemporary Iran on the grounds of the categories of religious and revolutionary elites. Moreover, the analysis of class formation serves to redirect our focus to the economic system of capitalism and paves the way for the rethinking of the origins of social and political power and resistance.

By linking the state institutional and ideological reorganisation to Iranian neoliberalisation, this book has revealed that the process has consolidated the institutional division of power (elected and appointed institutions) and led to the rearticulation of contesting 'liberal/democratic' and 'revolutionary' discourses of Islam. We also learned that both formal state institutions and civil society organisations have been battlegrounds for the struggles of the internationally oriented capital fraction and the military–bonyad complex for mastery and leadership in the society, including disputes over free elections, a free press, electoral fraud and the legality of the electoral preselection procedure. This new conceptualisation of the Iranian state and its institutional divisions of power by looking at the internal links between the process of class formation and the nature and form of the state fundamentally calls into question the conventional line of argument that justifies the institutional division of the state on the grounds of the existence of incompatible ideological stances of revolutionary elites. This approach further makes it unattainable to conceptualise the Iranian state as a government within a government.

Finally, this book has maintained that the internationalisation of capital/neoliberalism and geopolitical tensions are internally related to each other. It further characterised the relationship between major capitalist states as the dual tendency of imperial rivalry and cooperation and asserted that the dynamics of superpower relations offer peripheral powers the chance to deploy geopolitical disputes to their advantage. By situating Iran within the geoeconomic and geopolitical policies of the United States, the European Union, China and Russia in the Middle East in two periods (1990–2007 and the post-2008 era), we reached two main conclusions. First, to shape the processes of neoliberalism in the Middle East and Iran in line with the interests of their international capital, these global centres of power have deployed different policies while at the same time cooperating when collaboration has been conceived as necessary and ideal for all sides. Second, since the internationally oriented capital fraction has been the major advocate of closer links between Iran and the West, it has intervened in the disputes over the nuclear programme and international sanctions to facilitate the entrance of Western capital into Iran, particularly European capital. In contrast, by perceiving the economic rise of China and the return of the military power of Russia as an opportunity, the military–bonyad complex has constructed a combative stance on the nuclear programme and related sanctions and attempted to forge the anti-Western 'axis of resistance' in the region to block the integration of Iran into the circuit of Western capital. This approach deeply challenges the analyses of these geopolitical tensions through a containment lens (e.g., Waltz, 2012; Betts, Sagan, and Waltz, 2007) based on the artificial detachment between political economy and military-security interests or identity (e.g., Moshirzadeh, 2007; Mohammadnia, 2011) on the grounds of the separation of material and ideational structures. Furthermore, it overcomes the charge of subliminal Eurocentrism by incorporating the agency of the non-West in the study of geopolitics.

## Determining factors of future paths

The aggressive neoliberal reforms of the state and US sanctions as the prominent socioeconomic and geopolitical factors that have contributed to an explosive political and economic crisis in Iran in recent years are still in place. Whilst the outbreak of coronavirus was instrumental in the halt of the nationwide anti-state protests in late 2019, the effects of the COVID-19 pandemic in the midst of one of the toughest US sanction regimes have aggravated the ongoing crisis. The ecological catastrophes in Iran in recent years in the form of large wildfires, heatwaves, droughts and air pollution have added a new dimension to the crisis and have triggered major environmental protests for some time.[1] Against the backdrop of this multidimensional crisis of Iranian capitalism, we conclude our discussion by looking at three determining factors that could potentially influence the direction of the country in a considerable way in the coming years. These are the continuation of conflicts between the ruling class fractions within the state for power, the struggles from below, and the future of the Iranian nuclear deal.

The latest episode of the intra-class conflict within the state manifested itself in the management of the pandemic. In April 2020, the Iranian government under the presidency of Rouhani requested a $5 billion emergency loan from the IMF to fight COVID-19, which was supported by the European Union (Al-Shamahi, 2020). Predictably, the United States under the Trump administration blocked the loan, but considering the conditionality of the IMF loans, this shows the willingness of the internationally oriented capital fraction to deepen neoliberal restructuring and further integrate Iran into the Western-dominated world order. By contrast, in addition to pushing for the signing of the 25-year agreement with China, the supreme leader banned the import of US and British COVID-19 vaccines in favour of Chinese and Russian vaccines (Hafizi, 2021). At the same time, the supreme leader authorised and promoted homegrown vaccines by enterprises affiliated with the military–bonyad complex, leading to the development of CovIran Barakat by the Barakat Foundation (a subsidiary of the Setad), Noora by the IRGC and Fakhra by the Ministry of Defence, among others (Sinaee, 2022). With the election of Ebrahim Raisi as the new president in 2021, most of the state institutions are under the control of the military–bonyad complex. The greater assertiveness of the military forces, particularly the IRGC, in managing the economy and domestic and foreign policies points to a gradual decline of the power of the internationally oriented capital fraction within the state. That said, the past experiences invite caution because the crackdown of the 2009–11 Green Movement by the IRGC and the security forces was interpreted by many commentators and analysts as the final move to consolidate total state power in the hands of the military forces and revolutionary foundations. However, the victory of Rouhani in two presidential elections (2013 and 2017) with a huge mandate demonstrated the power of the internationally oriented capital fraction to mobilise the population against the military–bonyad complex. With the control of a big chunk of the economy and influence over some powerful state institutions such as the Expediency Discernment Assembly and the Supreme Council for National Security, it is unwise to write off the ability of the internationally oriented capital fraction to challenge the military–bonyad complex despite the recent erosion of the appeal of electoral politics as its optimal political game.

Until the Dey protests of 2017 and 2018, it can be argued that oppositional politics was centred on the vote, in which 'each ballot and electoral triumph' was interpreted as 'a step towards securing a politics less cruel, less absolute' (Malekzadeh, 2020). The internationally oriented capital fraction and its political representatives (initially reformists and later moderates) were pivotal in the creation, maintenance and continuation of this political game of the 'virtuous cycle of elections'. This managed electoral politics has been replaced by an emerging cycle of protest from below and violent counter-demonstration from above. Since the nationwide Aban uprising of 2019, protests by factory workers, teachers, farmers, pensioners, the unemployed and environmental, ethnic and women activists have continued. In accordance with the oppositional politics of recent years, these protests have occurred across the country in both big cities and provincial towns. In more recent months, specifically since September 2022, the 'Women, Life, Freedom' revolt has prompted a further cycle of nationwide demonstrations, which have been met with a brutal and systematic crackdown by the state. These recent protests share a great deal in common with the Dey and Aban protests in that young demonstrators, discontented with the deterioration of their living conditions, have targeted the entirety of the system (Engelbrecht and Fassihi, 2022). That said, the Women, Life, Freedom movement has been relatively more successful than previous uprisings in bridging the gap between class-oriented appeals and those centred on the rights of other marginalised groups such as women and ethnic minorities. Although the outcome of the ongoing unrest is difficult to forecast, it is certain that the Islamic Republic has not experienced such persistent resistance from below since its inception. More importantly, the revival of grassroots politics against electoral politics is likely to have long-term implications for the fate of the system.

The lifting of US sanctions can potentially mitigate the pressure from below. With Joe Biden in office, talks between Iran and the P5+1 to salvage the 2015 nuclear pact have resumed since April 2021. Like the previous US administrations since 2008, the Biden government has deployed wide-ranging economic sanctions and the 'leading from behind' strategy. In the context of the Middle East, the new US government has again encouraged the regional allies to take more responsibility and endeavoured to solve the Iranian crisis while restoring the wide-ranging sanctions of the Trump administration. Despite the resumption of the talks, reaching a new agreement seemed to be difficult since the initial demands of the new US administration were similar to the proposed 'grand bargain' or 'comprehensive deal' of the Trump administration. In contrast to the terms of negotiations during the Obama government,

Biden initially insisted on including Iran's missile programme and regional policy as part of the deal. This effort to reach a 'comprehensive' agreement move relatively satisfied the antagonists in the United States and the region, such as Israel and Saudi Arabia, but its rejection by the Iranian state hindered any real progress. In recent months, the global energy crisis following the Russian invasion of Ukraine has forced the Biden administration to drop these demands except for the removal of the IRGC from the list of terrorist organisations. While this has facilitated the grounds for the resumption of the JCPOA in full, two factors still delay bringing it to fruition. The invasion of Ukraine, which invited tough US and EU sanctions against Moscow, has altered the Russian position on Iran's nuclear deal. Accordingly, Russia has conditioned its approval on ' "written guarantees" from the United States that wide-ranging Western sanctions targeting Moscow over its invasion of Ukraine would not affect its economic and military cooperation with Iran' (DW, 2022a). In addition, Iran has demanded guarantees that the United States will not withdraw again from the deal (VOA News, 2022).

This does not mean reaching an agreement is impossible, especially given the EU's push because of the energy crisis and China's support, but the primary issue lies in the likelihood of the implementation of such a deal. On the US side, the resumption of the JCPOA that excludes Iran's missile ambition and regional interventions would attract some powerful opposition forces in the United States and the Middle East (i.e., Israel and Saudi Arabia). In addition to this, in the view of its opponents, the pact would enable China to further dominate Iran and the Middle East, contradicting the spirit of the 2021 and 2022 G7 summits that aimed to counter China's rise through the Western 'Partnership for Global Infrastructure and Investment' initiative (Reuters, 2021; DW, 2022b). Hence, the legal unfeasibility of a provision that guarantees that the United States will not pull out of the deal again indicates that future US administrations can withdraw from the JCPOA. On the Iranian side, while selling oil freely and reconnecting with the international financial systems would be welcomed, the military–bonyad complex has more incentives to tighten the links with China and Russia under the 'Look East' policy as a long-term guarantor of Iranian economic and political ambitions. Iran's robust support for the Russian invasion of Ukraine, its successful accession to full membership in the Shanghai Cooperation Organisation, and the invitation to join BRICS[2] underscore this preference (Aljazeera, 2022; Reals and Wassef, 2022). Thus, opening the Iranian market to Western capital as a pivotal element of the deal would emerge as a key sticking point since the Raisi administration could deliberately hamper the entrance of European and American investment in favour of the Chinese counterpart under the BRI and the 25-year agreement. This is not a far-fetched idea considering that the military–bonyad complex has historically situated itself close to China and Russia. In short, as a new nuclear deal and its full implementation are closely tied to the future of the world order and the rising tensions between the United States and the European Union on the one side and China and Russia on the other, the issue is likely to continue to influence the future of capitalism in Iran.

The Islamic Republic has tenaciously defied regular predictions of its impending collapse since 1979, despite the war with Iraq, Western pressure and sanctions and resistance from below. So far, the system has largely coped with the pressure from below, either through incorporating the material needs and demands of the working class and the poor or deploying brutal coercive measures that have become more routine in recent years. Moreover, as much as the ongoing changes in the global capitalist order could exacerbate the ongoing crisis, they may open up new avenues for the survival and strength of the Islamic Republic state, which were not present during the post-Cold War US triumphalist era. At any rate, it remains to be seen whether the struggles from below will lead to the overthrowing of the Islamic Republic or whether the system will maintain its integrity and influence in the region by moving more decisively towards the emerging China/Russia block. Nevertheless, any of these outcomes will have drastic implications for the process of capital accumulation and state formation in Iran.

## Notes

1 While the escalating environmental crises in Iran can be attributed in part to the rapid industrialisation of global capitalism in the last century, a significant share of responsibility falls upon the Iranian oil and gas industry. Moreover, the process of Iranian neoliberalisation has played a crucial role in exacerbating the environmental crisis, particularly through the military–bonyad complex, which has promoted 'the intertwined processes of securitization and commodification or the association of nature'. This phenomenon is exemplified by the excessive construction of dams (Samiee, 2022).
2 BRICS is an informal group of states comprising Brazil, Russia, India, China and South Africa. It is often referred to as the first clear attempt of emerging economies to challenge the hegemony of the United States and Europe in the global economy. In August 2023, BRICS extended invitations to Saudi Arabia, Iran, Ethiopia, Egypt, Argentina, and the United Arab Emirates to become full members starting from January 2024. For more information about the organisation see the BRICS website: http://infobrics.org/ (accessed 19 September 2023).

# Bibliography

Abrahamian, E. (1980). 'Structural causes of the Iranian revolution', *MERIP Reports*, 87, 21–6.

Abrahamian, E. (1982). *Iran Between Two Revolutions*. Princeton, NJ: Princeton University Press.

Abrahamian, E. (1991). 'Khomeini: Fundamentalist or populist?' *New Left Review*, 1:186, 102–19.

Abrahamian, E. (1993). *Khomeinism: Essays on the Islamic Republic*. Berkeley and Los Angeles: University of California Press.

Abrahamian, E. (2008). *A Modern History of Iran*. Cambridge: Cambridge University Press.

Adesnik, D. and Ghasseminejad, S. (2018). *Foreign Investment in Iran: Multinational Firms' Compliance with U.S. Sanctions. Research Memo*. Washington, DC: The Foundation for Defense of Democracies. Available at: www.fdd.org/wp-content/uploads/2018/09/MEMO_CompaniesinIran.pdf (accessed 23 August 2022).

Adib-Moghaddam, A. (2006). 'The pluralistic momentum in Iran and the future of the reform movement', *Third World Quarterly*, 27:4, 665–74.

Afshar, H. (1981). 'An assessment of agricultural development policies in Iran', *World Development*, 9:11/12, 58–79.

Afshari, B. (1999). 'The conundrum of bonyad's taxes', *Aria*, 11 September.

*Āftāb-e Yazd* (2010). 'Gholammohsen Elham (Spokesman of the Guardian Council): They want to eliminate the supervision of the Council', 13 February. Archival research.

Ahmad, A. (2008). 'Islam, Islamism, and the West', *Socialist Register*, 44:44, 1–37.

Ahmadi, R. (2012). 'The gradual death of profits after assignments', *E'temād*, 12 July. Available at: www.magiran.com/article/2538894 (accessed 1 May 2022).

Ahmadian, H. and Mohseni, P. (2019). 'Iran's Syria strategy: The evolution of deterrence', *International Affairs*, 95:2, 341–64.

Ahmadian, H. and Mohseni, P. (2021). 'From detente to containment: The emergence of Iran's new Saudi strategy', *International Affairs*, 97:3, 779–99.

Aizhu, C. (2012). 'Despite delays, China seeks full Iran oil volume for third month', Reuters, 5 September. Available at: www.reuters.com/article/us-china-iran-crude-idUSBRE8840JU20120905 (accessed 30 August 2022).

Ajami, I. (1973). 'Land reform and modernisation of the farming structure in Iran', *Oxford Agrarian Studies*, 2:2, 1201–131.

Alamdari, K. (2005). *Why the Middle East lagged behind: The case of Iran*. Lanham, MD: University Press of America.

Alamdari, K. (2009). 'Election as a tool to sustain the theological power structure', in Parasiliti, A. (ed.), *The Iranian Revolution at 30*. Washington, DC: Middle East Institute, pp. 109–11.

Alexander, A. (2018). 'The contemporary dynamics of imperialism in the Middle East: A preliminary analysis', *International Socialism*, 159. Available at: http://isj.org.uk/contemporary-dynamics-of-imperialism/ (accessed 25 July 2022).

Alfoneh, A. (2010). 'The Revolutionary Guards' looting of Iran's economy', *Middle Eastern Outlook. American Enterprise Institute for Public Policy Research*, 3, 1–9.

Aljazeera (2017). 'US and Saudi Arabia sign arms deals worth almost $110bn', 20 May. Available at: www.aljazeera.com/news/2017/5/20/us-and-saudi-arabia-sign-arms-deals-worth-almost-110bn (accessed 19 August 2022).

Aljazeera (2018). 'Mike Pompeo speech: What are the 12 demands given to Iran?' 21 May. Available at: www.aljazeera.com/news/2018/5/21/mike-pompeo-speech-what-are-the-12-demands-given-to-iran (accessed 19 August 2022).

Aljazeera (2022). 'Iran applies to join BRICS group of emerging countries', 28 June. Available at: www.aljazeera.com/economy/2022/6/28/iran-applies-to-join-brics-group-of-emerging-countries (accessed 17 August 2022).

Al-Shamahi, A. (2020). 'Can the IMF overcome US roadblocks to give aid to Iran?' Aljazeera, 17 April. Available at: www.aljazeera.com/ajimpact/imf-overcome-roadblocks-give-aid-iran-200416233604121.html (accessed 23 September 2022).

Amirahmadi, H. (1990). *Revolution and Economic Transition: The Iranian Experience*. Albany: State University of New York Press.

Amirahmadi, H. (1995). 'Bunyad', in Esposito, J.L. (ed.), *Encyclopaedia of the Modern Islamic World (Vol.1)*. New York: Oxford University Press.

Amirshahi, F. (2017). 'Four decades of insurgency and counterinsurgency', Radio Farda, 30 December. Available at: www.radiofarda.com/a/commentary-antiriot-forces/28947629.html (accessed 23 August 2022).

Amnesty International (2017). 'Iran: Release imprisoned trade unionists and uphold workers' rights', 30 April. Available at: www.amnesty.nl/actueel/iran-release-imprisoned-trade-unionists-and-uphold-workers-rights (accessed 17 August 2022).

Amnesty International (2022). 'Iran: Details of 321 deaths in crackdown on November 2019 protests [July 2022 update]', 29 July. Available at: www.amnesty.org/en/documents/mde13/2308/2020/en/ (accessed 24 August 2022).

Amsden, A. (1989). *Asia's Next Giant: South Korea and Late Industrialisation*. New York: Oxford University Press.

Amsden, A. (1990). 'Third World industrialization: "Global Fordism" or a new model?' *New Left Review*, 1:182, 5–31.

Amuzegar, J. (1997). *Iran's Economy under the Islamic Republic*. London: I.B. Tauris.

Amuzegar, J. (2001). 'Iran's post-revolution planning: The second try', *Middle East Policy*, 8:1, 25–42.

Amuzegar, J. (2005a). 'Iran's Oil Stabilization Fund: A misnomer', *Middle East Economic Survey*, 48:47. Available at: www.payvand.com/news/05/nov/1221.html (accessed 7 April 2023).

Amuzegar, J. (2005b). 'Iran's third development plan: An appraisal', *Middle East Policy*, 12:3, 46–63.

Amuzegar, J. (2010). 'Iran's fourth plan: A partial assessment', *Middle East Policy*, 17:4, 114–30.

Amuzegar, J. (2012). 'The Islamic Republic of Iran: Facts and fiction', *Middle East Policy*, 19:1, 25–36.

Amuzegar, J. (2014). *The Islamic Republic of Iran: Reflections on an emerging economy*. London: Routledge.

Anievas, A. (2008). 'Theory of the global state: Globality as an unfinished revolution a theory of global capitalism: Production, class, and the state in a transnational world', *Historical Materialism*, 16:2, 190–206.

Anievas, A. and Nişancıoğlu, K. (2015). *How the West Came to Rule: The geopolitical origins of capitalism*. London: Pluto Press.

Anousheh, M. (2013). 'Interview with the head of Iranian Privatisation Organisation: If the economic transformation plan was implemented correctly', *E'temād*, 22 January. Available at: www.magiran.com/article/2664920 (accessed 1 May 2022).

Ansari, A.M. (2001). 'The myth of the White Revolution: Mohammad Reza Shah, "modernization" and the consolidation of power', *Middle Eastern Studies*, 37:3, 1–24.

Ansari, A.M. (2014). *Modern Iran*. Oxford/New York: Routledge.

Arazmi, A. (2017). 'Mostazafan Foundation from the beginning until now', BBC Persian, 20 December. Available at: www.bbc.com/persian/iran-features-42378588 (accessed 16 September 2022).

Arjomand, S.A. (1988). *The Turban for the Crown: The Islamic Revolution in Iran*. Oxford: Oxford University Press.

Arjomand, S.A. (2000). 'Civil society and the rule of law in the constitutional politics of Iran under Khatami', *Social Research*, 67:2, 281–301.

Arjomand, S.A. (2009). *After Khomeini: Iran under his successors*. Oxford: Oxford University Press.

Arjomandy, D. (2014). 'Iranian membership in the World Trade Organization: An unclear future', *Iranian Studies*, 47:6, 933–50.

Arman, B. (1994). [مروری بر کارکرد و ریشه های ناکامی خصوصی سازی در ایران] 'An overview of the function and causes of the failure of privatisation in Iran'], *Majles & Pazhuhesh*, 7, 27–42.

Arms Control Association (2013). *Solving the Iranian Nuclear Puzzle*. Washington, DC: ACA Research Staff. Available at: www.armscontrol.org/files/ACA_Iran_Briefing_Book_2013.pdf (accessed 20 May 2022).

Ashraf, A. (1970). 'Historical obstacle to the development of bourgeoisie in Iran', in Cook, M.A. (ed.), *Studies on the Economic History of the Middle East*. London: Oxford University Press, pp. 308–32.

Ashraf, A. (1981). 'The roots of emerging dual class structure in nineteenth-century Iran', *Iranian Studies*, 14:1–2, 5–27.

Ashraf, A. (1988). 'Bazaar-mosque alliance: The social basis of revolts and revolutions', *International Journal of Politics, Culture, and Society*, 1:4, 538–67.

Ashraf, A. (1989). 'Bazaar iii', *Encyclopaedia Iranica*. Available at: www.iranicaonline.org/articles/bazar-iii (accessed 1 June 2022).

Ashraf, A. (1991). 'State and agrarian relations before and after the Iranian Revolution, 1960–1990', in Kazemi, F. and Waterbury, J. (eds), *Peasants and Politics in the Modern Middle East*. Miami: Florida International University Press, pp. 277–311.

Ashraf, A. and Banuazizi, A. (1985). 'The state, classes and modes of mobilization in the Iranian revolution', *State, Culture, and Society*, 1:3, 3–40.

Ashraf, A. and Banuazizi, A. (2001). 'Iran's tortuous path toward "Islamic Liberalism"', *International Journal of Politics, Culture, and Society*, 15:2, 237–56.

Assadzadeh, A. and Paul, S. (2004). 'Poverty, growth, and redistribution: A study of Iran', *Review of Development Economics*, 8:4, 640–53.

Axworthy, M. (2012). 'Diplomatic relations between Iran and the United Kingdom in the early reform period, 1997–2000', in Ehteshami, A. and Zweiri, M. (eds),

*Iran's Foreign Policy: From Khatami to Ahmadinejad*. Reading: Ithaca Press, pp. 105–14.

Axworthy, M. (2013). *Revolutionary Iran: A history of the Islamic Republic*. London: Penguin Books.

Axworthy, M. (2016). *Iran: What everyone needs to know*. Oxford: Oxford University Press.

Ayubi, N.N. (1996). *Over-stating the Arab State: Politics and society in the Middle East*. London: I.B. Tauris.

Bahmani, M. (1998). بررسی امکانات و روشهای خصوصی سازی شرکتهای تحت پوشش بانکها در نظام بانکداری اسلامی [‘Appraisal of the possibilities and methods of privatisation of companies under the control of banks in the Islamic banking system’]. (No journal name and issue/volume numbers), 392–411. [The author of the book has a pdf copy of the article.]

Bajoghli, N. (2018). ‘Behind the Iran Protests’, *Jacobin Magazine*, 8 January. Available at: https://jacobin.com/2018/01/iran-protests-hasan-rouhani-green-movement (accessed 17 September 2022).

Baktiari, B. (1996). *Parliamentary Politics in Revolutionary Iran: The Institutionalization of Factional Politics*. Gainesville: University Press of Florida.

Banaji, J. (2010). *Theory as History: Essays on Modes of Production and Exploitation*. Leiden: Brill.

Barker, C. (2013). ‘Class struggle and social movements’, in Barker, C. et al. (eds), *Marxism and Social Movements*. Boston: Brill, pp. 39–61.

Barker, C., et al. (2013). ‘Marxism and social movements: An introduction’, in Barker, C. et al. (eds), *Marxism and Social Movements*. Boston: Brill, pp. 1–37.

Barrow, C.W. (2011). ‘(Re)reading Poulantzas: State theory and the epistemologies of structuralism’, in Gallas, A. et al. (eds), *Reading Poulantzas*. London: Merlin Press, pp. 27–40.

Bayat, A. (1987). *Workers and Revolution in Iran*. London: Zed Books.

Bayat, A. (1994). ‘Squatters and the state: Back street politics in the Islamic Republic’, *Middle East Report*, 191, 10–14.

Bayat, A. (2007). *Islam and Democracy: What is the real question?* Amsterdam: Amsterdam University Press.

Bayat, A. (2013). ‘The making of post-Islamist Iran’, in Bayat, A. (ed.), *Post-Islamism: The Changing Faces of Political Islam*. Oxford: Oxford University Press, pp. 35–65.

Bayat, A. (2018). ‘The fire that fuelled the Iran protests’, *The Atlantic*, 27 January.

BBC News (1998). ‘Business: The Company File from Anglo-Persian Oil to BP Amoco’, 11 August. Available at: http://news.bbc.co.uk/2/hi/business/149259.stm (accessed 15 July 2022).

BBC News (2004). ‘Iran MPs defy calls to end sit-in’, 14 February. Available at: http://news.bbc.co.uk/2/hi/middle_east/3395621.stm (accessed 15 July 2022).

BBC News (2018). ‘Six charts that explain the Iran protests’, 4 January. Available at: www.bbc.com/news/world-middle-east-42553516 (accessed 15 July 2022).

BBC Persian (2005). ‘The cost of opposing the most controversial figure of Ahmadinejad’ government’, 24 August. Available at: www.bbc.com/persian/iran/story/2005/08/050824_mf_afrough (accessed 18 July 2022).

BBC Persian (2013). ‘Mohammad Saidikia became the head of the Mostazafan Foundation’, 22 July. Available at: www.bbc.com/persian/iran/2014/07/140722_l51_mostazafan_foundation_saidikia (accessed 18 July 2022).

BBC Persian (2015a). 'The privatisation is a good opportunity for foreign investors', 24 July. Available at: www.bbc.com/persian/business/2015/07/150724_l45_nematzadeh_vienna_sanction (accessed 17 July 2022).

BBC Persian (2015b). 'Zarif: Economic relations with the West guarantee the enforcement of the nuclear deal', 4 August. Available at: www.bbc.com/persian/iran/2015/08/150804_l10_zarif_iran_nuclear_deal_scofr (accessed 17 July 2022).

BBC Persian (2016a). 'Astan Quds: What happens in the biggest endowment entity of the Islamic world?' 6 March. Available at: www.bbc.com/persian/iran/2016/03/160306_l26_l45_astan_ghods_razavi_chart_business_activities (accessed 19 July 2022).

BBC Persian (2016b). 'Nahavandian's trip to London: Is Iran the heaven of investment?' 11 March. Available at: www.bbc.com/persian/iran/2016/03/160311_me_iran_investment_opportunities (accessed 17 July 2022).

BBC Persian (2018a). 'Have there been any signs of protests before?' 2 January. Available at: www.bbc.com/persian/iran-42541340 (accessed 17 July 2022).

BBC Persian (2018b). 'Deputy commander of the IRGC is unaware of the assignment of its enterprises', 25 January. Available at: www.bbc.com/persian/iran-42819644 (accessed 17 July 2022).

BBC Persian (2018c). 'Europe's billion contracts under threat', 12 May. Available at: www.bbc.com/persian/world-44094069 (accessed 17 July 2022).

BBC Persian (2018d). 'Return of sanctions: fifty companies that left Iran because of U.S. retaliation', 4 November. Available at: www.bbc.com/persian/iran-features-46090538 (accessed 17 July 2022).

Beal, T. (2021). 'Sanctions as Instrument of coercion: Characteristics, limitations, and consequences', in Davis, S. and Ness, I. (eds), *Sanctions as War: Anti-imperialist perspectives on American geo-economic strategy*. Leiden: Brill, pp. 27–50.

Behdad, A. (2013). 'Interview with Gholamreza Anaraki part III: Hashemi's government and first steps of privatisation', *Donyā-ye Eqtesād*, 20 June. Available at: www.magiran.com/article/2757647 (accessed 22 September 2022).

Behdad, S. (1989). 'Winners and losers of the Iranian revolution: A study in income distribution', *International Journal of Middle East Studies*, 21:3, 327–58.

Behdad, S. (1996). 'The post-revolutionary economic crisis', in Rahnema, S. and Behdad, S. (eds), *Iran After the Revolution*. London: I.B. Tauris, pp. 97–128.

Behdad, S. (2000). 'From populism to economic liberalisation: The Iranian predicament', in Alizadeh, P. (ed.), *The Economy of Iran*. London: I.B. Tauris, pp. 100–44.

Behkish, M.M. (2010). اقتصاد ایران در بستر جهانی شدن [Iranian economy in the context of globalisation]. Tehran: Ney.

Behravesh, M. (2011). 'A crisis of confidence revisited: Iran-West tensions and mutual demonization', *Asian Politics & Policy*, 3:3, 327–47.

Betts, R., Sagan, S. and Waltz, K. (2007). 'A nuclear Iran: Promoting stability or courting disaster?' *Journal of International Affairs*, 60:2, 135–50.

Bieler, A. (2000). *Globalisation and Enlargement of the European Union: Austrian and Swedish social forces in the struggle over membership*. London: Routledge.

Bieler, A. (2001). 'Questioning cognitivism and constructivism in IR Theory: Reflections on the material structure of ideas', *Politics*, 21:2, 93–100.

Bieler, A. (2006). *The Struggle for a Social Europe: Trade unions and EMU in times of global restructuring*. Manchester: Manchester University Press.

Bieler, A. (2014). 'Transnational labour solidarity in (the) crisis', *Global Labour Journal*, 5:2, 114–33.

Bieler, A. and Morton, A.D. (2008). 'The deficits of discourse in IPE: Turning base metal into gold?' *International Studies Quarterly*, 52:1, 103–28.

Bieler, A. and Morton, A.D. (2013/14). 'The will-o'-the-wisp of the transnational state', *Journal of Australian Political Economy*, 72, 23–51.

Bieler, A. and Morton, A.D. (2015). 'Axis of evil or access to diesel? Spaces of new imperialism and the Iraq War', *Historical Materialism*, 23:2, 94–130.

Bieler, A. and Morton, A.D. (2018). *Global Capitalism, Global War, Global Crisis*. Cambridge: Cambridge University Press.

Block, F. (2001). 'Using social theory to leap over historical contingencies: A comment on Robinson', *Theory and Society*, 30:2, 215–21.

Borger, J. and Tait, R. (2010). 'The financial power of the Revolutionary Guards', *The Guardian*, 15 February. Available at: www.theguardian.com/world/2010/feb/15/financial-power-revolutionary-guard (accessed 22 July 2022).

Boroujerdi, M. and Rahimkhani, K. (2018). *Postrevolutionary Iran: A political handbook*. Syracuse, NY: Syracuse University Press.

Boroumand, L. and Boroumand, R. (2000). 'Illusion and reality of civil society in Iran: An ideological debate', *Social Research*, 67:2, 303–44.

Borszikp, O. (2014). 'International sanctions against Iran under President Ahmadinejad: Explaining regime persistence', *German Institute of Global and Area Studies*, Working paper 260, 1–25.

Bowen, W. and Kidd, J. (2004). 'The Iranian nuclear challenge', *International Affairs*, 80:2, 257–76.

Bozorgmehr, N. (2017). 'Iran cracks down on Revolutionary Guards business network', *Financial Times*, 14 September. Available at: www.ft.com/content/43de1388-9857-11e7-a652-cde3f882dd7b (accessed 20 July 2022).

Brenner, R. (1986). 'The social basis of economic development', in Roemer, J. (ed.), *Analytical Marxism*. Cambridge: Cambridge University Press, pp. 23–53.

Brenner, R. (2006). 'What is, and what is not, imperialism?' *Historical Materialism*, 14:4, 79–105.

Brewer, A. (1990). *Marxist Theories of Imperialism: A critical survey*. London: Routledge & Kegan Paul.

Bridenthal, R. (2021). 'Blowback to US sanctions policy', in Davis, S. and Ness, I. (eds), *Sanctions as War: Anti-imperialist perspectives on American geo-economic strategy*. Leiden: Brill, pp. 323–32.

Buchta, W. (2000). *Who Rules Iran? The structure of power in the Islamic Republic*. Washington, DC: Washington Institute for Near East Policy.

Burawoy, M. (2001). 'Neoclassical sociology: From the end of communism to the end of classes', *American Journal of Sociology*, 106:4, 1099–120.

Burns, J.F. (2000). 'Gunman in Iran seriously wounds a top reform figure', *New York Times*, 13 March. Available at: www.nytimes.com/2000/03/13/world/gunman-in-iran-seriously-wounds-a-top-reform-figure.html (accessed 5 August 2022).

*Burs*. (2013). «امور سهام تخصیصی و عدالت سازمان خصوصی سازی» دفتر رسمی گزارش :گزارش ویژه عدالت سهام ساله 8 کارنامه؛ شد منتشر [Special report: The official report of 'the Justice Shares Affairs Office of the Iranian Privatisation Organisation' published: Eight-year appraisal of the justice shares], 103, 48–55.

Burton, G. (2021). 'China's Three Level Game in the Middle East', *Asian Journal of Middle Eastern and Islamic Studies*, 15:2, 189–204.

Calabrese, J. (2018). 'China's "One Belt, One Road" (OBOR) initiative: envisioning Iran's role', in Ehteshami, A. and Horesh, N. (eds), *China's Presence in the Middle East*. Oxford: Routledge, pp. 174–91.

Callinicos, A. (2007). 'Does capitalism need the state system?' *Cambridge Review of International Affairs*, 20:4, 533–49.

Callinicos, A. (2009). *Imperialism and Global Political Economy*. London: Polity Press.

Callinicos, A. (2010). 'The limits of passive revolution', *Capital & Class*, 34:3, 491–507.

Capasso, M. (2021). 'IR, imperialism, and the Global South: From Libya to Venezuela', *Politics*, 1–16. doi: 10.1177/02633957211061232.

Carey, J.P.C. and Carey, A.G. (1976). 'Iranian agriculture and its development: 1952–1973', *International Journal of Middle East Studies*, 7:3, 359–82.

Celasun, O. (2003). 'Exchange rate regime considerations in an oil economy: The case of the Islamic Republic of Iran', *IMF*, Working Paper 03/26.

Chamber of Commerce, Industries, Mines and Agriculture (2016). مناطق آزاد تجاري [ و ویژه اقتصادي، بسترها و الزامات، چالش ها و راهكارها ['Free trade and special economic zones, conditions and requirements, challenges and solutions']. Official Report, Deputy for Economic Affairs of Iran. Available at: https://research.chambertrust. ir//0311-كلان-و-خرد-نظري-اقتصاد-/2اقتصادي-بازرگاني-و-اقتصاد/item/296-ویژه-و-تجاري-آزاد-مناطق اقتص ادي،-بست رها-و-الزا مات،-چالش-ها-و-راهكا رها-بولتن-بررسی-مسائل-روز-اقت صاد-ایران-آبان-1395.html (accessed 9 September 2022).

Chang, H. (2002). *Kicking away the ladder? Economic development in historical perspective*. London: Anthem.

Clawson, P. and Rubin, M. (2005). *Eternal Iran: Continuity and chaos*. London: Palgrave Macmillan.

Codato, A. and Perissinotto, R.M. (2011). 'Marxism and elitism: Two opposite social analysis models?' *Revista Brasileira de Ciências Sociais*, 5, 1–12.

Connell, R. and Dados, N. (2014). 'Where in the world does neoliberalism come from?' *Theory and Society*, 43:2, 117–38.

Cox, J. (2022). 'China holdings of U.S. debt fall below $1 trillion for the first time since 2010', CNBC, 10 July. Available at: www.cnbc.com/2022/07/18/china-holdings-of-us-debt-fall-below-1-trillion-for-the-first-time-since-2010.html (accessed 1 May 2022).

Dabashi, H. (2011a). 'Iran's Green Movement as a civil rights movement', in Hashemi, N. and Postel, D. (eds), *The People Reloaded: The Green Movement and the struggle for Iran's future*. New York: Melville House, pp. 22–5.

Dabashi, H. (2011b). 'Iran's greens and the American civil rights movement: An interview with Cornel West', in Hashemi, N. and Postel, D. (eds), *The People Reloaded: The Green Movement and the struggle for Iran's future*. New York: Melville House, pp. 284–8.

Dadkhah, K. (2003). 'Iran and the global financial markets', in Mohammadi, A. (ed.), *Iran Encountering Globalisation*. London: Routledge, pp. 86–106.

Dannreuther, R. (2012). 'Russia and the Middle East: A cold war paradigm?' *Europe-Asia Studies*, 64:3, 543–60.

Darvish-Tavangar, A. (1997). 'The economic foundation of the Imam's thoughts', *Resālat*, 1 June.

Davenport, K., Himball, D.G. and Thielmann, G. (2015). 'Solving the Iranian nuclear puzzle: The Joint Comprehensive Plan of Action', Arms Control Association. Available at: www.armscontrol.org/reports/Solving-the-Iranian-Nuclear-Puzzle-The-Joint-Comprehensive-Plan-of-Action/2015/08 (accessed 1 February 2022).

Davidson, N. (2009). 'Putting the nation back into "the international"', *Cambridge Review of International Affairs*, 22:1, 9–28.

Davidson, N. (2010a). 'Many capitals, many states: Contingency, logic or mediation?' in Anievas, A. (ed.), *Marxism and World Politics*. London: Routledge, pp. 77–93.

Davidson, N. (2010b). 'From deflected permanent revolution to the law of uneven and combined development', *International Socialism*, 128. Available at: http://isj.org.uk/from-deflected-permanent-revolution-to-the-law-of-uneven-and-combined-development/ (accessed 27 January 2022).

Davidson, N. (2016). 'Debating the nature of capitalism: An engagement with Geoffrey Hodgson', *Competition & Change*, 20:3, 204–18.

Davidson, N. (2017). 'Crisis neoliberalism and regimes of permanent exception', *Critical Sociology*, 43:4–5, 615–34.

Davies, W. (2018). 'The neoliberal state: Power against "politics"', in Cahill, D. et al. (eds), *The SAGE Handbook of Neoliberalism*. London: SAGE, pp. 273–83.

Davis, S. and Ness, I. (2021). 'Introduction: Why are economic sanctions a form of war?', in Davis, S. and Ness, I. (eds), *Sanctions as War: Anti-imperialist perspectives on American geo-economic strategy*. Leiden: Brill, pp. 1–24.

Dehghanpisheh, B. and Stecklow, S. (2013). 'Assets of Ayatollah II: Khamenei's conglomerate thrived as sanctions squeezed Iran', Reuters, 12 November. Available at: www.reuters.com/investigates/iran/#article/part2 (accessed 10 June 2022).

Delafrouz, M.T. (2014). دولت و توسعه اقتصادی: اقتصاد سیاسی توسعه در ایران و دولت های توسعه گرا [State and economic development: The political economy of development in Iran and developmental states]. Tehran: Āgah.

Dinmore, G. (2000). 'Upturn in Iran may aid Khatami: The president is trying to move his country away from a command-led economy', *Financial Times*, 22 August, p. 10.

Dinmore, G. (2001a). 'Private Iran bank gains licence', *Financial Times*, 5 September, p. 7.

Dinmore, G. (2001b). 'Iran shifts to single rial exchange rate', *Financial Times*, 24 December, p. 6.

Dinmore, G. (2002). 'Iran finally passes law on outside investment economic reforms', *Financial Times*, 5 June, p. 10.

*Donyā-ye Eqtesād* (2017). 'The head of Iranian Privatisation Organisation stated: A new narrative from the ambiguous aspects of privatisation', 11 July. Available at: www.magiran.com/article/3590562 (accessed 22 September 2022).

Draper, H. (1978). *Karl Marx's Theory of Revolution (Vol II): The politics of social classes*. London: Monthly Review.

Drenou, A.T. (2012). 'Iran: Caught between European Union–United States rivalry?' in Ehteshami, A. and Zweiri, M. (eds), *Iran's Foreign Policy: From Khatami to Ahmadinejad*. Reading: Ithaca Press, pp. 73–88.

Dryburgh, L. (2008). 'The EU as a global actor? EU policy towards Iran', *European Security*, 17:2–3, 257–8.

Duménil, G. and Lévy, D. (2004). *Capital Resurgent: Roots of the neoliberal revolution*. Cambridge, MA: Harvard University Press.

DW (2022a). 'Is Russia sabotaging the Iran nuclear deal over Ukraine sanctions?' 9 March. Available at: www.dw.com/en/is-russia-sabotaging-the-iran-nuclear-deal-over-ukraine-sanctions/a-61064382 (accessed 17 September 2022).

DW (2022b). 'G7: Western democracies unite to face China and Russia', 28 June. Available at: www.dw.com/en/g7-western-democracies-unite-to-face-china-and-russia/a-62293032 (accessed 25 August 2022).

*E'temād* (2010). 'Majid Ansari in an extensive interview with ILNA: Our revolution was a reformist revolution', Interview with ISNA, 2 February. Available at: www.magiran.com/article/2036219 (accessed 1 May 2022).

*E'temād* (2013). 'Spokesperson of the IRGC in an interview with E'temād: The IRGC competitor in construction projects is the national-religious group (melli-mazhabi-hā)', 17 September. Available at: www.magiran.com/article/2814077 (accessed 1 May 2022).

*E'temād* (2014). 'The commander of the Ghorb: The IRGC does not occupy the place of the private sector in developmental projects', 12 October. Available at: www.magiran.com/article/3041565 (accessed 1 May 2022).

*E'temād-e Melli* (2008). 'Proactive supervision, operation of the Guardian Council and the subject of candidates approval process in an E'temād- e Melli interview with Ayatollah Bayat- e Zanjani', 14 January. Available at: https://bayat.info/و-نگهبان-شوراي-عملكرد-،استصوابي-نظارت/ (accessed 13 September 2022).

Ehsani, K. (1994). 'Tilt but don't spill: Iran's development and reconstruction dilemma', *Middle East Report*, 191, 16–20.

Ehteshami, A. (1995). *After Khomeini: The Iranian second republic.* London: Routledge.

Ehteshami, A. (2017). *Iran: Stuck in transition.* London: Routledge.

Ehteshami, A. and Zweiri, M. (2007). *Iran and the Rise of its Neoconservatives: The politics of Tehran's silent revolution.* London: I.B. Tauris.

Eltagouri, M. (2018). 'Tens of thousands of people have protested in Iran. Here's why', *Washington Post*, 3 January.

Engelbrecht, C. and Fassihi, F. (2022). 'What's Driving the Protests in Iran?' *New York Times*, 22 September. Available at: www.nytimes.com/2022/09/22/world/middleeast/iran-protests.html (accessed 23 September 2022).

England, A. and Bozorgmehr, N. (2019). 'Iran-US tensions: Trump gambles on curbing Tehran's reach', *Financial Times*, 9 May. Available at: www.ft.com/content/6b47d1dc-7179-11e9-bf5c-6eeb837566c5 (accessed 10 February 2022).

Erdbrink, T. (2015). 'Iran prepares to lure foreign investors after nuclear deal', *New York Times*, 21 August. Available at: www.nytimes.com/2015/08/22/world/middleeast/after-nuclear-deal-with-west-iran-gears-up-to-cash-in.html (accessed 26 March 2022).

Esfahani, H.S. and Pesaran, M.H. (2009). 'The Iranian economy in the Twentieth Century: A global perspective', *Iranian Studies*, 42:2, 177–211.

*Ettelā'āt* (1997). 'Interview with Mohammad Khatami: The horizons of religious thought', 5 August. Archival Research.

*Ettelā'āt* (1998a). 'Mohammad Khatami: The Islamic Revolution, the precursor of another civilisation', 2 February. Archival Research.

*Ettelā'āt* (1998b). 'Mohammad Khatami: The Islamic Revolution and the flagship of another civilisation', 4 February. Archival Research.

Evans, P. (1995). *Embedded Autonomy: States and industrial transformation.* Princeton, NJ: Princeton University Press.

Eyal, G., Szelenyi, I. and Townsley, E. (2001). *Making Capitalism Without Capitalists.* London: Verso.

Fakiolas, T.E. and Fakiolas, E.T. (2006). 'Europe's "Division" over the war in Iraq', *Perspectives on European Politics and Society*, 7:3, 298–311.

Farhi, F. (2011). 'Tehran's delayed spring?' *Globalizations*, 8:5, 617–21.

Fars News Agency (2015). 'What is the Executives of Construction Party position on the economy?' 11 March. Available at: www.farsnews.ir/news//13931219000 911/حوزه-در-سازندگي-كارگزاران-حرف8C%80%E2% (accessed 9 September 2022).

Farzin, H. (1996). 'The political economy of foreign exchange reform', in Rahnema, S. and Behdad, S. (eds), *Iran After the Revolution*. London: I.B. Tauris, pp. 174–202.

Farzin, M.R. (2004). تأملی در جایگاه و نقش بنیاد مستضعفان در عرصه های اقتصادی و اجتماعی ['A reflection on the place and role of the Mostazafan Foundation in the economic and social arenas'], *Goftogu*, 39, 75–83.

Farzin, Y.H. (1995). 'Foreign exchange reform in Iran: Badly designed, badly managed', *World Development*, 23:6, 987–1001.

Fathollah-Nejad, A. (2017). *Rouhani's Neoliberal Doctrine Has Failed Iran*, Middle East Institute, 18 May. Available at: www.mei.edu/publications/rouhanis-neoliberal-doctrine-has-failed-iran (accessed 14 August 2022).

Fathollah-Nejad, A. (2020). 'The Islamic Republic of Iran four decades on: The 2017/18 protests amid a triple crisis'. Brookings Doha Center. Available at: www.brookings.edu/research/the-islamic-republic-of-iran-four-decades-on-the-2017-18-protests-amid-a-triple-crisis/ (accessed 13 September 2022).

Fekri, M. (2014). 'Interview with Pour Hosseini: Unusual intervention for halting the process of privatisation', *E'temād*, 17 May. Available at: www.magiran.com/article/2951697 (accessed 1 May 2022).

Ferrier, R. (1991). 'The Iranian oil industry', in Avery, P., Hambly, G.R.G. and Melville, C. (eds), *The Cambridge History of Iran (Vol. 7)*. Cambridge: Cambridge University Press, pp. 639–704.

Fesharaki, F. (1985). 'Iran's petroleum policy: How does the oil industry function in revolutionary Iran?' in Afshar, H. (ed.), *Iran: A Revolution in Turmoil*. London: Palgrave Macmillan, pp. 99–120.

Figueroa, W. (2022). 'China and Iran since the 25-year agreement: The limits of cooperation', The Diplomat, 17 January 2022. Available at: https://thediplomat.com/2022/01/china-and-iran-since-the-25-year-agreement-the-limits-of-cooperation/ (accessed 8 June 2022).

*Financial Times* (1997). 'State foundations dominate economy', 17 July.

*Financial Times* (2002). 'First foreign takeover of Iranian group', 21 March, p. 9.

*Financial Times* (2006). 'Iran to privatise but cling to big oil companies', 3 July.

*Financial Times* (2019a). 'Germany says Iran nuclear deal is key in regional stability', 8 May. Available at: www.ft.com/video/de3c2b9f-89ad-400a-ad5f-3b886f804909 (accessed 3 July 2022).

*Financial Times* (2019b). 'Iran nuclear decision raises tension with US', 8 May. Available at: www.ft.com/content/e2b1cd28-71aa-11e9-bf5c-6eeb837566c5 (accessed 3 July 2022).

Fischer, M.J. (2003). *Iran: From religious dispute to revolution*. London: University of Wisconsin Press.

Fitzpatrick, M. (2006). 'Assessing Iran's nuclear programme', *Survival*, 48:3, 5–26.

Fleming, S. and Manson, K. (2018). 'Donald Trump pulls US out of Iran nuclear deal', *Financial Times*, 8 May. Available at: www.ft.com/content/fb369232-52d1-11e8-b3ee-41e0209208ec (accessed 4 July 2022).

Foran, J. (1994). 'The Iranian Revolution of 1977–79: A challenge for social theory', in Foran, J. (ed.), A *Century of Revolution: Social movements in Iran*. Minneapolis: University of Minnesota Press, pp. 160–88.

Forozan, H. (2015). *The Military in Post-Revolutionary Iran: The evolution and roles of the Revolutionary Guards*. London: Routledge.

Fowler, S. (2018). 'Iran's chain murders: a wave of killings that shook a nation', BBC, 2 December. Available at: www.bbc.com/news/world-middle-east-46356725 (accessed 9 July 2022).

Gallagher, K.S. and Qi, Q. (2021). 'Chinese overseas investment policy: Implications for climate change', *Global Policy*, 12:3, 260–72.

Gerges, F.A. (2013). 'The Obama approach to the Middle East: The end of America's moment?' *International Affairs*, 89:2, 299–323.

Ghadimi, A. (2017). 'What is a "khosolati" firm and why is Rouhani against it?' BBC Persian, 24 May. Available at: www.bbc.com/persian/iran-features-39993711 (accessed 14 August 2022).

Ghadimi, A. (2018). 'What is the justice shares and how much is it worth?', BBC Persian, 12 January. Available at: www.bbc.com/persian/iran-features-42649658 (accessed 14 August 2022).

Ghafari, R. (1995). 'The economic consequences of Islamic fundamentalism in Iran: The political economy of Islamic Republic of Iran 1979–1994', *Capital & Class*, 19:2, 91–115.

Ghafouri, G. (2015). 'Iran and China relations', *Jām-e-Jam*, 15 February. Available at: https:// jameja monl ine.ir/ fa/ news/ 770 751/چین-و-ایران-بات مناس (accessed 17 August 2022).

Ghamari-Tabrizi, B. (2008). *Islam and Dissent in Postrevolutionary Iran*. London: I.B. Tauris.

Ghaninejad, M. (2017). اقتصاد و دولت در ایران [*Economy and State in Iran*]. Tehran: Donyā-ye Eqtesād.

Gharchedaghi, L. (2017). 'Why has disagreement between Rouhani and the IRGC intensified?' BBC Persian, 19 July. Available at: www.bbc.com/persian/iran-features-40646325 (accessed 29 June 2022).

Ghasemi, F. (2016). جمهوری اسلامی: از بازرگان تا روحانی [*The Islamic Republic: From Bazargan to Rouhani*]. H&S Media.

Ghasimi, M.R. (1992). 'The Iranian economy after the revolution: An economic appraisal of the five-year plan', *International Journal of Middle East Studies*, 24:4, 599–614.

Ghobadzadeh, N. and Rahim, L.Z. (2012). 'Islamic reformation discourses: Popular sovereignty and religious secularisation in Iran', *Democratization*, 19:2, 334–51.

Global Slavery Index (2018). 'Annual Report'. Available at: www.globalslaveryindex.org/2018/findings/global-findings/ (accessed 13 June 2022)

Golkar, S. (2011). 'Liberation or suppression technologies? The internet, the Green Movement and the regime in Iran', *International Journal of Emerging Technologies and Society*, 9:1, 50–70.

Gordon, J. (2013). 'Crippling Iran: The UN Security Council and the Tactic of Deliberate Ambiguity', *Georgetown Journal of International Law*, 44:3, 973–1006.

Gramsci, A. (1971). *Selections from the Prison Notebooks*. Q. Hoare and G. Nowell-Smith (eds and trans.). London: Lawrence and Wishart.

Gramsci, A. (1995). *Further Selections from the Prison Notebooks*. D. Boothman (ed. and trans.). London: Lawrence and Wishart.

Haadi-Zenouz, B. (2003). تجربه سیاستهای صنعتی در ایران 80 – 1374 [*The Practice of Industrial Policies in Iran (1374– 80)*]. Tehran: Islamic Parliament Research Center Press.

Habibi, A. and Khoshpour, H. (1996). ارزیابی عملکرد سیاست خصوصی‌سازی شرکتهای دولتی در ایران (۱۳۶۸-۱۳۷۴) ['Appraisal of the policy of privatisation of the state-owned enterprises in Iran (1989–1995)'], *Journal of Barnāmeh & Budjeh*, 7, 41–68.

Habibi, N. (2014). 'The economic legacy of Mahmoud Ahmadinejad', Crown Centre for Middle East Studies, Working Paper 5. Available at: www.brandeis.edu/economics/RePEc/brd/doc/Brandeis_WP69.pdf (accessed 9 September 2022).

Hafezi, P. (2021). 'Iran leader bans import of U.S., UK COVID-19 vaccines, demands sanctions end', Reuters, 8 January. Available at: www.reuters.com/article/health-coronavirus-iran-int-idUSKBN29D0YC (accessed 23 September 2022).

Hafezi, P. and Barbuscia, D. (2020). 'Currency crisis impoverishes Iranians, strains economic defenses', Reuters, 7 July. Available at: www.reuters.com/article/us-iran-economy-rial-analysis-idUSKBN2480M3 (accessed 24 August 2022)

Hafezi, P. and Charbonneau, L. (2015). 'Iranian nuclear deal set to make hard-line Revolutionary Guards richer', Reuters, 6 July. Available at: www.reuters.com/article/us-iran-nuclear-economy-insight/iranian-nuclear-deal-set-to-make-hardline-revolutionary-guards-richer-idUSKCN0PG1XV20150706 (accessed 12 August 2022).

Hakimian, H. (2011). 'Iran's free trade zones: Back doors to the international economy?' *Iranian Studies*, 44:6, 851–74.

Hall, S. (1977). 'The "political" and the "economic" in Marx's theory of classes', in Hunt, A. (ed.), *Class & Class Structure*. London: Lawrence and Wishart, pp. 16–60.

Hall, S. (1986). 'The problem of ideology – Marxism without guarantees', *Journal of Communication Inquiry*, 10:2, 28–44.

Halliday, F. (1979). *Iran: Dictatorship and development*. Harmondsworth: Penguin Books.

Halliday, F. (1987). 'The Iranian revolution and its implications', *New Left Review*, 1:166, 29–37.

*Hamshahri* (1996). 'Interview with Mohsen Rafigh-Doust: Government economic policies, development and poverty alleviation', 20 June. Archival Research.

*Hamshahri* (1997). 'Political renovation of society is a necessity of our era (evaluation of the programme of the elect president)', 24 July. Archival Research.

*Hamshahri* (1998). 'Interview with Mohsen Armin: Civil society does not have any conflict with religious beliefs', 19 January. Archival Research.

*Hamshahri Online* (2017). 'Rouhani in Yazd: People decide if they want dignity or the shadow of ominous war', 29 April. Available at: www.hamshahrionline.ir/news/397 368 /مردم-بگویند-عزت-می-خواهند-یا-سایه-شوم-جنگ-ایجاد-شغل-را-عملی-اتی (accessed 11 May 2022).

Handjani, A. (2018). 'Commentary: The best way to respond to Iran protests', Reuters, 2 January. Available at: www.reuters.com/article/us-handjani-iran-commentary/commentary-the-best-way-to-respond-to-iran-protests-idUSKBN1ER1FK (accessed 18 April 2022).

Hanieh, A. (2010). 'The internationalisation of Gulf capital and Palestinian class formation', *Capital & Class*, 35:1, 81–106.

Hanieh, A. (2011). *Capitalism and Class in the Gulf Arab States*. London: Palgrave McMillan.

Hanieh, A. (2013). *Lineages of Revolt: Issues of contemporary capitalism in the Middle East*. Chicago, IL: Haymarket Books.

Hanieh, A. (2015). 'Overcoming methodological nationalism: spatial perspectives on migration to the Gulf Arab States', in Khalaf, A., AlShehabi, O. and Hanieh, A. (eds), *Transit States: Labor, migration and citizenship in the Gulf*. London: Pluto Press, pp. 57–76.

Hanieh, A. (2018). *Money, Markets, and Monarchies: The Gulf Cooperation Council and the political economy of the contemporary Middle East.* Cambridge: Cambridge University Press.

Harris, K. (2013). 'The rise of the subcontractor state: Politics of pseudo-privatization in the Islamic Republic of Iran', *International Journal of Middle East Studies*, 45;1, 45–70.

Harris, K. (2017). *A Social Revolution: Politics and the welfare state in Iran.* Oakland: University of California Press.

Harris, K. and Kalb, Z. (2018). 'How years of increasing labour unrest signalled Iran's latest protest wave', *Washington Post*, 19 January.

Harrop, W.S. (2009). 'Muhammad Khatami: A dialogue beyond paradox', in Parasiliti, A. (ed.), *The Iranian Revolution at 30.* Washington, DC: Middle East Institute, pp. 115–18.

Harvey, D. (2003). *The New Imperialism.* Oxford: Oxford University Press.

Harvey, D. (2004). 'The 'new' imperialism: Accumulation by dispossession', *Socialist Register*, 40, 63–87.

Harvey, D. (2005). *A Brief History of Neoliberalism.* Oxford: Oxford University Press.

Harvey, D. (2006). *The Limits to Capital.* London: Verso.

Harvey, D. (2010). *A Companion to Marx's Capital Vol.1.* London: Verso.

Harvey, D. (2020). *The Anti-Capitalist Chronicles.* London: Pluto Press.

Hashemi, N. (2014). 'Renegotiating Iran's post-revolutionary social contract: The Green Movement and the struggle for democracy in the Islamic Republic', in Kamrava, M. (ed.), *Beyond the Arab Spring: The evolving ruling bargain in the Middle East.* Oxford: Oxford University Press, pp. 191–216.

Hesam, F. (2002). قانون کار؛ تبلور سیاست اجتماعی در حوزه روابط کار ['The labour law: The crystallisation of social policy in the labour relations'], *Goftogu*, 35, 21–33.

Heydarian, R.J. (2015). 'Iran after Sanctions: An Emerging Economy Giant? An Iranian nuclear agreement could be an economic game changer', *The Diplomat*, 8 April. Available at: https://thediplomat.com/2015/04/iran-after-sanctions-an-emerging-economy-giant/ (accessed 1 August 2022).

Higgins, A. (2007). 'Inside Iran's holy money machine', *Wall Street Journal*, 2 June. Available at: www.wsj.com/articles/SB118072271215621679 (accessed 24 July 2022).

Hill, D., Wald, N. and Guiney, T. (2016). 'Development and neoliberalism', in Springer, S., Birch, K. and MacLeavy, J. (eds), *The Handbook of Neoliberalism.* London: Routledge, pp. 130–42.

Hirsch, J. and Wissel, J. (2011). 'The transformation of contemporary capitalism and the concept of a transnational capitalist class: A critical review in neo-Poulantzian perspective', *Studies in Political Economy*, 88:1, 7–33.

Hobson, J.M. (2007). 'Is critical theory always for the white West and for Western imperialism? Beyond Westphilian towards a post-racist critical IR', *Review of International Studies*, 33:S1, 91–116.

Hobson, J.M. (2012). *The Eurocentric Conception of World Politics: Western international theory, 1760–2010.* Cambridge: Cambridge University Press.

Holloway, J. (1996). 'The Abyss opens: The rise and fall of Keynesianism', in Bonefeld, W. and Holloway, J. (eds), *Global Capital, National State and the Politics of Money.* Basingstoke: Palgrave Macmillan, pp. 7–34.

Hooglund, E.J. (1973). 'The khwushnishin population of Iran', *Iranian Studies*, 6:4, 229–45.

Hooglund, E.J. (1982). *Land and Revolution in Iran, 1960–1980.* Austin: University of Texas Press.

Hosseini, M. (2017). 'Asadollah Asgar-Owladi's criticism of Raisi's and Qalibaf's election promises in an interview with "*E'temād*": these are all slogans', *E'temād*, 11 May. Available at: www.magiran.com/article/3557208 (accessed 1 May 2022).

Hourcade, B. (2004). وقف و مدرنیته در ایران: کشت و صنعت آستان قدس رضوی. ['Endowment and modernity: Cultivation and industry of the Imam Reza Shrine Foundation'], *Goftogu*, 39, 85–109.

Hovsepian-Bearce, Y. (2015). *The Political Ideology of Ayatollah Khamenei: Out of the mouth of the Supreme Leader of Iran.* New York: Routledge.

Human Rights Activists News Agency (2022). 'A Statistical Look at the Situation of Iranian Workers over the Past Year', 29 April. Available at: www.en-hrana.org/a-statistical-look-at-the-situation-of-iranian-workers-over-the-past-year/ (accessed 21 August 2022).

Human Rights Watch (2013). 'Iran: Government Trampling Workers' Rights Campaign Highlights Labour Concerns on International Workers' Day', 30 April. Available at: www.hrw.org/news/2013/04/30/iran-government-trampling-workers-rights (accessed 11 August 2022).

Ilias, S. (2010). 'Iran's economic conditions: US policy issues'. Congressional Research Service Report for Congress. Available at: https://msuweb.montclair.edu/~lebelp/ShayerahIliasIranEconomicConditionsCRS2010.pdf (accessed 17 August 2022).

ILNA (2017). 'Minister of Roads and Urban Development: The Compassion Housing Project increased house prices by 500 Per cent', 10 October. Available at: www.ilna.ir/بخش-اقتص ادی- 4/ 544 -890مسکن-مهر-قیمت-خانه-را-درصد-افز ایش-داد-ثبات- قیمت-زمین-در-دولت-یازدهم (accessed 11 August 2022).

IMF DataMapper. Available at: www.imf.org/external/datamapper/NGDP_RPCH @WEO/OEMDC/ADVEC/WEOWORLD (accessed 13 September 2022).

IMF (1998). 'Islamic Republic of Iran: Recent economic developments', Staff Country Report no. 98/27. Available at: www.imf.org/en/Publications/CR/Issues/2016/12/30/Islamic-Republic-of-Iran-Recent-Economic-Developments-2564 (accessed 13 September 2022).

IMF (2006). 'Islamic Republic of Iran: Staff report for the 2005 Article IV Consultation'. Country Report no. 06/154. Available at: www.imf.org/en/Publications/CR/Issues/2016/12/31/Islamic-Republic-of-Iran-Staff-Report-for-the-2005-Article-IV-Consultation-19177 (accessed 13 September 2022).

*Irān* (2010). 'The end of the attempt to limit the power of the Guardian Council', 13 March. Available at: www.magiran.com/article/2056117 (accessed 13 September 2022).

*Irān* (2016). 'The obstacles to the effective presence of the private sector in the national economy', 27 July. Available at: www.magiran.com/article/3401143 (accessed 13 September 2022).

Iran Data Portal (no date a). 'The Guardian Council letter, no. 1234', dated 1/3/1370 [5/22/1991]. Interpretation of Article 99. Available at: https://irandataportal.syr.edu/interpretation-of-article-99 (accessed 13 September 2022).

Iran Data Portal (no date b). 'The general policies pertaining to Principle 44 of the Constitution of the Islamic Republic of Iran'. Available at: https://irandataportal.syr.edu/the-general-policies-pertaining-to-principle-44-of-the-constitution-of-the-islamic-republic-of-iran (accessed 13 September 2022).

Iran Online (2017). 'The Imam Reza Shrine Foundation is not exempted from withholding and value-added taxes', 9 May. Available at: www.ion.ir/news/215279/ (accessed 13 September 2022).

IRNA (2017). 'Ex-UK FM Straw sees Iran-West relationship missed opportunity', 31 October. Available at: https://en.irna.ir/news/82714939/Ex-UK-FM-Straw-sees-Iran-West-relationship-missed-opportunity (accessed 11 August 2022).

Islamic Parliament Research Center (2016). [بیکاری، اشتغال و بازار کار 'Unemployment, Employment, and the Labour Market']. Report no. 14978. Available at: https://rc.majlis.ir/fa/report/show/985478 (accessed 13 September 2022).

Islamic Parliament Research Center (2017a). واکاوی افزایش اشتغال در سال های 1394 و 1395 ['Probing the employment increase in 2015 and 2016']. Report no. 15431. Available at: https://rc.majlis.ir/fa/report/show/1026394 (accessed 13 September 2022).

Islamic Parliament Research Center (2017b). تحلیل الگوی اشتغال در بخش صنعت ایران (با بررسی طرح کارانه اشتغال برای جوانان (کاج)) ['An analysis of the pattern of employment in the Iranian industrial sector'], report no. 15521. Available at: https://rc.majlis.ir/fa/report/show/1031525 (accessed 13 September 2022).

ISNA (2021). '97 per cent of work contracts are temporary/the number of job seekers is several times bigger than the number of job opportunities', 6 May. Available at: www.isna.ir/ news/ 140002 1610 589/۹۷--افراد-تعداد-است-موقت-کار-های-قرارداد-درصد جویای-کار-چندین (accessed 13 September 2022).

Issawi, C. (1991). 'European economic penetration, 1872–1921', in Avery, P., Hambly, G.R.G. and Melville, C. (eds), *The Cambridge History of Iran (Vol. 7)*. Cambridge: Cambridge University Press, pp. 590–607.

Jafari, P. (2009). 'Rupture and revolt in Iran', *International Socialism*, 124:1, 95–136. Available at: https://isj.org.uk/rupture-and-revolt-in-iran/ (accessed 16 August 2022).

Jafari, p. (2021). 'Impasse in Iran: Workers versus authoritarian neoliberalism', in Azzellini, D. (ed.), *If Not Us, Who?* Hamburg: VSA Verlag, pp. 143–9.

Jahanbakhsh, F. (2001). *Islam, Democracy and Religious Modernism in Iran, 1953–2000: From Bāzargān to Soroush (Vol. 77)*. Leiden: Brill.

Jahanbegloo, R. (2011a). *Civil Society and Cemocracy in Iran*. New York: Lexington Books.

Jahanbegloo, R. (2011b). 'Iran and the democratic struggle in the Middle East', *Middle East Law and Governance*, 3:1–2, 126–35.

Jamārān News (2022). 'Only 4 per cent of workers in Iran have job security! – 96% of contracts are temporary', 5 May. Available at: www.jama ran.news/-جی-بخش پلاس- /70 1550 -562فقط-درصد-کارگران-در-ایران-امنیت-شغلی-دارند-درصد-قراردا دها-موقت-است (accessed 13 September 2022).

Jām-e jam Online (2004). 'Different comments regarding the Turkcell contract', 24 September. Available at: https://jamejamonline.ir/fa/news/48784/ (accessed 13 September 2022).

*Jomhuri-ye Eslāmi* (1997a). 'People are thirsty for social justice', 5 August. Archival Research.

*Jomhuri-ye Eslāmi* (1997b). 'The necessity of serious fight against the bonanza phenomenon Part I', 6 August. Archival Research.

*Jomhuri-ye Eslāmi* (1997c). 'The necessity of serious fight against the bonanza phenomenon Part II', 7 August. Archival Research.

*Jomhuri-ye Eslāmi* (1997d). 'The necessity of serious fight against the bonanza phenomenon Part III', 9 August. Archival Research.

Joyner, D.H. (2016). *Iran's Nuclear Program and International Law: From confrontation to accord*. Oxford: Oxford University Press.

Kadivar, M.A. et al. (2021). 'Labor organizing on the rise among Iranian oil workers', *Middle East Report Online*, 25 August. Available at: https://merip.org/2021/08/labor-organizing-on-the-rise-among-iranian-oil-workers/ (accessed 21 August 2022).

Kamel, M.S. (2018). 'China's belt and road initiative: Implications for the Middle East', *Cambridge Review of International Affairs*, 31:1, 76–95.

Kamrava, M. (2001). 'The civil society discourse in Iran', *British Journal of Middle Eastern Studies*, 28:2, 165–85.

Kamrava, M. (2003). 'Iranian Shiism under debate', *Middle East Policy*, 10:2, 102–12.

Kamrava, M. (2008). *Iran's Intellectual Revolution*. Cambridge: Cambridge University Press.

Kanovsky, E. (1998). 'Iran's sick economy: Prospects for change under Khatami', in Clawson, P.L. (ed.), *Iran under Khatami: A political, economic, and military assessment*. Washington, DC: Washington Institute for Near East Policy, pp. 57–70.

Karbassian, A. (2000). 'Islamic revolution and the management of the Iranian economy', *Social Research*, 67:2, 621–40.

Karlin, M. and Wittes, T.C. (2019). 'America's Middle East purgatory: The case for doing less', Foreign Affairs, January/February 2019. Available at: www.foreignaffairs.com/articles/middle-east/2018-12-11/americas-middle-east-purgatory?cid=nlc-fa_fatoday-20181220 (accessed 2 August 2022).

Karshenas, M. (1990a). *Oil, State and Industrialisation in Iran*. Cambridge: Cambridge University Press.

Karshenas, M. (1990b). 'Oil income, industrialisation bias, and the agricultural squeeze hypothesis: New evidence on the experience of Iran', *Journal of Peasant Studies*, 17:2, 245–72.

Karshenas, M. and Pesaran, H. (1995). 'Economic reform and the reconstruction of the Iranian economy', *Middle East Journal*, 49:1, 89–111.

Karuka, M. (2021). 'Hunger politics: Sanctions as siege warfare', in Davis, S. and Ness, I. (eds), *Sanctions as War: Anti-imperialist perspectives on American geo-economic strategy*. Leiden: Brill, pp. 51–62.

Katouzian, H. (1981). *The Political Economy of Modern Iran: Despotism and pseudo-modernism, 1926–1979*. London: Macmillan Press.

Katouzian, H. (1999). *Musaddiq and the Struggle for Power in Iran*. London: I.B. Tauris.

Katouzian, M.A. (1974). 'Land reform in Iran: A case study in the political economy of social engineering', *Journal of Peasant Studies*, 1:2, 220–39.

Katouzian, M.A. (1978). 'Oil versus agriculture: A case of dual resource depletion in Iran', *Journal of Peasant Studies*, 5:3, 347–69.

Katz, C. (2022). *Dependency Theory After Fifty Years: The continuing relevance of Latin American critical thought*. Leiden: Brill.

Katzman, K. (2006). 'Iran's bonyads: Economic strengths and weaknesses', Emirates Centre for Strategic Studies and Research, 6 August. Available at: www.ecssr.ae/en/reports_analysis/irans-bonyads-economic-strengths-and-weaknesses/ (accessed 18 August 2022).

Kaussler, B. (2008). 'European Union constructive engagement with Iran (2000–2004): An exercise in conditional human rights diplomacy', *Iranian Studies*, 41:3, 269–95.

Kaussler, B. (2013). *Iran's Nuclear Diplomacy: Power politics and conflict resolution*. Abingdon: Routledge.

*Kayhan* (2011). 'General Jafari's account of the prominent role of Khatam-al Anbiya Headquarter in the management of the sanctions', 8 August. Available at: www.magiran.com/article/2333035 (accessed 13 September 2022).

*Kayhan* (2016). 'Kayhan evaluates: Repeating the bitter experience of Turkcell in a new contact of the Ministry of Energy', 2 November. Available at: www.magiran.com/article/3457869 (accessed 13 September 2022).

*Kayhan* (2017). 'Exclusive report: Government debt to the IRGC exceeded 230 trillion rials', 5 July. Available at: www.magiran.com/article/3586985 (accessed 13 September 2022).

Kazemi, F. (1980). *Poverty and Revolution in Iran*. New York: New York University Press.

Kazemi, F. and Abrahamian, E. (1978). 'The nonrevolutionary peasantry of modern Iran', *Iranian Studies*, 11:1–4, 259–304.

Kazemian, M. (1999). 'Removing the proactive supervision is the realisation of [the Slog] Iran for all Iranians', *Khordad*, 10 May. Archival Research.

Keddie, N. (1991). 'Iran under the late Qajars, 1848–1992', in Avery, P., Hambly, G.R.G. and Melville, C. (eds), *The Cambridge History of Iran (Vol. 7)*. Cambridge: Cambridge University Press, pp. 174–212.

Keddie, N. (2003). *Modern Iran: Roots and results of revolution*. New Haven, CT: Yale University Press.

Kerr, S., England, A. and Bozorgmehr, N. (2019). 'Iran's economy slumps as US sanctions pile on the pain', *Financial Times*, 29 April. Available at: www.ft.com/content/ac599cf4-6a72-11e9-80c7-60ee53e6681d (accessed 21 July 2022).

Keshavarzian, A. (2007). *Bazaar and State in Iran: The politics of the Thran marketplace*. Cambridge: Cambridge University Press.

Khairollahi, A. (2018). اقتصاد سیاسی »بحران« تأمین اجتماعی در ایران ['The political economy of the "crisis" of social security in Iran'], *Naqd-e Eqtesād-e Siāsi*, 5, 1–50.

Khajehpour, B. (2000). 'Domestic political reforms and private sector activity in Iran', *Social Research*, 67:2, 577–98.

Khalaj, M. (2019). 'Revolutionary Guards drill into Iran's gas potential', *Financial Times*, 21 March. Available at: www.ft.com/content/ff6184bc-4af0-11e9–8b7f-d49067e0f50d (accessed 3 June 2022).

Khalatbari, F. (1994). 'The Tehran Stock Exchange and privatization of public sector enterprises in Iran', in Coville, T. (ed.), *The Economy of Islamic Iran: Between state and market*. Paris: Peeters.

Khomeini, R. (2008). صحیفه نور جلد بیستم *[Sahife' Noor Vol 20]*. Tehran: Mo'sseseh-e Tanzim va Nashr-e Āsār-e Emām. The Institute for Compilation and Publication of Imam Khomeini's Works.

*Khordād* (1999). '116 conservative MPs legalised proactive supervisory power', 11 August. Archival Research.

Khosrokhavar, F. (2011). 'The Green Movement in Iran: Democratization and secularization from below', in Jahanbegloo, R. (ed.), *Civil Society and Democracy in Iran*. New York: Lexington Books, pp. 39–78.

Khosrokhavar, F. (2012). 'The Green Movement', in Hooglund, E. and Stenberg, L. (eds), *Navigating Contemporary Iran: Challenging economic, social and political perceptions*. London: Routledge.

Khuzestani, J.M. (1999). 'The role of the proactive supervision at the service of totalitarians', *Sobh-e Emrouz*, 11 May. Archival Research.

Kiely, R. (2007). *The New Political Economy of Development: Globalization, imperialism, hegemony*. Basingstoke: Palgrave Macmillan.

Kiely, R. (2010). *Rethinking Imperialism*. Basingstoke: Palgrave Macmillan.

Klein, N. (2007). *The Shock Doctrine: The rise of disaster capitalism*. London: Penguin.

Kohli, A. (2004). *State-Directed Development: Political power and industrialization in the global periphery*. Cambridge: Cambridge University Press.

Konings, M. (2012). 'Neoliberalism & the state', *Alternate Routes: A Journal of Critical Social Research*, 23, 85–98.

Kozhanov, N. (2018). *Russian Policy Across the Middle East: Motivations and methods*. London: Chatham House, Royal Institute of International Affairs.

Kulaai, A. and Mazarei, Y. (2016). (نوسازی و تحزب (مطالعه موردی: دولت هاشمی رفسنجانی) ['Modernisation and political party building: The case study of the Hashemi Rafsanjani administration'], *Siāsat*, 46:2, 403–22.

Kurzman, C. (2012). 'The Arab Spring: Ideals of the Iranian Green Movement, methods of the Iranian revolution', *International Journal of Middle East Studies*, 44:1, 162–5.

Labor Law of Iran (1990). English Translation (the International Labour Organization). Available at: www.ilo.org/dyn/natlex/natlex4.detail?p_lang=en&p_isn=21843 (accessed 17 September 2022)

Lacher, H. (2002). 'Making sense of the international system', in Rupert, M. and Smith, H. (eds), *Historical Materialism and Globalization*. London: Routledge, pp. 147–64.

Lambton, A. (1991). *Landlord and Peasant in Persia: A study of land tenure and land revenue administration*. London: I.B. Tauris.

Lautenschlager, W. (1986). 'The effects of an overvalued exchanged rate on the Iranian economy, 1979–84', *International Journal of Middle East Studies*, 18:1, 31–52.

Law of the First Economic, Social and Cultural Development of the Islamic Republic of Iran (1990). Available at: http://rc.majlis.ir/fa/law/show/91755 (accessed 13 September 2022).

Law of the Fourth Economic, Social and Cultural Development of the Islamic Republic of Iran (2004). Available at: https://rc.majlis.ir/fa/law/show/94202 (accessed 13 September 2022).

Law of the Second Economic, Social and Cultural Development of the Islamic Republic of Iran (1994). Available at: https://rc.majlis.ir/fa/law/show/92488 (accessed 13 September 2022).

Law of the Third Economic, Social and Cultural Development of the Islamic Republic of Iran (2000). Available at: https://rc.majlis.ir/fa/law/show/93301 (accessed 13 September 2022).

Luxemburg, R. (1913/1951). *The Accumulation of Capital*. London: Routledge and Kegan Paul.

Mahdavi, M. (2011a). 'The civil society approach to democratization in Iran: The case for bringing it back carefully', in Jahanbegloo, R. (ed.), *Civil Society and Democracy in Iran*. New York: Lexington Books, pp. 79–93.

Mahdavi, M. (2011b). 'Post-Islamist trends in post-revolutionary Iran', Comparative Studies of South Asia, *Africa and the Middle East*, 31:1, 94–109.

Mahdi, A.A. (2004). 'The Iranian women's movement: A century long struggle', *The Muslim World*, 94:4, 427–48.

Malekzadeh, S. (2020). 'Why this time the protests in Iran are different', *Responsible Statecraft*, 17 January. Available at: https://responsiblestatecraft.org/2020/01/17/why-this-time-the-protests-in-iran-are-different/ (accessed 23 September 2022).

Maloney, S. (2000a). 'Agents or obstacles? Parastatal foundations and challenges for Iranian development', in Alizadeh, P. (ed.) *The Economy of Iran: Dilemmas of an Islamic state*. London: I.B. Tauris, pp. 145–76.

Maloney, S. (2000b). بنیادها و خصوصی سازی در ایران ['Foundations and Privatisation in Iran'], *Goftogu*, 28, 83–111.

Maloney, S. (2015). *Iran's Political Economy Since the Revolution*. Cambridge: Cambridge University Press.

Martin, R. (2013). *Constructing Capitalism: Transforming business systems in Central and Eastern Europe*. Oxford: Oxford University Press.

Marx, K. (1867/1990). *Capital, Vol. I*. London: Penguin Books.

Marx, K. (1885/1992). *Capital, Vol. II*. London: Penguin Books.

Matin, K. (2007). 'Uneven and combined development in world history: The international relations of state-formation in Premodern Iran', *European Journal of International Relations*, 13:3, 419–47.

Matin, K. (2012a). 'International relations in the making of political Islam: Interrogating Khomeini's 'Islamic government'', *Journal of International Relations and Development*, 16:4, 455–82.

Matin, K. (2012b). 'Democracy without Capitalism: Retheorizing Iran's Constitutional Revolution', *Middle East Critique*, 21:1, 37–56.

Matin, K. (2013a). *Recasting Iranian Modernity*. London: Routledge.

Matin, K. (2013b). 'Redeeming the universal: Postcolonialism and the inner life of Eurocentrism', *European Journal of International Relations*, 19:2, 353–77.

Matin-Asgari, A. (2022). 'The Iranian protests are the latest phase in a long cycle of popular unrest', *Jacobin*, 1 December. Available at: https://jacobin.com/2022/12/iran-protest-revolution-history-anti-imperialism-islamic-republic (accessed 27 March 2023).

Mazarei, A. (1996). 'The Iranian economy under the Islamic Republic: Institutional change and macroeconomic performance (1979–1990)', *Cambridge Journal of Economics*, 20:3, 289–314.

McLachlan, K.S. (1991). 'Economic development, 1921–1979', in Avery, P., Hambly, G.R.G. and Melville, C. (eds), *The Cambridge History of Iran (Vol. 7)*. Cambridge: Cambridge University Press, pp. 608–38.

McMichael, P. (1990). 'Incorporating comparison within a world-historical perspective: An alternative comparative method', *American Sociological Review*, 55:3, 385–97.

McMichael, P. (2000). 'World-systems analysis, globalization, and incorporated comparison', *Journal of World-Systems Research*, 6:3, 668–89.

McMichael, P. (2014). *Development and Social Change: A global perspective*. London: Sage.

Mehr News Agency (2017). 'Story of ten years anti-deprivation effort of the Barakat Foundation in the country', 11 December. Available at: www.mehrnews.com/news/4169408/روایت-۱۰-سال-تلاش-بنیاد-برکت-برای-محرومیت-زدایی-در-کشور (accessed 16 July 2022).

Mezzadri, A. (2019). 'On the value of social reproduction: Informal labour, the majority world and the need for inclusive theories and politics', *Radical Philosophy*, 2:4, 33–41.

Moaddel, M. (1986). 'The Shi'i ulama and the state in Iran', *Theory and Society*, 15:4, 519–56.

Moaddel, M. (1991). 'Class struggle in post-revolutionary Iran', *International Journal of Middle East Studies*, 23:3, 317–43.

Moaddel, M. (1993). *Class, Politics, and Ideology in the Iranian Revolution*. New York: Columbia University Press.

Moaddel, M. (1996). 'The social bases and discursive context of the rise of Islamic fundamentalism: The cases of Iran and Syria', *Sociological Inquiry*, 66:3, 330–55.

Moghadam, V. (1987). 'Socialism or anti-imperialism: The Left and revolution in Iran', *New Left Review*, 1:166, 5–28.

Mohammadnia, M. (2011). 'A holistic constructivist approach to Iran's foreign policy', *International Journal of Business and Social Science*, 2:4, 279–94.

Mohandesi, S. (2013). 'Class consciousness or class composition?' *Science & Society*, 77:1, 72–97.

Mohebi, M. (2014). *The Formation of Civil Society in Modern Iran: Public intellectuals and the state*. New York: Palgrave Macmillan.

Mohebian, A. (1998). 'Civil society and the logic of the Western infiltration', *Resālat*, 7 February. Archival Research.

Mohseni, P. (2016). 'Factionalism, privatization, and the political economy of regime transformation', in Brumberg, D. and Farhi, F. (eds), *Power and Change in Iran: Politics of contention and conciliation*. Bloomington: Indiana University Press, pp. 37–69.

Mohseni, P. and Kalout, H. (2017). 'Iran's axis of resistance rises', *Foreign Affairs*, 24 January. Available at: www.foreignaffairs.com/iran/irans-axis-resistance-rises (accessed 1 August 2022).

Momeni, F. (2014). اقتصاد ایران در دوران تعدیل ساختاری [*Iran's economy during the structural adjustment era*]. Tehran: Naghsh va Negār.

Momeni, F. and Naeb, S. (2017). تحولات تکنولوژی و آینده توسعه در ایران [*Technological transformation and the future of development in Iran*]. Tehran: Nahādgarā.

Morady, F. (2010). 'Iran: Islamic republic or God's kingdom? The election, protest, and prospects for change', *Research in Political Economy*, 26, 69–97.

Morady, F. (2011). 'Who rules Iran? The June 2009 election and political turmoil', *Capital and Class*, 35:1, 39–61.

Morady, F. (2020). *Contemporary Iran: Politics, economy, religion*. Bristol: Bristol University Press.

Morgana, M.S. (2019). 'Talking to workers: From Khomeini to Ahmadinejad, how the Islamic Republic's discourse on labor changed through May Day speeches (1979–2009)', *Iranian Studies*, 52:1–2, 133–58.

Morgana, M.S. (2020). 'Precarious workers and neoliberal narratives in post-revolutionary Iran: Top-Down Strategies and Bottom-Up Responses', Middle East Institute, 28 January. Available at: www.mei.edu/publications/precarious-workers-and-neoliberal-narratives-post-revolutionary-iran-top-down (accessed 16 August 2022).

Morgana, M.S. (2021). 'Trajectories of resistance and shifting forms of workers' activism in Iran', *International Labor and Working-Class History*, 1–20. doi: 10.1017/S0147547921000077.

Mortazavi, S.Z. (1996). 'Social justice in confrontation with American Islam', *Jomhuri-ye eslāmi*, 11, 12, 13, 15 June (4 parts). Archival Research.

Morton, A.D. (2007). 'Disputing the geopolitics of the states system and global capitalism', *Cambridge Review of International Affairs*, 20:4, 599–617.

Morton, A.D. (2010). 'The continuum of passive revolution', *Capital & Class*, 34:3, 315–42.

Morton, A.D. (2013a). *Revolution and the State in Modern Mexico: The political economy of uneven development*. Lanham, MD: Rowman & Littlefield.

Morton, A.D. (2013b). 'The limits of sociological Marxism?' *Historical Materialism*, 21:1, 129–58.

*Mosharekat* (2001). 'Theoretical foundation of the Islamic Revolution', 25 June. Archival Research.

Moshirzadeh, H. (2007). 'Discursive foundations of Iran's nuclear policy', *Security Dialogue*, 38:4, 521–43.

Moslem, M. (2002). *Factional Politics in Post-Khomeini Iran*. Syracuse, NY: Syracuse University Press.

Movasaghi, A. (2006). اقتصاد سیاسی ایران در دوره جمهوری اسلامی ['Political economy during the Islamic Republic Era']. *Siāsat*, 71, 311–54.

Mozaffari, M. (1991). 'Why the bazar rebels', *Journal of Peace Research*, 28:4, 377–91.

Nabavi, S.M. and Malayeri, M.H. (1996). درآمدی بر سیاست گزاری صنعتی در ایران ['An introduction to the industrial policymaking in Iran'], *Majles & Rāhbord*, 21, 16–44.

Nahvi, R. (2018). 'Casualisation of labourers in the triangle of danger', *Hamdeli*, 30 January. Available at: https://hamdelidaily.ir/index.php?newsletternumber=799 &page=4 (accessed 18 August 2022).

Najmabadi, A. (1987). *Land Reform and Social Change in Iran*. Salt Lake City: University of Utah Press.

Namazi, B. (2000). 'The legal aspects of doing business in Iran', *International Financial Law Review*, 19:2, 23–7.

Nasr, V. (2000). 'Politics within the Late-Pahlavi State: The Ministry of Economy and industrial policy 1963–69', *International Journal of Middle East Studies*, 32:1, 97–122.

Negri, A. and Hardt, M. (2000). *Empire*. Cambridge, MA: Harvard University Press.

Nellis, J. (1999). 'Time to rethink privatization in transition economies?' *World Bank. International Finance Corporation Discussion Paper*, IFD 38.

*Neshat* (1999). 'Mostazafan Foundation and structural problems', 24 July. Archival Research.

*New York Times* (1992). 'Iran allows foreigners to buy its companies', 28 June. Available at: www.nytimes.com/1992/06/29/business/iran-allows-foreigners-to-buy-its-companies.html (accessed 10 May 2022).

*New York Times* (2018). 'How corruption and cronyism in banking fuelled Iran's protests', 22 January. Available at: www.nytimes.com/2018/01/20/world/middleeast/iran-protests-corruption-banks.html (accessed 16 September 2022).

Niblock, T. (2020). 'China and the Middle East: A global strategy where the Middle East has a significant but limited place', *Asian Journal of Middle Eastern and Islamic Studies*, 14:4, 481–504.

Nikfar, M. (2001). 'A government with a crisis every nine days', *Hambastegi*, 6 June. Archival Research.

Nili, M. Darghagi, H. and Fatemi, S.F. (2012). بهره وری صنعت ایران: بررسی توان رقابت پذیری بنگاه های صنعتی [*The productivity of industry in Iran: Evaluation of the competitiveness of industrial enterprises*]. Tehran: Donyā-ye Eqtesād.

Nomani, F. and Behdad, S. (2006). *Class and Labour in Iran*. Syracuse, NY: Syracuse University Press.

Nomani, F. and Behdad, S. (2008). 'The rise and fall of Iranian classes in the post-revolutionary decades', *Middle Eastern Studies*, 44:3, 377–96.

Nomani, F. and Behdad, S. (2009). 'What a revolution! Thirty years of social class reshuffling in Iran', *Comparative Studies of South Asia, Africa and the Middle East*, 29:1, 84–104.

Nomani, F. and Behdad, S. (2012). 'Labour rights and the democracy movement in Iran: Building a social democracy', *Northwestern Journal of International Human Rights*, 10:4, 212–30.

Nowruzi, S. (2016). 'Will the knot of oil contracts be opened by the Setad?', BBC Persian, 5 October. Available at: www.bbc.com/persian/iran-features-37562382 (accessed 27 July 2022).

Oborne, P. and Morrison, D. (2013). 'US scuppered deal with Iran in 2005, says then British Foreign Minister', Open Democracy, 23 September. Available at: www.opendemocracy.net/david-morrison-peter-oborne/us-scuppered-deal-with-iran-in-2005-says-then-british-foreign-minister\ (accessed 27 July 2022).

Ollman, B. (1976). *Alienation: Marx's Conception of Man in Capitalist Society*. Cambridge: Cambridge University Press.

Ollman, B. (1993). *Dialectical Investigations*. London: Routledge.

Ollman, B. (2003). *Dance of the Dialectics: Steps in Marx's method*. Urbana: University of Illinois Press.

Ollman, B. (2015). 'Marxism and the philosophy of internal relations; or, how to replace the mysterious "paradox" with "contradictions" that can be studied and resolved', *Capital & Class*, 39:1, 7–23.

Omidvar, K. (2008). 'The Mostazafan Foundation, new trader of oil', BBC Persian, 24 June. Available at: www.bbc.com/persian/business/story/2008/06/080624_ge-iran-oil (accessed 3 August 2022).

Omidvar, K. (2012). 'Does the IRGC confiscate the state assets?' BBC Persian, 28 May. Available at: www.bbc.com/persian/business/2012/05/120528_ka_khatam_sepah (accessed 3 August 2022).

Ong, A. (2006). *Neoliberalism as Exception: Mutations in citizenship and sovereignty*. Durham and London: Duke University Press.

Oveisy, F. and Amini, B. (2018). 'The Iran protests: A third path to political change?' Socialist Project, 17 January. Available at: https://socialistproject.ca/2018/01/iran-protests-third-path-political-change/ (accessed 13 September 2022).

Pahlavi, M.R. (1980). *Answer to History*. New York: Stein and Day.

Panitch, L. and Gindin, S. (2004). 'Global capitalism and American empire', *Socialist Register*, 40, 1–42.

Panitch, L. and Gindin, S. (2012). *The Making of Global Capitalism*. London: Verso.

Papan-Matin, F. (Trans.) (2014). 'The Constitution of the Islamic Republic of Iran (1989 Edition)', *Iranian Studies*, 47:1, 159–200.

Parkhideh, A. (2008). صنعت و تجربه سیاست‌گذاری صنعتی در ایران قبل و بعد از انقلاب اسلامی. [*Industry and the experience of industrial policymaking in Iran before and after the Islamic Revolution*]. Tehran: Markaz-e Asnād-e Enqlāb-e Eslāmi.

Parsa, M. (1994). 'Mosque of last resort: State reform and social conflict in the early 1960s', in Moghadam, V. and Foran, J. (eds), *A Century of Revolution: Social movements in Iran*. Minneapolis: University of Minnesota Press, pp. 135–59.

Parsa, M. (2009). 'State, class, and ideology in the Iranian Revolution', *Comparative Studies of South Asia, Africa and the Middle East*, 29:1, 3–17.

Pesaran, M.H. (1982). 'The system of dependent capitalism in pre-and post-revolutionary Iran', *International Journal of Middle East Studies*, 14:4, 501–22.

Pickard, J. and Mance, H. (2016). 'Sajid Javid to lead high-level export push to Iran', *Financial Times*, 9 March. Available at: www.ft.com/content/66ea3cbc-e552-11e5-a09b-1f8b0d268c39 (accessed 16 August 2022).

Poulantzas, N. (1973). *Political Power and Social Classes*. London: New Left Books.

Poulantzas, N. (1978). *Classes in Contemporary Capitalism*. London: Verso.

Pozo-Martin, G. (2007). 'Autonomous or materialist geopolitics?' *Cambridge Review of International Affairs*, 20:4, 551–63.

Prapanchi, M. (2005). 'Turkcell: we will leave Iran; the Majles: goodbye', BBC Persian, 1 February. Available at: www.bbc.com/persian/iran/story/2005/02/printable/050201_mj-mp-iran-turkcell (accessed 16 September 2022).

*Problematica* (2015). 'Interview with Mohsen Hakimi (Labour Activists): Experiences and Prospect of Independent Labour Organisations', 14 December.

Radio Farda (2017). 'IRGC commander's sharp response to Rouhani', 27 June. Available at: https://en.radiofarda.com/a/iran-rouhani-irgc-response-on-economy/28581813.html (accessed 16 August 2022).

Radio Farda (2018). 'Enemies fomenting labour discord, says Khamenei', 27 February. Available at: https://en.radiofarda.com/a/iran-khamenei-says-enemies-foemnting-labor-discord/29065673.html (accessed 16 August 2022).

Radio Farda (2019). 'Resolution of the Majles: The Imam Reza Shrine Foundation and economic entities of the revolutionary institutions must pay taxes', 23 February. Available at: www.radiofarda.com/a/iran-parliament-approved-organizations-under-khamenei-supervision-must-pay-taxes/29786821.html (accessed 30 August 2022)

Rahnema, S. (1996). 'Continuity and change in industrial policy', in Rahnema, S. and Behdad, S. (eds), *Iran After the Revolution*. London: I.B. Tauris, pp. 129–42.

Raja News (2015). 'Interview with H.R. Taraghi: Behind the scenes of the formation of the Executives of Construction Party', 3 May. Available at: www.rajanews.com/news/210036 (accessed 16 August 2022).

Rakel, E.P. (2007). 'Conglomerates in Iran: the political economy of Islamic Foundations', in Hogenboom, B. and Jilberto, A.E.F. (eds), *Big Business and Economic Development: Conglomerates and economic groups in developing countries and transition economies under globalisation*. London: Routledge, pp. 109–33.

Rakel, E.P. (2008). *Power, Islam, and Political Elite in Iran*. Boston: Brill.

Rakel, E.P. (2009). 'The political elite in the Islamic Republic of Iran: From Khomeini to Ahmadinejad', *Comparative Studies of South Asia, Africa and the Middle East*, 29:1, 105–25.

Ramazani, R.K. (2012). 'Iran's foreign policy: Independence, freedom and the Islamic Republic', in Ehteshami, A. and Zweiri, M. (eds), *Iran's Foreign Policy: From Khatami to Ahmadinejad*. Reading: Ithaca Press, pp. 1–16.

Ranjipour, A. (2017). 'A calamity named the Compassion Housing Project', BBC Persian, 22 November. Available at: www.bbc.com/persian/blog-viewpoints-42079543 (accessed 16 August 2022).

Rasa, H. (2016). 'The Six Majles; sit-in, protest', BBC Persian, 24 February. Available at: www.bbc.com/persian/iran/2016/02/160214_ir94_6th_majlis (accessed 16 August 2022).

Razaghi, E. (1997). آشنایی با اقتصاد ایران [*Introduction to the Iranian economy*]. Tehran: Ney.

Razavi Economic Organisation website. Available at: https://globe.razavi.ir/en/ 69789/razavi-economic-organization (accessed 13 September 2022).

Razavi-Faqih, S. (2002). 'The manifest of the Islamic Revolution', *Nvwruz*, 3 February. Archival Research.

Reals, T. and Wassef, K. (2022). 'Iran supreme leader lauds Putin for starting Ukraine war and says if he hadn't, "dangerous" NATO would have', CBS News, 20 July. Available at: www.cbsnews.com/news/russia-ukraine-war-iran-vladimir-putin-khamenei-nato-us/ (accessed 25 August 2022).

Reisinezhad, A. (2015). 'The Iranian Green Movement: Fragmented collective action and fragile collective identity', *Iranian Studies*, 48:2, 193–222.

*Resālat* (1995). 'Economic discipline and the cliff of consumerism and luxurism', 10 July. Archival Research.

*Resālat* (1996). 'Preserving values, a fundamental principle', 14 May. Archival Research.

*Resālat* (1997a). ' "Construction" requires clean hands', 24 February. Archival Research.

*Resālat* (1997b). 'Avoiding luxurism', 16 March. Archival Research.

*Resālat* (1997c). 'Cost for the government, profit for individuals: This is not privatisation', 11 August. Archival Research.

*Resālat* (2009). 'Ayatollah Yazdi: Creation of a parallel entity for supervising elections is illegal and irrational', 31 May. Available at: www.magiran.com/article/ 1870167 (accessed 16 August 2022).

*Resālat* (2017a). 'Aladdin Broujerdi: The Ghorb is the most capable economic and developmental group in the Country', 25 January. Available at: www.magiran. com/article/3505493 (accessed 16 August 2022).

*Resālat* (2017b). 'Fatah (the head of Relief Committee): 6 per cent of the country's population is under the protection of the Relief Committee', 10 September. Available at: www.magiran.com/article/3595386 (accessed 16 August 2022).

*Resālat* (2017c). 'Fattah: 12 million people live in absolute poverty', 18 September. Available at: www.magiran.com/article/3630390 (accessed 16 August 2022).

Reuters (2017). 'Factbox – Iran's deals with foreign firms since easing of sanctions', 15 October. Available at: www.reuters.com/article/uk-iran-nuclear-economy-deals-factbox-idUKKBN1CK0CZ (accessed 17 August 2022).

Reuters (2021). 'China denounces G7 statement, urges group to stop slandering country', 14 June. Available at: www.reuters.com/world/china/china-denounces-g7-statement-urges-group-stop-slandering-country-2021-06-14/ (accessed 17 August 2022).

Reuters (2022). 'Iran to start accepting Russian Mir payment cards soon – official', 27 July. Available at: www.reuters.com/business/finance/iran-start-accepting-russian-mir-payment-cards-soon-official-2022-07-27/ (accessed 17 August 2022).

Rezaei, F. and Moshirabas, S.K. (2018). 'The Revolutionary Guards: From spoiler to accepter of the nuclear agreement', *British Journal of Middle Eastern Studies*, 45:2, 138–55.

Richards, H. (1975). 'America's Shah Shahanshah's Iran', *MERIP Reports*, 40, 3–26.

Ritter, D.P. (2015). *The Iron Cage of Liberalism: International politics and unarmed revolutions in the Middle East and North Africa*. Oxford: Oxford University Press.

Robinson, W. (2001). 'Social theory and globalization: The rise of a transnational state', *Theory and Society*, 30:2, 157–200.

Robinson, W. (2004). *A Theory of Global Capitalism*. Baltimore, MD and London: Johns Hopkins University Press.

Robinson, W. and Harris, J. (2000). 'Towards a global ruling class? Globalization and the transnational capitalist class', *Science & Society*, 64:1, 11–54.

Roccu, R. (2017). 'Passive revolution revisited: From the prison notebooks to our "great and terrible world"', *Capital & Class*, 41:3, 537–59.

Rosenberg, J. (2005). 'Globalization theory: A post mortem', *International Politics*, 42:1, 2–74.

Rosenberg, J. (2006). 'Why is there no international historical sociology?' *European Journal of International Relations*, 12:3, 307–40.

Rostami, A. (1999). 'Political game regarding the Mostazafan Foundation', *Resālat*, 7 September. Archival Research.

Rostami-Povey, E. (2010). *Iran's Influence: A religious-political state and society in its region*. London: Zed Books.

Rundle, C. (2012). 'Iran–United Kingdom relations since the revolution: Opening doors', in Ehteshami, A. and Zweiri, M. (eds), *Iran's Foreign Policy: From Khatami to Ahmadinejad*. Reading: Ithaca Press, pp. 89–104.

Sabet-Sadie, S. (2012). 'Iranian–European relations: A strategic partnership?', in Ehteshami, A. and Zweiri, M. (eds), *Iran's Foreign Policy: From Khatami to Ahmadinejad*. Reading: Ithaca Press, pp. 55–72.

Sabouniha, A. (2017). 'Privatisation', in Nili, M. et al. (eds), اقتصاد ایران به کدام سو می‌رود؟ [*Which direction is Iran's economy moving?*].Tehran: Donyā-ye Eqtesād, pp. 501–58.

Sadeghi-Boroujerdi, E. (2023). Iran's uprisings for 'Women, Life, Freedom': Over-determination, crisis, and the lineages of revolt, *Politics*, 1–15. doi: 10.1177/02633957231159351.

Sadeghi-Brojeni, K. (2011). نئولیبرالیسم در بوته ی نقد [*Neoliberalism under critical scrutiny*]. H&L Media.

Sadjadpour, K. (2008). *Reading Khamenei: The world view of Iran's most powerful leader*. Washington, DC: Carnegie Endowment for International Peace.

Sadri, M. (2001). 'Sacral defense of secularism: The political theologies of Soroush, Shabestari, and Kadivar', *International Journal of Politics, Culture, and Society*, 15:2, 257–70.

Saeidi, A.A. (2004). 'The Accountability of para-governmental organizations (bony-ads): The case of Iranian foundations', *Iranian Studies*, 37:3, 479–98.

Sahimi, M. (2021). 'A century of economic blackmail, sanctions and war against Iran', in Davis, S. and Ness, I. (eds), *Sanctions as War: Anti-imperialist perspectives on American geo-economic strategy*. Leiden: Brill, pp. 165–89.

Samiee, M. (2022). 'Beyond rentier state and climate conflict: Clashing environmental imaginaries and ecological oppression in Iran', in Dunlap, A. and Brock, A. (eds), *Enforcing Ecocide: Power, policing & planetary militarization*. Cham, Switzerland: Palgrave Macmillan.

Saull, R. (2012). 'Rethinking hegemony: Uneven development, historical blocs, and the world economic crisis', *International Studies Quarterly*, 56:2, 323–38.

Schimmel, A. (2022). 'Sufism'. *Encyclopaedia Britannica*. Available at: www.britannica.com/topic/Sufism (accessed 13 September 2022).

Schirazi, A. (1993). *Islamic Development Policy: The agrarian question in Iran*. Boulder, CO: Lynne Rienner.

Sedaghat, P. (2017). اقتصاد سیاسی نابرابری درآمدی در ایران ['The political economy of income inequality in Iran'], *Naqd-e Eqtesād-e Siāsi*, 5, 10–19.

Selwyn, B. (2009). 'An historical materialist appraisal of Friedrich List and his modern-day followers', *New Political Economy*, 14:2, 157–80.

Selwyn, B. (2014). *The Global Development Crisis*. Cambridge: Polity.

Selwyn, B. (2016). 'Elite development theory: A labour-centred critique', *Third World Quarterly*, 37:5, 781–99.

Sevastopulo, D. et al. (2019). 'US to eliminate sanctions waivers on Iran oil imports', *Financial Times*, 22 April. Available at: www.ft.com/content/b45dcb40-649c-11e9-9adc-98bf1d35a056 (accessed 18 August 2022).

Shaddel, M. (2018). 'How Rouhani's neoliberal policies provoked unrest in Iran', Open Democracy, 1 February. Available at: www.opendemocracy.net/en/north-africa-west-asia/how-rouhani-s-neoliberal-policies-provoked-unrest-in-iran/ (accessed 18 August 2022).

*Shargh* (2010). 'Interview with Ahmad Khorram: Two views prevent the attraction of FDI', 21 August, p. 4. Available at: www.magiran.com/article/2174481 (accessed 18 August 2022).

*Shargh* (2013). 'The spokesman of the IRGC in conversation with Shargh declares: Revisiting the IRGC relationships with the governments of Hashemi, Khatami, and Ahmadinejad', 22 July. Available at: www.magiran.com/article/2780581 (accessed 18 August 2022).

*Shargh* (2016). 'Everything about the Ghorb', 31 December. Available at: www.magiran.com/article/3489891 (accessed 20 August 2022).

*Shargh* (2017a). 'New campaign of Rostam', 21 February. Available at: www.magiran.com/article/3520654 (accessed 20 August 2022).

*Shargh* (2017b). 'The Ghorb's reaction to the contract with the Total', 8 July. Available at: www.magiran.com/article/3588211 (accessed 20 August 2022).

*Shargh* (2017c). 'Empire of "Khosoolatiha"', 21 November. Available at: https://www.magiran.com/article/3664708 (accessed 18 August 2022).

Shariatinia, M. and Azizi, H. (2019). 'Iran and the Belt and Road Initiative: Amid hope and fear', *Journal of Contemporary China*, 28:120, 984–94.

Shariatmadari, H. (2017). 'If there wasn't that duality', *Kayhan*, 7 August. Available at: www.magiran.com/article/3605535 (accessed 20 August 2022).

Sharltouki, A. (2016). 'Mashhad: a mutiny that suppressed', BBC Persian, 31 August. Available at: www.bbc.com/persian/blogs/2016/08/160831_l44_nazeran_mashhad_mutiny (accessed 20 August 2022).

Siavoshi, S. (1992). 'Factionalism and Iranian politics: The post-Khomeini experience', *Iranian Studies*, 25:3/4, 27–49.

Sick, G. (2011). 'Iran's foreign policy: A revolution in transition', in Keddie, N. and Matthee, R. (eds.), *Iran and the Surrounding World: Interactions in culture and cultural politics*. Seattle, WA: University of Washington Press, pp. 355–76.

Simpson, K. (2016). *US Nuclear Diplomacy with Iran: From the War on Terror to the Obama Administration*. London: Rowman & Littlefield.

Sinaee, M. (2022). 'Iran developed too many COVID vaccine varieties, mostly unused', Iran International, 26 April. Available at: www.iranintl.com/en/202204267681 (accessed 23 September 2022).

Skocpol, T. (1979). *States and Social Revolutions: A comparative analysis of France, Russia and China*. Cambridge: Cambridge University Press.

Skocpol, T. (1982). 'Rentier state and Shi'a Islam in the Iranian revolution', *Theory and Society*, 11:3, 265–83.

Smith, B. (2004). 'Collective action with and without Islam: Mobilizing the Bazaar in Iran', in Wiktorowicz, Q. (ed.), *Islamic Activism: A social movement theory approach*. Bloomington: Indiana University Press, pp. 185–204.

Smith, N. (2006). 'The geography of uneven development', in Dunn, B. and Radice, H. (eds), *100 Years of Permanent Revolution*. London: Pluto, pp. 180–95.

Sodaie, A. (2016). 'Why the Majles report regarding the Martyrs' Foundation corruption was not read?', BBC Persian, 25 May. Available at: www.bbc.com/persian/iran/2016/05/160525_l45_shahid_foundation_corruption_investigation (accessed 20 August 2022).

Soleimani, K. and Mohammadpour, A. (2020). 'The Securitisation of Life: Eastern Kurdistan Under the Rule of a Perso-Shi'i State', *Third World Quarterly*, 41:4, 663–82.

Soltani, S.A. (2005). قدرت، گفتمان و زبان: سازوکارهای جریان قدرت در جمهوری اسلامی ایران. [*Power, discourse and language: Mechanisms of power in the Islamic Republic of Iran*]. Tehran: Ney.

Soroush, A., Sadri, M. and Sadri, A. (2000). *Reason, Freedom & Democracy: Essential writings of Abdolkarim Soroush*. Oxford: Oxford University Press.

Statistical Center of Iran (1996/1997). *Statistical Yearbook*. Available at: www.amar.org.ir/صفحه-نخست/آرشیو-تازه های-نشر/agentT ype/ ViewT ype/ Pro pert yTyp eID/ 1735 (accessed 13 September 2022).

Statistical Center of Iran (2015/2016). *Statistical Yearbook*. Available at: www.amar.org.ir/صفحه-نخست/آرشیو-تازه های-نشر/agentT ype/ ViewT ype/ Pro pert yTyp eID/ 1735/ currentpage/2 (accessed 13 September 2022).

Statistical Center of Iran, Censuses for 1986, 1991, 1996, 2006, 2011 and 2016. Available at: www.amar.org.ir/سرشم اری-عمومی-نفوس-و-مسکن/نتایج-سرشم اری (accessed 16 September 2022).

Stecklow, S., Dehghanpisheh, B. and Torbati, Y. (2013). 'Assets of the Ayatollah I: Khamenei controls massive financial empire built on property seizures', Reuters, 11 November. Available at: www.reuters.com/investigates/iran/#article/part1 (accessed 21 August 2022).

Stepanova, E. (2018). 'Russia and conflicts in the Middle East: Regionalisation and implications for the west', *The International Spectator*, 53:4, 35–57.

Stork, J. (1975). *Middle East Oil and the Energy Crisis*. New York: Monthly Review Press.

Sukidi (2005). 'The travelling idea of Islamic Protestantism: A study of Iranian Luthers', *Islam and Christian–Muslim Relations*, 16:4, 401–12.

Sundquist, V. (2013a). 'Iranian democratization, part I: A historical case study of the Iranian Green Movement', *Journal of Strategic Security*, 6:1, 19–34.

Sundquist, V. (2013b). 'Iranian democratization, part II: The Green Movement – revolution or civil rights movement?', *Journal of Strategic Security*, 6:1, 35–46.

Tahmasebi-Birgani, V. (2010). 'Green women of Iran: The role of the women's movement during and after Iran's presidential election of 2009', *Constellations*, 17:1, 78–86.

Taiar, J. (1996a). 'Cultural camisado of the enemy to all aspects of the society', *Kayhan*, 6 March. Archival Research.

Taiar, J. (1996b). 'Dependent intellectuals, the channels of cultural infiltration of the enemy', *Kayhan*, 10 March. Archival Research.

Takeyh, R. (2004). 'Iran builds the bomb', *Survival*, 46:4, 51–63.

Tansel, C.B. (2015). 'Deafening silence? Marxism, international historical sociology and the spectre of Eurocentrism', *European Journal of International Relations*, 21:1, 76–100.

Tansel, C.B. (2016). 'Geopolitics, social forces, and the international: Revisiting the "Eastern Question"', *Review of International Studies*, 42:3, 492–512.

Tarock, A. (2001). 'The muzzling of the liberal press in Iran', *Third World Quarterly*, 22:4, 585–602.

Tasnim News Agency (2017). 'Child labour statistics range from 3 to 7 million', 27 September. Available at: www.tasnimnews.com/fa/news/1396/07/05/1531608/ آمار-کودکان-کار-ایران-بین-3-تا-7-میلیون-است (accessed 21 August 2022).

Taylor, I. (2017). 'Transnationalizing capitalist hegemony: A Poulantzian reading', *Alternatives*, 42:1, 26–40.

Teschke, B. (2003). *The Myth of 1648*. London: Verso.

Teschke, B. and Lacher, H. (2007). 'The changing "logics" of capitalist competition', *Cambridge Review of International Affairs*, 20:4, 565–80.

Thaler, D.E. et al. (2010). *Mullahs, Guards, and Bonyads: An exploration of Iranian leadership dynamics*. Santa Monica, CA: National Defense Research Institute.

*The Economist* (1997). 'Dual control: So many ways of pulling strings', 18 January.

*The Economist* (2001). 'A mess: How not to build a private sector', 19 July.

*The Iran Primer* (2020). 'Fact sheet: Protests in Iran (1979–2020)'. *United States Institute for Peace*. 21 January. Available at: https://iranprimer.usip.org/blog/ 2019/dec/05/fact-sheet-protests-iran-1999-2019-0 (accessed 24 August 2022).

Thompson, E.P. (1963). *The Making of the English Working Class*. New York: Vintage.

Thompson, E.P. (1978). 'Eighteenth-Century English society: Class struggle without class?' *Social History*, 3:2, 133–65.

Torati, Y., Stecklow, S. and Dehghanpisheh, B. (2013). 'Assets of the Ayatollah III: To expand Khamenei's grip on the economy, Iran stretched its laws', Reuters, 13 November. Available at: www.reuters.com/investigates/iran/#article/part3 (accessed 23 August 2022).

Trade Promotion Organisation of Iran. *Annual reports*. Available at: https://tpo.ir/ (accessed 23 August 2022).

Trotsky, L. (1936/1972). *The Revolution Betrayed*. New York: Pathfinder Press.

UN Security Council (2006). 'Resolution 1737'. Available at: www.iaea.org/sites/ default/files/unsc_res1737-2006.pdf (accessed 13 September 2022).

UN Security Council (2007). 'Resolution 1747'. Available at: www.iaea.org/sites/ default/files/unsc_res1747-2007.pdf (accessed 13 September 2022).

UN Security Council (2008). 'Resolution 1803'. Available at: www.iaea.org/sites/ default/files/unsc_res1803-2008.pdf (accessed 13 September 2022).

US Treasury Department (2012). 'Treasury submits report to Congress on NIOC And NITC', 24 September. Available at: https://home.treasury.gov/news/press-releases/tg1718 (accessed 3 February 2022).

UNCTADStat. Available at: https://unctadstat.unctad.org/wds/TableViewer/table View.aspx?ReportId=96740 (accessed 16 September 2022).

Vahdat, F. (2011). 'Theorizing civil society in contemporary Iran', in Jahanbegloo, R. (ed.), *Civil Society and Democracy in Iran*. New York: Lexington Books, pp. 25–38.

Vakilli, V. (1997). *Debating Religion and Politics: The political thought of Abdolkarim Soroush*. New York: Council on Foreign Relations.

Valadbaygi, K. (2021). 'Hybrid neoliberalism: Capitalist development in contemporary Iran', *New Political Economy*, 26:3, 313–27.

Valadbaygi, K. (2022). 'Neoliberalism and state formation in Iran', *Globalizations*, 1–15. doi: 10.1080/14747731.2021.2024391.

Valibeigi, M. (1994). 'The private sector in Iran's post-revolutionary economy', *Journal of South Asian and Middle Eastern Studies*, 17:3, 1–18.

van der Linden, M. (2008). *Workers of the World: Essays toward a global labor history*. Leiden: Brill.

Vaziri, M. (2013). *Iran as Imagined Nation* (second edition). Piscataway, NJ: Gorgias Press.

Virdee, S. (2019). 'Racialized capitalism: An account of its contested origins and consolidation', *Sociological Review*, 67:1, 3–27.

VOA News (2022). 'US calls Iranian demand to end nuclear probes "unreasonable"', 22 September. Available at: www.voanews.com/a/us-calls-iranian-demand-to-end-nuclear-probes-unreasonable-/6759826.html (accessed 23 September 2022).

Wade, R. (1990). *Governing the Market: Economic theory and the role of government in East Asian industrialization*. Princeton, NJ: Princeton University Press.

Waltz, K. (2012). 'Why Iran should get the bomb', *Foreign Affairs*, 91:4, 2–5.

Warnnar, M. (2013). *Iranian Foreign Policy During Ahmadinejad: Ideology and actions*. New York: Palgrave Macmillan.

Webb, M.S. (2016). 'Is Iran really one of the world's best investments?' *Financial Times*, 11 March. Available at: www.ft.com/content/7349a988-e6f7-11e5-bc31-138df2ae9ee6 (accessed 23 August 2022).

Weinbaum, M.G. (1977). 'Agricultural policy and development politics in Iran', *Middle East Journal*, 31:4, 434–50.

White, G. (1988). *Developmental States in East Asia*. London: Macmillan.

Williams, A. and Bozorgmehr, N. (2019). 'US designates Iran's Revolutionary Guard a foreign terrorist organisation', *Financial Times*, 8 April. Available at: www.ft.com/content/3a4a9672-5a0a-11e9-939a-341f5ada9d40 (accessed 23 August 2022).

Wood, E.M. (2016). *Democracy against Capitalism: Renewing historical materialism*. London: Verso.

World Bank, DataBank, World Development Indicators. Available at: https://databank.worldbank.org/source/world-development-indicators (accessed 16 September 2022).

World Bank, World Development Indicators database. Available at: https://data.worldbank.org/indicator/SL.TLF.TOTL.FE.ZS?end=2021&locations=IR&start=1990&view=chart (accessed 28 March 2023).

Wu, B. (2021). 'China and New Middle East', *Journal of Balkan and Near Eastern Studies*, 23:3, 443–57.

Yacoubian, A. (2021). 'Iran's increasing reliance on China', *The Iran Primer*, United States Institute of Peace. Available at: https://iranprimer.usip.org/blog/2019/sep/11/irans-increasing-reliance-china (accessed 23 August 2022).

Yaghmaian, B. (2002). *Social Change in Iran*. Albany: State University of New York Press.

Ye, M. (2022). 'Ten years of the Belt and Road: Reflections and recent trends', Global Development Policy Center, 6 September. Available at: www.bu.edu/gdp/2022/09/06/ten-years-of-the-belt-and-road-reflections-and-recent-trends/?utm_content=220278315&utm_medium=social&utm_source=twitter&hss_channel=tw-905477617775771654 (accessed 7 September 2022)

Yeganeh, B. (2007). 'The casualties of gasoline: From Tehran to Yasuj', Radio Farda, 1 July. Available at: www.radiofarda.com/a/f3_petrol_rationing_protest/400289.html (accessed 23 August 2022).

Yeganeh, C. (1985). 'The agrarian structure of Iran: From land reform to revolution', *State, Culture, and Society*, 1:3, 67–84.

Yeganeh, H. (2015). *Making Sense of Iranian Society, Culture, and Business.* New York: Business Expert Press.

Yetiv, S.A. and Lu, C. (2007). 'China, global energy, and the Middle East', *Middle East Journal*, 61:2, 199–218.

Yıldız, E. (2021). 'Of nuclear rials and golden shoes: Scaling commodities and currencies across sanctions on Iran', *International Journal of Middle East Studies*, 53:4, 604–19.

Zhang, K.H. (2009). 'Rise of Chinese multinational firms', *Chinese Economy*, 42:6, 81–96.

Zia-Ebrahimi, R. (2016). *The Emergence of Iranian Nationalism: Race and the politics of dislocation.* New York: Columbia University Press.

# Index

Page numbers in *italics* refer to figures and those in **bold** refer to tables.

EU authorised representative for GPSR:
Easy Access System Europe, Mustamäe tee 50,
10621 Tallinn, Estonia
gpsr.requests@easproject.com

www.ingramcontent.com/pod-product-compliance
Lightning Source LLC
Chambersburg PA
CBHW052000270326
41929CB00015B/2725